Violin For Dummies®

Tuning Your Violin with a Pi...

D0732136

- ✔ Play G below middle C on the piano (see the figure...
- ✔ Pluck the G string of your violin — the one on the f...
- ✔ If the violin's G sounds lower than the piano's G, turn the fine tuner to the right. If the violin's G is higher than the piano's, turn the tuner to the left.
- ✔ Repeat these steps for the D, A, and E strings of your violin.

"Middle C"

C D E F G A B C D E F G A B C D E F G A B C D E

Bow Hold Tips

- ✔ Hold the bow quite lightly in your right hand, keeping your fingers flexible, and a generally rounded shape in all fingers and the thumb.
- ✔ Your fourth finger is curved, with its tip resting on top of the bow stick just above the outer right end of the frog.
- ✔ The inside tip of your thumb is snuggled underneath the bow stick and into the corner where the top left edge of the frog ebony meets the wood of the stick.
- ✔ Your middle finger and your ring finger tips are lying flat against the outside of the frog, with the ring finger tip close to, or actually covering the inlaid eye on the side of the frog.
- ✔ Your middle finger is opposite the thumb.
- ✔ Your index finger leans gently on the stick between the top and middle joints, with its outer side contacting the bow.
- ✔ Keep all fingers in a natural distance from one another, close to the distances you see if you let your hand hang by your side.
- ✔ Good bowing depends on keeping plenty of flexibility in your fingers, wrist, elbow, and shoulder joints so that you can move with ease.

Stick

Eye

Frog

For Dummies: Bestselling Book Series for Beginners

Violin For Dummies®

Violin Hold Tips

- Stand in a well-balanced posture, with your feet about shoulder width apart, as you swing the violin up into playing position.

- Ensure that the back edge of the violin, just under the chinrest, sits on your left collarbone and that the violin's ribs touch the left side of your neck about halfway between the center of your throat and the outer side of your neck.

- Hold the instrument more or less parallel to the floor. Most players find it helpful to use a shoulder rest to keep the violin comfortably lodged in playing position.

- After you place your jaw on the chinrest, keep your left hand in a rounded shape at the scroll end of the violin's neck, so that the fingertips hover over the strings, ready to drop onto their spots. The very tip of your left thumb peeks over the fingerboard opposite your index finger; you can see a straight line flowing along the outside forearm from your elbow to your knuckles.

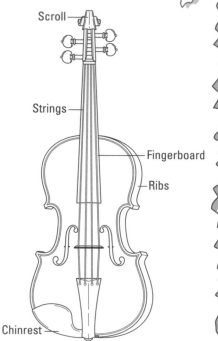

Scroll

Strings

Fingerboard

Ribs

Chinrest

Notes in First and Third Position

Here are the locations on the fingerboard of the most frequently played notes for first and third positions. See Chapter 5 for information on how to apply the fingerboard guides.

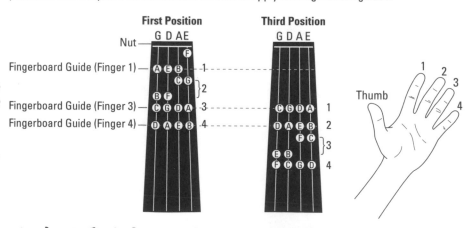

First Position

Third Position

Nut

G D A E

G D A E

Fingerboard Guide (Finger 1)

Fingerboard Guide (Finger 3)

Fingerboard Guide (Finger 4)

Thumb

For Dummies: Bestselling Book Series for Beginners

by Katharine Rapoport

WILEY

John Wiley & Sons Canada, Ltd.

Violin For Dummies®
Published by
John Wiley & Sons Canada, Ltd.
6045 Freemont Blvd.
Mississauga, ON L5R 4J3
www.wiley.com

For general information on John Wiley & Sons Canada, Ltd., including all books published by Wiley Publishing Inc., please call our warehouse, Tel. 1-800-567-4797. For reseller information, including discounts and premium sales, please call our sales department, Tel. 416-646-7992. For press review copies, author interviews, or other publicity information, please contact our marketing department, Tel. 416-646-4584, Fax 416-236-4448.

For authorization to photocopy items for corporate, personal, or educational use, please contact in writing The Canadian Copyright Licensing Agency (Access Copyright). For an Access Copyright license, visit www.accesscopyright.ca or call toll free 1-800-893-5777.

For technical support, please visit www.wiley.com/techsupport.

Library and Archives Canada Cataloguing in Publication Data

Rapoport, Katharine
 Violin for dummies / Katharine Rapoport.
Accompanied by a CD-ROM.
ISBN 978-0-470-83838-9
  1. Violin—Methods—Self-instruction. 2. Violin—Instruction and study.
3. Violin—Studies and exercises. 4. Music theory—Elementary works.
I. Title.
MT278.R219 2007   787.2'193   C2007-905868-X

Printed in Canada

1 2 3 4 5 TRI 11 10 09 08 07

WILEY

About the Author

Katharine Rapoport enjoys an eclectic career as a freelance violinist and violist in Toronto. After graduating from Cambridge University and the Guildhall School of Music, London, she spread her musical wings and spent seven more years performing and studying in Italy, Germany, Switzerland, Poland, and Austria before moving across the pond.

She has performed in just about every situation, from elegant Baroque opera on original instruments to cutting edge new music, from *La Bohème* to *Lès Miz*, from educational recordings to Viagra jingles. Her solo work includes concerto appearances with orchestras and sonata partnerships with pianists, and she also performs with a variety of chamber ensembles.

Her teaching has ranged from showing a two year-old how to unpack his violin case for the very first time to preparing outstanding young professionals for recitals, auditions, and competitions. She currently teaches at the University of Toronto, working with students who plan to make music their career, teaching violin and viola performance, and coaching chamber music ensembles. Many of her former students are now enjoying full-time careers in music, playing with major orchestras and chamber ensembles in Canada, the United States, and England, teaching and involving themselves in all aspects of music.

In her "spare" time, she takes on an assortment of projects for the Royal Conservatory of Music in Toronto: conducting the RCM Chamber Orchestra, compiling and editing violin publications for the Conservatory's examination system, devising their string syllabi, and going across Canada to examine and adjudicate young string players. She is frequently on faculty at summer chamber music and orchestral programs.

Dedication

Dedicated to my husband Alexander, my son Leo, and all my family; and to my students, who taught me how to teach.

Author's Acknowledgments

Special thanks to:

Robert Hickey, my patient and perspicacious editor, who envisioned and carried through this huge project; Heather Ball (developmental editor) and Andrea Douglas (copy editor) of the eagle eyes, well-organized brains and good humor; Ian Koo, for the amazing photographic work, and to the rest of the wonderful team at Wiley.

Dan and Carol Kushner, without whom VFD wouldn't have arrived at my door in the first place.

Joanne Martin, Patricia Shand and Marena Smith for ideas and feedback on pedagogical practicalities.

My teachers Yfrah Neaman, Bruno Giuranna, Hatto Beyerle, Arrigo Pelliccia, Franco Rossi, Alain Meunier, Burton Kaplan, Jennifer Glass and Nicola LeFanu, from whom I learned so much, and to the late greats whose legacy gives us all a precious violin inheritance, including Leopold Mozart, Leopold Auer, and some people not called Leopold, such as Carl Flesch, Joseph Szigeti, Ivan Galamian, Paul Rolland, and Shinichi Suzuki, whose ideas continue to inspire new generations of players.

My friends, colleagues and students Maxine Byam, Ron Hay, Anne Lindsay, George Meanwell, Mary McGeer, Barbara Morris, Elizabeth Morris, Michal and Pasia Schonberg, and James Tinsley, who read, advised, brainstormed.

Alistair Grieve and David Tamblyn at the Soundpost, Toronto; Jaak Liivoja-Lorius; Darragh McGee at Long and McQuade, Toronto; Quentin Playfair; Michael and Rosa Remenyi and Derrick Rathwell at Remenyi House of Music for their valuable expertise on violin and bow-making, repairing and accessories. Long and McQuade and the Soundpost kindly provided the items for the photoshoot.

The helpful staff at Atelier Grigorian in Toronto and at HMV shops in Vancouver and London, whose knowledge and willingness to help me find some great recordings made my task much easier and more fun.

And finally, my "in house" team, Alexander Rapoport, my husband, for advice on harmony (I'm lucky to have a composer around the place!), and Leo Rapoport, my son, for the idea of providing readers with video clips of the main actions.

Publisher's Acknowledgments

We're proud of this book; please send us your comments through our Dummies online registration form located at www.dummies.com/register/.

Some of the people who helped bring this book to market include the following:

Acquisitions, Editorial, and Media Development

Editor: Robert Hickey

Developmental Editor: Heather Ball

Copy Editor: Andrea Douglas

Media Development Specialist: Laura Atkinson

Cover and interior photos: Ian Koo

Cartoons: Rich Tennant
(www.the5thwave.com)

Composition Services

Vice-President Publishing Services: Karen Bryan

Project Manager: Elizabeth McCurdy

Project Coordinator: Lindsay Humphreys

Layout and graphics: Ronda David-Burroughs, Stephanie D. Jumper, Laura Pence, Barbara Moore, Rashell Smith

Proofreaders: Laura L. Bowman

Indexer: Belle Wong

Special Help

Zoë Wykes, Q Music

John Wiley & Sons Canada, Ltd.

    Bill Zerter, Chief Operating Officer

    Jennifer Smith, Vice-President and Publisher, Professional and Trade Division

Publishing and Editorial for Consumer Dummies

    Diane Graves Steele, Vice President and Publisher, Consumer Dummies

    Joyce Pepple, Acquisitions Director, Consumer Dummies

    Kristin A. Cocks, Product Development Director, Consumer Dummies

    Michael Spring, Vice President and Publisher, Travel

    Kelly Regan, Editorial Director, Travel

Publishing for Technology Dummies

    Andy Cummings, Vice President and Publisher, Dummies Technology/General User

Composition Services

    Gerry Fahey, Vice President of Production Services

    Debbie Stailey, Director of Composition Services

Contents at a Glance

Table of Contents

Introduction

*V*iolins have fascinated humans ever since they began their existence in primitive forms. The violin's shape is so stunningly beautiful, and its tone so evocative — like a human voice, but with a magical take on the sound. Watching violinists play allows us a peek into a secret world where physical ability and artistic expression meet to make beautiful music.

I first fell in love with the violin when I was in grade school in London, England. One day, my music teacher, Miss Simpson, brought to class a fascinating-looking case. She opened it up to show us the most exquisite item I had ever seen — a violin. She played a few notes on this beautiful instrument, and I was hooked for life. After listening to my persistent requests for a violin of my own, my parents figured it was more than a passing fancy, so they set me up for some violin lessons with my neighbors' daughter. I even used her old ¾-size violin, which cost the shocking sum of £10! The musical bug kept me busy through high school and university, and it has never worn off, even after many years of pursuing a full-time career in music.

Why This Book Is for You

I talk to so many people — audience members after I play a concert, friends, colleagues, people who see me carrying my violin case on the subway — who all tell me the same thing: "I wish I knew how to play the violin." *Violin For Dummies* is for all of you (and for all the people I don't know personally, but who I know are out there) who have the same desire.

Even if you've never picked up a violin, let alone tried to play one, this book tells you what you need to know to make some music. I take you from the first moment you look at your instrument right on through the stages of an exciting journey to playing the violin. And the journey is fun — I guarantee it.

No matter how skilled you are with the violin (or even if you have no skills yet), this book has something for you. If you're new to the instrument and want to play, you can follow the chapters in order. If you have some violin background and are looking for some tips on sharpening your skills, you can zone in on areas where you want some advice and skip over the places where you know how to manage.

If you're a more advanced musician, or even a music teacher, you may want to use *Violin For Dummies* for reference. I give you extra teaching ideas, and you can find some new tricks and approaches to playing that really work.

Foolish Assumptions

Because you're reading this book, I can make quite a few assumptions about you already:

- You have a violin.

  If you don't have a violin, you're preparing to buy, rent, or borrow one, along with a few necessary bits of equipment. I tell you about all the equipment you need, plus some violin accessories that are just really cool.

- You love all kinds of music, and you want to play music yourself.

- You want to study the violin seriously and quite thoroughly, but you don't want to be bored out of your mind in the process — that's why I sprinkle so many fun songs for you to play throughout the book.

- You're not necessarily familiar with reading music, but you want to give it a try. That curiosity is just what you need, because I ease you into reading musical notation until you can read it as well as you're reading this right now.

- You're eager to add words like *pizzicato* and *purfling* to your vocabulary. I give you all the basic violin and music terminology you need to sound very knowledgeable.

- You have access to a CD player to listen to and play along with the songs I provide. And likely, you even have access to a computer so that you can watch the moves in action on the CD-ROM.

How This Book Is Organized

No matter how you choose to read *Violin For Dummies* (jumping between chapters or reading systematically from cover to cover), the book is organized into handy sections so that you always know where you are on your musical journey. This book takes you through the first steps all the way to more-advanced playing techniques, and it even covers some essentials of music theory. Or, if you're looking for a particular topic, the book's organization helps you find it faster than you can say "Paganini."

Part 1: So You Want to Play the Violin

Part I introduces you to the world of the violin by telling you the names of the parts of the violin and bow. (Say "Pleased to meet you!") After you've said hello, I show you how to tune your violin and hold it comfortably (and properly) so that you can begin to play.

Part II: Getting Started: The Basics

In this part, I tell you how to hold and manage the bow with your right hand to draw a sound out of the violin. After the bowing's going (and flowing!), you put both hands to work together by using the left-hand fingers to make many different notes.

Part III: Reading Music for the Violin

You can manage quite a bit of playing by ear and with the handy charts I show you in Part II, but eventually you'll want to read music on your own, which is exactly what this part is about. After you're able to read music, you can figure out any new pieces you meet. I show you the main aspects of musical notation: notes, rhythms, meters (not the parking kind!), and other musical signs.

Part IV: Musicianship and Harmony

All kinds of elements go into even the simplest-sounding piece of music. Read this part to understand how music works when all the parts sound together. I talk about scales, key signatures, and harmony so that you know what's going on around you as you play.

Part V: Taking It Up a Notch: Techniques and Styles

The violin is hardly a one-note wonder. This instrument has lots of character, and I want to show it off. The music that you play becomes quite a lot fancier in Part V, where you find out about some very slick moves with the bowing and the fingering. You also enjoy a brief visit to the worlds of fiddling, jazz music, and gypsy violin, and I give you a few tips about how to sound authentic when you play in these characteristic styles.

Part VI: Getting into Gear, Staying in Gear

Read this part to find out about renting or buying a good violin, and taking proper care of your instrument and bow. I also talk about neat accessories, some of which may look rather strange to you at first. I explain what the accessories do and let you know which ones are must-haves and which are ones to lust after unrequitedly at the music store.

Part VII: The Part of Tens

Your family probably tells you that you're the world's greatest violinist. But you know you can always find ways to discover more about the violin. This part lists famous violinists of yesterday and today, and mentions some of their recordings for you to enjoy. For even more fun with your violin, I tell you ways to join in on musical activities with other players and how to find a good teacher to take you on the next step of your violin journey.

The CD-ROM

The CD-ROM that comes with *Violin For Dummies* contains audio recordings of every song and exercise in the book in MP3 format, so you can put this disk in your computer or upload the files to your MP3 player and play along. It also includes short video clips of many of the key movements you need to know to play the violin, enabling you to see just what I'm writing about. I fill you in on how to use the CD-ROM at the back of the book, in the appendix.

Icons Used in This Book

Flipping through the book, you'll no doubt notice some little pictures in the margins. I hope they grab your attention, because that's their job. Whenever you see one of these icons, look for the following kinds of information:

A Tip icon tells you stuff that makes life a whole lot easier, and that may even make playing the violin a whole lot easier. So my tip to you is to watch for the Tip icon.

A Remember icon tells you to keep in mind something you probably already know.

When you see the Warning icon, take special notice of the information. This icon tells you that you need to watch out for a possible problem or difficulty.

Technical Stuff icons give you useful information and even some impressive jargon about the theory behind a particular section. But this information isn't crucial, and it doesn't affect what you're actually doing. So if you're not in a technical frame of mind, you can come back to this icon later, or skip hastily to the next bit.

This icon reminds you that *Violin For Dummies* is more than just a book: It's also an audio-visual experience. The book's companion CD-ROM contains MP3 files of the songs and even provides video clips of the moves I describe, so you can know if you're doing them right. Whenever you see this icon, check out the CD-ROM to hear and see things in action.

Where to Go from Here

Well, in most books, page 1 is a good place to start. But this book is different. You don't have to read *Violin For Dummies* in strict order, from the first page to the last page. You won't miss the punch line if you turn to check out some question about violin playing that's been bugging you for 37 years and then flip back to the previous section afterwards.

Of course, you're also very welcome to start with the basics in Chapter 1 and then move gradually through the book to the more advanced material, because the book does build up systematically, skill by skill, chapter by chapter.

Whatever your musical background, you can use this book as your guide to the world of violins. So sit back (or rather, sit up straight, in case you want to pick up your violin) and get ready to make some music.

Part I

So You Want to Play the Violin

The 5th Wave   By Rich Tennant

"I can let you have this one for $50 dollars, no strings attached."

In this part . . .

You don't have to be a professional violinist to play well and enjoy the violin. You don't have to be a child prodigy, and you don't have to buy a million-dollar violin to sound good. But you do have to take it step by step. In Chapter 1, I give you an overview of just about everything you can expect to discover as a violinist, every step of the way. Then it's time to pick up your instrument. Check out Chapter 2 to familiarize yourself with the names and functions of all the parts of the violin. That chapter also shows you how to tune your instrument so it sounds like it should. Chapter 3 is all about how to hold the violin comfortably.

Chapter 1

Introducing the Violin

*Y*ou don't have to be a professional musician to enjoy playing the violin. Learning to play for your own enjoyment — for the joy of making music — can be really satisfying. If you've always wanted to play but have never had the chance, or if you've taken some lessons or played a bit at school, this book is for you: It starts right from the first time you open your case and takes you step-by-step to playing real music on your violin.

Bring On the Violin!

The violin is a member of the *string family,* which also claims the illustrious viola, the magnificent cello, and the imposing double bass as its own, actually totaling 16 strings among them — or even 17, as some basses actually have five strings! People also often include such instruments as the guitar and the harp in the string family, but these relatives lack an essential accoutrement: Players don't need a bow to make sounds. So the string family (just like so many human families nowadays) has become known by another name too: *bowed strings.* All of the bowed strings' family members bear a distinct resemblance. The overall shape of the instruments is similar, and their sound is instantly recognizable.

The smallest member of the string family, the violin, is an instrument that's familiar to people all over the world. Just because the violin's the smallest in size, however, doesn't mean it's the least important or least powerful — quite the contrary. The violin's special soprano voice can express a whole gamut of emotions, even those beyond the power of mere words. The violin can produce tone colors and intensities like the greatest of painters, and it has fascinated and moved players and listeners alike for generations.

Making a violin requires great skill, honed through a long apprenticeship, to get more than 70 component parts put together into one beautiful instrument. But most violinists wouldn't know their *scroll* (the beautifully carved whorl of wood at the end of the violin farthest from the player) from their *saddle* (the small ebony ridge that supports the whole course of the strings). This unawareness isn't surprising; although most people are pretty familiar with cars, they can't name auto parts either.

Plenty of very experienced violinists aren't able to name all the component parts of a violin, mainly because many parts are completely hidden inside the violin after it's put together. They *are* able to name the key ones, though. I discuss the key parts of the violin in Chapter 2 as I take you on a tour of your violin. I also discuss in Chapter 2 some different violin-making processes, and I walk you through the steps for getting your violin safely out of its case when you begin your playing session, and for putting it away again when you're done.

Tuning up

After being properly introduced to the violin, you need to tune your instrument before you begin to play. Each string has its own set note that you tune to, so that when you put down your fingers, you get the sound you expect.

Tuning the violin can be potentially quite intimidating: Those four strings need a checkup tuning every time you start your daily playing session, and they occasionally slip out of tune even during a practice session. This frequent tuning seems a bit unfair. After all, pianists don't have to tune for themselves; they just have to call in the tuner a couple of times a year. And flautists use a fairly simple process to adjust the tuning of their flutes. On the violin, some aspects of tuning can be pretty tricky, so I offer tips on how to tune — and how to deal with managing the tricky stuff too (see Chapter 2).

Eventually, the process becomes second nature, and violinists don't mind tuning their instruments, because they sound good when the strings are in tune. And think of those pianos with several notes slipping out of tune, and the tuner not due for months — pianists have to grit their teeth and wait! Violinists can fix out-of-tune strings right away.

Holding on

In addition to your violin being undoubtedly the most elegant of instruments, another part of its appeal is how debonair violinists look when they're actually playing. Great violinists often look like their instrument is an extension of themselves — but this seemingly effortless posture actually involves a lot of practice.

Apart from looking great, taking time to get the instrument comfortably lodged and balanced prevents your playing from becoming a literal pain in the neck. Your arm and finger functions also work optimally when all their muscles are free to move as needed, with no excess tension or creaky joints. Chapter 3 shows you how to hold the violin really well, along with providing a few tips on finding useful accessories to help you in your quest for balance and comfort.

Bowing Out Some Sounds

The violin may get most of the glory, but its renown wouldn't be possible without its slender companion, the bow. The bow's job is to activate the vibrations of the strings so that your violin can sing out. When you look at the narrow bow stick, which is only about 29 inches long, and its ribbon of powdery-white horsehair, it seems quite amazing how much sound a bow can draw out of the strings, and in how many different ways.

Taking a close look at the bow

The bow doesn't have as many components as does its more celebrated case-mate, but it has its own quirks and nuances. How can you not appreciate something with a part named "frog"? I introduce you to the frog and more prosaically named parts of the bow (no toads or princesses) in Chapter 4, which also tells you how to care for your bow so that it stays in tip-top condition.

Although your bow doesn't require tuning, it does need its own type of attention before and after every use — and just like the violin, it needs special attention paid to how it's held. You get an introduction to holding the bow properly and you actually bow out a few tunes at the end of Chapter 4.

Getting both your hands in on the action

Remember trying to pat your head and rub your tummy at the same time (or is it the other way around?). Playing the violin is a good exercise for your brain and hand coordination because your two hands move very differently to make sounds happen. If you're an adult taking up the violin for the first time, you can earn extra points for all that new brain activity.

Your left hand has a lot of responsibilities on the violin, making notes both by landing and by lifting fingers on and off the four strings. Fingers also have to move horizontally and laterally to reach various notes on different strings. Eventually, the left hand also moves to different locations farther up the strings to find those impressive high notes. Chapter 5 gets your left hand actions off on the right track, showing you the finger-numbering system for the violin and the way to successfully land your fingers on the strings without getting a pilot's license.

But all that left-hand work can't make an impact if the bow doesn't stroke the strings — and that's where your right hand gets to work on its important job: to hold your bow just right. When you assemble all your bowing skills, the bow can make a whole range of sounds, from singing sweetly in lyrical music to hammering out sounds in passionate passages. Chapter 6 sets you on the right path by bringing your hands together to bow and finger the notes simultaneously. You make music by using some simple charts, and you finish up with songs that pull all your skills into action.

Reading between the Lines

The first songs you meet in this book don't require the ability to read music, because they're written out in handy charts. The charts allow you to play simple songs right away as you begin to play your violin. However, when you find out how to read actual musical notation, you can play more advanced music and enjoy a wealth of songs and pieces.

Printed musical notation is a shorthand system that communicates a whole world of playing instructions to musicians. These instructions include information about which notes to play, and at what speed and rhythm; how loud or soft the music needs to be; and a wealth of other visual information that helps you to make the sounds right. As an added advantage, the ability to read music allows you to understand music that's been written for any instrument or singer, not just for the violin.

Knowing the notes

Reading music is a bit like reading a language written with a different alphabet than the one you're used to: Printed music has similarities to what you already know; you just need to get to know the new system. The notes belong on those famous five lines, with the lines functioning much like a ladder: the higher the notes climb the ladder, the higher the sound you get. Notes have slightly different appearances according to their time values. Various symbols give musicians information about the volume, how to "attack" the notes (just with a bow, no arrow necessary), and so on.

To crack the secret code, see Chapter "007" (or Chapter 7, if you're not the espionage type), which takes you through the symbols and signs and shows you how to make them into actual sounds.

Getting rhythm

All the melodies in the world would be a lot less listenable if it weren't for rhythm. Dancers would trip over one another, soldiers would fall over like dominoes, and toe-tappers would be toe-tally frustrated. Rhythm gives life and energy to music and lets you dance to the tunes of many different drummers (or violinists).

Chapter 8 introduces you to the most important elements of rhythm and shows you how to count your way through the different values. In Chapter 9, you put those rhythms together into different measures so you know when to waltz and when to polka.

Digging Deeper into Music

Reading notes on the page and knowing the time values of the notes is just the start of playing music. After you learn those basics, doors open to the big leagues.

Scales and key signatures

I know that scales often inspire dread because they used to be drilled and repeated endlessly in the bad ol' days. But scales are really the building blocks to music, enabling musicians to find their way around just about any piece. Knowing your scales well gives you fluency and confidence, and there's nothing wrong with those attributes. Chapter 10 covers some of the most essential scales for a violinist.

After you know some scales, you have the picks to unlock *key signatures*. These little signs, containing up to seven sharps or flats, occur at the very start of each piece of music and are repeated as reminders at the start of every line throughout the piece. A key signature is a way of telling musicians exactly which notes to play in a particular piece. Chapter 11 shows you how to read and recognize the different key signatures.

Harmony

Although violins usually play the melody one note at a time, one of the advantages of a string instrument is that its four strings enable players to play up to four notes at once, when needed. But just as pickles and ice cream don't mix, not all notes work well together. Chapter 12 combines some of these notes into sweet harmonies, so you don't marry dill and vanilla.

Getting Stylish

The violin is well loved for its versatility and for the panoply of sounds it can make, from the gentle singing of a slow, peaceful lullaby to the dazzling cascade of brilliance in a virtuoso showpiece. You probably already have a great desire to tackle some fancy tricks and to coax all kinds of exotic sounds out of your violin. The good news is that you can begin to do some pretty neat things as you look into the chapters that deal with the development of fancier techniques and styles.

Dazzling technique

After you master some different ways of playing with the bow, you can add new dash and panache to your sounds. Even the names of the different bowings sound very fancy. When you bump into your friends, you can casually let drop that you're playing *spiccato,* and then after a suitable pause for effect, you can let them know that this is a bow stroke where the bow bounces off the strings of the violin.

Seeing the words *brush stroke* may make you wonder what a violinist is doing with a brush, but you don't have to transform into Chagall to play your violin — you just add an artistic brushing movement to your bow strokes, bringing a whole new palette of sounds to your fingertips. Chapter 13 introduces you to a choice menu of bowings, some in the meat-and-potato department, and some definitely in the sinful dessert category!

In Chapter 14, you go through a similar journey of discovery with your left hand, getting your fingers to dance across the strings (almost doing a violin version of the Highland fling) and do other neat moves. Not only do your fingertips lift and land on one string, but they also slide and hop to different spots on that same string, ready to leap across to another string at any time. Sometimes two different fingers play on two different strings at once. Just when you have those fingers in line, you find out how to move your left hand to high positions (and back again) so that you can play high notes or make slinky-sounding slides.

Multicultural music

The violin is like a chameleon — it's at home just about anywhere. In addition to the more classical styles of playing, many other cultures all over the world have their own unique styles featuring the violin and its relatives — from the Chinese two-string *erhu,* which has a ravishing and magical vocal sound, to the Indian *surangi,* a very expressive and exotic instrument with three gut strings to play on and a whole array of metal strings that vibrate sympathetically.

But you don't need to get hold of an erhu or a sarangi to play in different styles. Chapter 15 takes you on a visit to some different musical styles that you can play with your very own violin. You can fit right in, whether you're at a ceilidh, at a smoky jazz club, or in a gypsy caravan.

A Violin of Your Own

As you embark on your important and exciting violin project, you may be quite sure you're going to love the violin, so you may want to buy one right away. However, you may feel cautious about jumping in, so you may be considering renting an instrument for a while. Either option can be a very successful way to get started.

Finding the right instrument with the right price tag for you, whether it's through buying or renting a violin, is a personal decision that affects your enjoyment and progress. You want to feel satisfied with the instrument you play, so your violin needs to sound good enough. Chapter 16 discusses some of the issues to consider before you make a decision about what's best.

After you're equipped with all the gear, you can find out how to take good care of it and do the necessary maintenance. Keeping your violin and bow in tip-top condition takes only a few simple steps. Chapter 17 covers these in detail (even talking about what to do if an accident occurs to your violin), discussing daily care, changing strings, and traveling safely with your violin in hand.

Chapter 2

Getting Started with the Violin

. . . .

In This Chapter

▶ Taking a look at the parts of the violin

▶ Figuring out how violins work

▶ Getting your violin out of the case

▶ Tuning your violin like a pro

▶ Dealing with pegs and fine tuners

. . . .

*W*ith all of its different component parts and its beautiful, delicate-looking body, the violin can be a bit intimidating at first. So this chapter begins by telling you how to go about getting to know your instrument, introducing you to the names of the most important parts of your violin, talking about how violins work to make a sound, and taking you through the steps for the very first time you take the violin out of its case.

Even after you get to know the names of the most important parts of your violin, you still need to tune it before you start to play. Tuning looks pretty simple when you go to a symphony orchestra concert. You hear a sudden hush at the appointed hour. The oboe plays an A, and then the whole orchestra tunes to that note, either all together or in turn: woodwinds, brass, and strings. The tuning process takes a short time, probably less than half a minute. However, these are professional players who have been tuning for years. The musicians have all warmed up and tuned up their instruments in the green room offstage, so they just do a checkup before they perform the concert. Most orchestras tune again before each piece they play, because the heat generated by the stage lights and the warm bodies of the audience in the hall causes their instruments to go a bit out of tune. Of course, for a beginner, it can take a lot of trial and error to learn to tune each string.

In this chapter, I tell you all you need to know about tuning your violin, so that next time you want to play, you can crack open your case with confidence.

Examining the Violin

More than 70 parts go into making a complete violin. The main parts that I refer to throughout the book are labeled in Figure 2-1 and explained here.

- **Back:** One of the most important parts of the violin, for both aesthetic and acoustic properties. The back of the violin can be made of one or two pieces, and it's arched for strength and tone power.

- **Bass bar:** A slim strip of wood glued under the table of the violin on the side of, and running more or less parallel to, the lower strings. The bass bar reinforces the strength of the violin's top and enriches the tone of the lower notes.

- **Body:** The sounding box of the violin has evolved over ages to produce the best sound and use the most convenient playing shape. The "waist" of the violin is actually a necessary indentation, so that the bow can move freely across the strings without bumping into the body of the instrument.

- **Bridge:** The only piece of unvarnished wood on the violin, it sits on top, about halfway down the body, placed exactly between the little cross-bars of the violin's f-holes. The strings run over the top of the bridge, which then transfers their vibrations to the main body of the violin for amplification. The bridge is slightly rounded to match the shape of the fingerboard and to enable the player to bow on one string at a time.

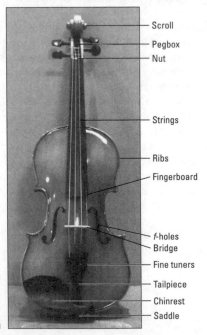

Scroll
Pegbox
Nut

Strings

Ribs
Fingerboard

f-holes
Bridge
Fine tuners
Tailpiece
Chinrest
Saddle

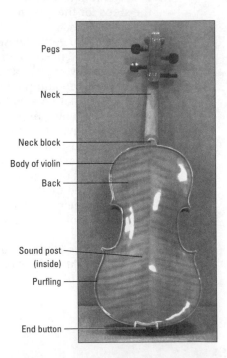

Pegs

Neck

Neck block
Body of violin
Back

Sound post (inside)
Purfling

End button

Figure 2-1: The violin.

- **Chinrest:** The spot on which your jaw rests when you're playing (come to think of it, it should be called a "jaw rest"). Chinrests are usually made of ebony that has been carved into a cupped shape to fit the left side of your jaw. Your chinrest is attached just to the left of the tailpiece by a special metal bracket. You can choose from a variety of models to fit your chin shape and neck length most comfortably (see Chapter 3 for more about choosing chinrests).

- **End Button:** A small circular knob made of ebony, to which the tailpiece is attached by a loop.

- **F-holes:** The openings on either side of the bridge. They're called f-holes because they're shaped like the italic letter *f.*

- **Fine tuners:** Small metal screws fitted into the tailpiece and used for minor tuning adjustments.

- **Fingerboard:** A slightly curved, smooth piece of ebony that's glued on top of the neck of the violin, under most of the length of the strings.

- **Neck:** The long piece of wood to which the fingerboard is glued. The neck connects the body of the violin to the pegbox and scroll.

- **Nut:** A raised ridge at the pegbox end of the fingerboard that stops the strings from vibrating beyond that point. A "nut" is also what you call the person at the end of the violin.

- **Pegbox:** The rectangular part of the scroll immediately adjoining the nut end of the fingerboard, before all the fancy carving begins, where each of the four pegs fits snugly sideways into its individual hole.

- **Pegs:** Four pieces of wood, usually ebony, shaped for ease of turning and fitted into round holes in the pegbox. The player turns the peg to tighten or loosen each string when tuning the violin.

- **Purfling:** An inlay running around the edge of the top and back of the violin's body. The purfling is both decorative and functional because it protects the main body of the violin from cracks that can occur through accidental bumps. Of all the parts of the violin, "purfling" is the most fun to say.

- **Ribs:** The sides of the violin. The *luthier* (a fancy word for violin maker) bends the wood, curving it to fit the outline of the top and back of each instrument.

- **Saddle:** An ebony ridge over which the tailpiece loop passes. The saddle protects the body of the violin from becoming damaged and prevents rattling sounds, which would occur if the tailpiece was to contact the top of the violin when it's vibrating with sound.

Peering inside your violin

The world inside your violin contains some structural essentials that you can't see unless you take the violin apart — and I don't recommend doing that! Take my word for it: The corners are reinforced by small, triangular blocks of wood called *corner blocks*. The violin maker also fits an extra block of wood (the *neck block*) to strengthen the joint where the neck joins the body of the violin.

Something that you *can* see inside many violins is the maker's label, usually glued to the back of the instrument and visible if you peek into the f-holes. Don't be too excited if the label says *Stradivarius* or *Guarnerius:* Imitation is the sincerest form of flattery — many workshop and factory instruments are modeled on "Strad" patterns.

- ✔ **Scroll:** Named after the rolled-up paper scrolls that were sent instead of envelopes in the old days, the scroll forms the very end of the pegbox. Carving a scroll requires artistic vision and great expertise, so creative violin makers see the scroll as an opportunity to display their best work. Occasionally, you meet a violin with a lion's head scroll, or some other fanciful shape, the result of a maker's whimsy.

- ✔ **Sound post:** Enhances the volume and tone of the violin by transferring the sound vibrations to the back of the instrument after the bow makes a string sound near the bridge. If you peek into the f-hole near the E string (your thinnest string), you see a small round column of unvarnished wood, about the circumference of a pencil, which fits vertically from the top to the back of the violin.

- ✔ **Strings:** The four metal-wrapped wires (often made with silver or aluminum ribbon spiraling smoothly around a gut or synthetic core material) that you bow on (or pluck) to produce the notes of the violin.

- ✔ **Tailpiece:** A flared-shaped piece of wood into which the top end of each string is attached. The tailpiece itself is attached to the end button by a gut or synthetic loop.

- ✔ **Top (or Table):** The "face" of the violin. The top is very important to the character and quality of the violin's sound as well as to its general appearance.

How Violins Work

Chances are good that although you may be fascinated by the anatomy of the violin, you're more interested in making some music with it. So how does this instrument work? I'm glad you asked.

String vibration and string length

Whether you stroke the strings with your bow or pluck them like a guitarist, the strings are set into motion, and they make a sound the moment they start to vibrate. Although the strings are all the same length, they produce different pitches (see "Tuning the Violin," later in this chapter, for more about pitch) when they vibrate, because they're tightened to different degrees of tension. The tighter the tension, the higher the pitch. You've probably twanged a rubber band and noticed that the sound it produces gets higher as you stretch it. The thickness of a string also affects its pitch, as you can see if you look inside a grand piano, where the bass strings (for the lower notes) are dramatically thicker than the treble strings (for the higher notes). On a violin, you can see a less dramatic, but quite noticeable, difference in the strings' thickness, and you can feel greater tension as the pitch of the strings gets higher.

A violinist changes the sounding pitch on any string by putting down a finger, which shortens the *vibrating length* of the string (that's the part of the string that stretches between the player's fingertip and the bridge of the violin), making the pitch go higher accordingly. To get all those notes, you need lots of cooperation between the strings and your left-hand fingers! Figure 2-2 shows you two different vibrating lengths on a string.

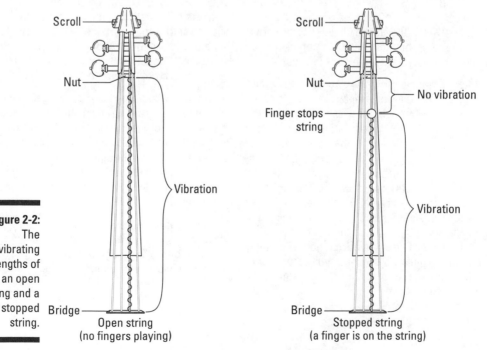

Figure 2-2: The vibrating lengths of an open string and a stopped string.

Discovering how violins are made

Your violin may look a lot like any other violin, but it could have arrived in your hands from any one of these three building processes:

Handmade by a luthier: First the luthier selects the wood — most frequently maple or sycamore for the back, ribs, and neck, and spruce for the top. The *seasoning process,* getting the wood into the right condition for violin making, takes eight to ten years. Seasoning is best done in fresh air, because hurrying the process with kiln-drying usually leads to problems with cracks and warping later. Sometimes, the luthier actually bites on the wood to tell if it's ready!

The seasoned wood is sectioned into slabs from which the body of the violin is carved. The luthier uses a pattern to determine the proper dimensions. Usually, these patterns are based on models of the great makers' works, such as violins by *Stradivarius,* the Latin name of Antonio Stradivari (1644–1737), or *Guarnerius,* the Latin name for Giuseppe Guarneri del Gesù (1698–1744). The luthier planes the corner blocks to fit the mold and then carves the top block in readiness for the neck joint cut.

After setting up the basic structure, the luthier prepares the ribs and shapes them up. Using the ribs as a reference, the violin maker cuts the outline of the table and back before starting work on the *arching* — the curved shape of these parts — using a curved chisel and scrapers. With the outside shape complete, the *plates,* as they are called, can be reduced to the correct thickness from the inside. The luthier uses precise calculations to determine the thickness of the top and bottom of the instrument, to combine structural strength and beauty of tone — and the thickness will vary according to the maker and the nature of the wood being used.

When the top and bottom of the violin are done, the luthier cuts out the f-holes and fits and shapes the bass bar. Then come the neck and scroll, formed from one solid block of flamed maple wood. A bit of saw and chisel work gives the scroll its rough outline, and a gouge is the main instrument for carving the details of the scroll. The surface of the scroll emerges with the help of a scraper, and finally, the luthier reams the peg holes.

The luthier machines the ebony fingerboard to a rough finish before shaping it to the right contours. When satisfied with the fingerboard, the violin maker crafts the neck joint and fits the neck to the body of the violin. Using a knife, the luthier shapes the neck into a rounded shape, so it's comfortable for the left hand, and then files it.

The violin's surface is smoothed and scraped before it's varnished. The varnish on fine instruments is quite delicate and soluble, based on oils and spirits, to protect the instrument and to enhance its sound (although the varnish on school instruments is usually plastic-based to withstand a more adventurous existence).

Finally, the luthier spends a good deal of time setting up the new instrument so that it's ready to play. Generally, *setup* refers to all those parts that are the interface between the violin and the player, such as the bridge, the nut, the sound post, the tailpiece, and the fingerboard. A good instrument can become useless if the setup is poorly done.

Luthiers can take several months to make a violin, and they usually work on several instruments at once, finishing up to ten in a year. A handmade violin can last for centuries.

Made in a workshop: In a workshop environment, the instruments are still handmade, but with several artisans preparing different violin parts at once, the process is considerably faster. Depending on the quality of materials and workmanship, the results can still be very good, but the violins have less of an individual stamp than do those made by a single luthier.

Made in a factory: Industrial violin making came into existence around the turn of the twentieth century. One factory Web site boasts of manufacturing 6,000 violins per month! These violins are assembled from machine-cut parts, and the front, back, and ribs are often steam-pressed to achieve their shapes. Factory-made violins are much more affordable than their handmade counterparts. If you try out a few factory-made student violins, you notice that they may all look similar, but they can sound very different. One can sound much better than another, just by the luck of the draw, or a fortunate chunk of wood.

Factory-made violins tend to have a shorter playing life than that of a handmade violin. Generally, a factory-made violin's value depreciates, like a car, the older it gets, while handmade violins appreciate over the years and eventually become precious antiques.

You probably know that the smaller instruments of the string family, the violins and violas, are higher in pitch than cellos and basses. The smaller instruments make higher sounds because the length of their strings is shorter. An everyday example of this phenomenon is that a child's voice, which emerges from a small person, is usually much higher than a fully grown adult's. Or think of how tapping a sherry glass produces a higher sound than tapping a large goblet does.

Using both hands to make a sound

If you want to play a note on the piano, you just press a finger down on any key, and hey, presto, a note sounds! The violin normally requires both hands working together to create sound. Your left-hand fingers are in charge of creating the notes you play. You use your left-hand fingertips to press down on the string (to *stop* the string, as it's called). The right hand strokes the string with the bow. As soon as the bow sets the string in motion, you can hear the note being played. You can even change fingers during the same bow stroke to make different notes in smooth or rapid passages.

How the bow helps

The bow is the feature that gives the violin family its unique individual stamp in the larger family of instruments whose notes are generated from making strings sound. Other instruments with strings include the piano, in which felted hammers strike the strings, and guitars, where the player plucks the instrument with a finger or a pick. Stroking the strings with a bow allows string players to sustain and connect the sounds, a feature that fills pianists with envy! Furthermore — and I say "furthermore" to sound important, because this is a really good bit about violins — you can even make those sounds get louder or softer, or change in all kinds of ways, during the course of one bow stroke. We violinists do expression to the max!

Taking the Violin Out of Its Case

After all this talk about the violin, I bet you're dying to get your hands on one. But handling a violin is serious stuff. Because a violin is a delicate instrument, violin players have to be pretty careful about how they tote around their instruments. Most violin cases have two latches *and* a lock, which shows you how precious their cargo is!

Taking the violin out of its case (and putting it away again safely) is a skill; mastering the art ensures that your instrument will have a long and happy life. To open the case, follow these steps (you can also check out Figure 2-3 and the CD-ROM, which shows the process in action):

1. **Place the violin case on a stable flat surface, such as a table or a sofa, with the lid facing the ceiling, and then turn the latch-and-handle side to face you.**

   Note: You may have to unzip the case's cover first, which usually has two zips that pull away to either side of the case's handle. Pull the zips all the way around to the back of the case so that the lid is able to open fully.

2. **Open the latches first, then release the lock and lift the lid.**

   Because the cases are very snugly built, the top can be a bit sticky to lift, in which case (no pun intended!), you hold firmly on the handle while you lift the lid.

3. **After you open the case, lift off the covering blanket (if you have one) and undo the strap or the ribbon that safely holds your violin around its neck in the case, before you lift out the violin.**

4. **Hold the violin around its neck to lift it from the case — don't grab the body, because that's not good for the varnish.**

   I recommend putting the velvet cloth that covers the violin onto the table and next to the case; this way, you can place the instrument onto the cloth.

5. **Release the bow from the case by turning the toggle, taking the bow by the frog end (the name for the piece of ebony wood below the stick at the right end of the bow) with your right hand, and then sliding it gently to the right until the tip (the pointy end) of the bow is out of its loophole (I talk more about the bow in Chapter 4).**

   Never twist the stick while doing this — bows are strong, but they can't always resist sideways twists.

Figure 2-3:
Taking the
violin and
bow out of
the case.

At the end of a playing session, just reverse the preceding steps to put your violin and bow away (you can watch the process on the CD-ROM):

1. **Slide the stick back into the case, tip first, into the loop at the left end of the case's lid. Secure the frog by turning the case's toggle from a horizontal position, where you can fit the bow stick back in its spot, to a vertical position, which holds the frog safely in place.**

2. **Remove the shoulder rest or cushion from under the violin, and then place the instrument back in the case, tying it in safely at the neck and covering it with its velvet cloth.**

   The shoulder rest or cushion can be packed in the case too, so long as it's not scratching or pressing on the violin. Often, it can fit into the end compartment near the scroll.

   Cases are designed to protect the violin and to fit quite snugly, but take care not to pad the top of your violin overenthusiastically — although adding a folded cloth on top of your violin before closing the case might seem like a dandy idea, you can end up squashing the bridge and cracking the top of the instrument.

3. **Gently close the case's lid, and then make sure that the latches are closed securely, so the violin doesn't accidentally fall out and get damaged.**

Violins are made of natural materials that are sensitive to temperature and humidity changes. Follow these tips to help your violin have a long and happy life:

- ✔ Keep your violin at about room temperature.

- ✔ Store the case away from high-traffic areas so that it doesn't get knocked around.

- ✔ Always close and latch the case when you finish playing, to protect your violin from falls.

- ✔ Keep your violin away from radiators, air ducts, and direct sunlight, and avoid leaving it for long stays (or almost any stays!) in car trunks, especially in very hot or very cold weather.

- ✔ Most important of all, keep your violin in a humidity of 40–60 percent whenever possible, and if you're traveling to a different climate, take care to preserve the humidity in the violin's case at a similar level. (I talk more about humidifiers for violins in Chapter 17.) Allow the violin to adjust to the new climate gradually over several days or even weeks.

Tuning the Violin

You know that tuning is something you need to do, but what exactly does it mean? The word *tuning* refers to the adjustment of the strings of the violin (or of any stringed instrument, such as the guitar, harp, or piano) to their proper pitches. (Check out the sidebar "Pitch" to find out more.) Just about all musical instruments need a tuning session before the music begins.

String players spend quite a bit of time tuning their instruments before they begin to play each day, and sometimes they need to tune again after a while, if a string has slipped slightly out of tune. All sorts of factors can affect the pitch of each string — temperature and humidity changes, drafts, playing loud music where the bow pushes heavily on the string — so you need to know how to tune effectively, right from the start.

You may be wondering how to know when your violin needs tuning. Well, a big clue may be that everyone in the house is walking around wearing earplugs! But seriously, you're able to tell because the songs sound strange when your violin's out of tune. Sometimes, a peg slips a whole lot and the string looks really loose — in which case, you can tighten it to look like the other strings before you begin to tune it to an exact pitch.

Just to help you along a bit, you can listen to the correct tuning of each string — G, D, A, E — on the CD-ROM (Track 1).

Pitch

Pitch isn't a term you just throw around. Rather, pitch has become clearly defined over the ages and is now fairly consistent throughout the world.

Today, pitches are internationally defined by the _frequency_ (number of vibrations per second) of each sound in the musical scale, from the lowest to the highest note. The present standard, which was adopted in 1939, is that A above middle C — the violin's A string is the international standard — has 440 vibrations per second.

In the olden days, a whole panoply of pitches existed, and they caused plenty of confusion. In Bach's time, even the tuning of organs in two churches in the same area could use different pitches. Poor old Bach, in addition to writing a complete new cantata for every Sunday service

and looking after Mrs. Bach and the 20 kids, would have to sit down and rewrite various orchestral parts to suit the pitch of the new church organ.

As you might expect, music history includes several attempts to improve this random pitch situation. The first official ruling came from the Paris Academy in 1859 (The Paris Academy was so fond of making rulings, you'd think they would've gotten into the business of manufacturing music manuscript paper!). The violin's A was set at 435 cycles per second, a little lower than today's A. In 1885, a conference held in Vienna called the standard _international pitch,_ and it prevailed until the 1939 adjustment to A-440, still in use today.

Violinists tune their instruments by tightening or loosening the tension of each string until it sounds at the correct pitch. Turning the pegs or the fine tuners is the way to tune your strings. **_Remember:_** The tighter the string, the higher the pitch.

The whole business is made more fiddly (heh, heh) by the fact that most beginners don't have much dexterity in managing the pegs, which can be tricky little monsters. First-time violinists may also need help in finding the right pitch for each string. No problem; this book is here to help you.

Working the pegs and fine tuners

A beginner violinist eventually becomes best buddies with the pegs and fine tuners, but at first, using them feels pretty strange, and they don't always behave perfectly. This section shows you how to manage pegs and fine tuners when they're being good; the "Troubleshooting Guide to Dealing with Pegs and Fine Tuners" section (near the end of this chapter) helps you when they're being naughty. I recommend doing some trial runs with the pegs and fine tuners before you actually start tuning to specific notes, so that you get a feel for the process without the pressure of doing it precisely right away.

Fine-tuning your violin

The easiest way for a beginner to tune the violin is by using the fine tuners, which work well if the strings need only a little adjustment in tension to get in tune. When turning your fine tuners, remember this great rhyme:

"Righty, tighty; lefty, loosey."

You usually need to turn a fine tuner for one or two complete turns before you can hear a change in the pitch of the note. So don't be afraid to turn them freely — you can always turn them back again, if you don't like what you hear!

Tuning is ordinarily done with the bow sounding the open strings. But for now, I show you how to tune your violin using your right hand to pluck each string, because it's easier to manage (and because you haven't yet used the bow).

Sit in a chair, and then place the violin on your left knee, scroll end up. Hold the violin with your left hand around the neck (of the violin, that is!), with the front of the violin facing you (refer to "Examining the Violin," earlier in this chapter, where I name the violin's parts). With your right hand, pluck each string with your thumb, a bit like a guitarist. Turn the fine tuners using your right thumb and index finger together: right = tight (clockwise), and left = loose (counterclockwise — or anticlockwise to Brits!). Check out Figure 2-4 to see how to turn the fine tuners, and check out the CD-ROM to see fine tuners in use.

Tuning with pegs

The most important thing for beginners to know about tuning is that turning the peg even a quarter-turn makes a considerable difference to the string's pitch. So turn only a little bit at a time — about one-eighth of a turn is a good starting point. If you think of the circular turning of the peg as hands on a clock face, each "hour" you turn makes the string sound distinctly different.

Tuning with pegs is a lot more fiddly than tuning with fine tuners. But you're finding out how to fiddle, after all! Pegs are slightly narrower at the far end from the "handle" bit that you turn, a design that helps them stay in place by being wedged in with a slight push as you tune.

Sometimes pegs can feel stuck in place, and in that case, it helps to loosen the string by a quarter-turn before you attempt to tighten it. As with your first acquaintance with fine tuners, I recommend that you hold the violin facing you on your knee, with the scroll end up, for your first peg-tuning adventure! To keep things simple, the bow doesn't play any part in this initial process. It's fine to pluck the string gently with your free thumb to hear the pitch.

For peg tuning, you can choose any string to tune first, *except* the E string, which rarely requires this kind of tuning, due to being made of hardier steel wire, which is less susceptible to pitch changes. Also, it's your tightest string, and therefore, it's likely to break without too much encouragement.

Figure 2-4:
Tuning with
the fine
tuners.

If you're right-handed, you may be most comfortable holding the violin's neck with your left hand and making adjustments to the Λ string peg (see Figure 2-5) with your right hand.

For lefties, you can hold the violin's neck securely with your right hand and tune the D or G string by turning the pegs with your left hand. Having your dominant hand turn the peg at first helps build your confidence and strength.

To make the pitch higher, turn the peg so that its top edge moves toward the scroll end of the violin. To make the pitch lower, turn the top edge of the peg toward the body of the violin. You can see what turning the pegs looks like on the CD-ROM.

Playing the violin is one activity where left-handed people are at an advantage, because, eventually, you bow the violin with your right hand on the bow, you operate the fine tuners and pegs with your left hand, and you do all the fiddly fingering stuff with your left-hand fingers. For once, the world favors left-handers!

Figure 2-5:
Tuning with
the pegs.

Tuning with the piano

If you happen to have a piano hanging around the place, tuning with the piano works very well. You can play the note you want and then press the sustaining pedal with your right foot so that the note goes on sounding while you tune your violin string to match. Pianos stay in tune for much longer than violins; they need a professional tuning about every six months, usually at the major season changes. And of course, digital pianos don't need to be tuned.

The names of the violin's open strings from lowest to highest (the thickest string to the thinnest string) are G, D, A, and E. Figure 2-6 shows which notes you play if you have a piano or keyboard to match the violin and get it in tune.

"Middle C"

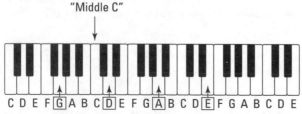

Figure 2-6:
Tuning with
the piano.

C D E F G A B C D E F G A B C D E F G A B C D E

Finding a musician-guru

If you happen to know an experienced musician (even if this person doesn't play the violin), asking for a little help in the early stages of finding out how to tune your violin is useful. Musicians are almost always happy to share their expertise — if you don't call them at 2 a.m.! Getting a second pair of ears to listen with you can be good for your confidence, and soon, you're able to tune by yourself.

Play G below middle C on the piano. Sing or hum that note. Pluck the G string of your violin — the one on the far left when the violin faces you — and then sing that pitch. Many violinists have some choir singing experience from school or church or being in a teenage rock group, so they can tell if their violin's G is lower or higher than the desired pitch by singing and then comparing the two pitches. If singing isn't your forte, press down the right sustaining pedal of the piano with your foot so that the piano G hangs on a lot longer while you compare with your plucked string.

If the violin's G sounds lower than the piano's G, turn the fine tuner to the right. And yes, if the violin's G is higher than the piano's, turn the tuner to the left.

You may need to make up to three full turns of the fine tuner to change pitch to the next note.

Using an electronic tuner

In addition to using the piano to tune your violin (refer to the previous section), another tuning method that works well for most violinists is using an electronic tuner — it's cool and high-tech too (check out Intellitouch tuners, for example). You can see an example of an electronic tuner in Figure 2-7. A basic electronic chromatic tuner costs about $25 in a music store, and they're easy to use:

1. **Switch the tuner on.**

2. **Pluck the violin's G string.**

3. **Watch the gauge on the tuner, where you see a little needle moving around.**

   The needle registers the pitch and tells you if your note is too low or too high.

4. **Make the adjustments to the violin string using the fine tuners (tighten if the note is too low, or loosen if it's too high).**

5. **Pluck the string again.**

   The tuner keeps telling you how you're doing as you adjust, until the little needle of the tuner is on target (pointing to the middle of the gauge).

6. **When the needle stays in the center of the gauge — bingo!**

   Your violin is in tune.

7. **Continue through the D, A, and E strings using Steps 3 through 6.**

Using a pitch pipe

If you're lucky, your violin outfit may be equipped with a pitch pipe (like the one shown in Figure 2-8). All sorts of pitch pipes are available at specialist music stores — some are geared to suit guitars or choirs, and others are especially for violins. A pitch pipe is a very low-tech and handy item to keep in a compartment of your violin case because it's light and portable and can be activated by your breath. The pitch pipe isn't the most reliable tuning device ever — because the notes it produces vary somewhat in pitch according to how hard you blow — but it does give you a good idea of the sound of each string.

Figure 2-7:
An
electronic
tuner.

Chromatic tuners

Chromatic tuners first appeared on the market around 1975 and are probably the most popular and effective tuners available today. Before that, precision tuning had not been generally available to musicians. Chromatic tuners are probably the best way to go for beginners, because they allow you to tune accurately. These tuners may cost a bit more than a machine that merely generates a fixed pitch, but they're worth the expenditure.

Toward the end of the '70s, tuners began to feature an electronic meter (not unlike an old car speedometer) that had a quartz oscillator needle to show how close your tuning was to the desired pitch.

By 1985, compact LED meter tuners were generally available, some with a metronome incorporated — and you can't beat that!

Chromatic tuners are really useful to your violin tuning process, because they also tell you what note you're playing right now. This feature lets you figure out how to get to the note you want, just like a map helps you to get somewhere only if you know where you are right now.

Finding the best chromatic tuner for tuning your violin may take a few visits to different music stores, but it's worth the effort. Look for three main features:

✔ Needle indicator

✔ Lights or signs to tell you when you tune your string too high or too low

✔ Lights to indicate the name of the note you're playing

Blowing into a pitch pipe, you can produce each of the violin's four pitches: G, D, A, and E. Starting with the lowest string, G, play the G on the pitch pipe (each pipe has the note's name on it), and then continue through the D, A, and E strings, tuning each string to match the pitch pipe's sound.

Using a tuning fork

This nifty invention dates from 1711, when John Shore, a Royal trumpeter and lutenist, figured out that he and his mates sounded a lot more dignified when they were well in tune with each other. This pocket-sized piece of metal consists of a handle (stem) and two tines. A quick rap, preferably not on the knuckles, sets the tines vibrating.

Today, many musicians keep a tuning fork (shown in Figure 2-9) in the violin case, for ease of tuning the A string. With a little experience, you can get the other strings to the correct pitch after you have tuned the violin's A to the tuning fork's A.

Figure 2-8:
A pitch pipe.

The sound fades rather quickly with a regular tuning fork, so scientists invented electrically driven versions (after electricity came along, of course) to sustain the sound for longer periods of time. Nowadays, most electronic metronomes have a setting that sounds a sustained A for tuning purposes.

To make the tuning fork sound, hold it by the stem, tap the tines firmly on your knee, and then touch the very end of the stem lightly on the top of your violin to amplify the sound. You hear a pure and ethereal-sounding A, which is the pitch to which you tune your violin's A string. You can also hear the note of a tuning fork by tapping the fork and then holding it next to your ear, but the sound is less clear.

Figure 2-9:
You can't
eat dinner
with a
tuning fork.

Troubleshooting Guide to Dealing with Pegs and Fine Tuners

No matter how much you baby your violin, it still goes out of tune. And sometimes, your little buddies — the pegs and fine tuners — stubbornly refuse to do their job. So I list some of the most common problems you face, as well as the solutions.

Peg problems

Sometimes pegs are hard to turn or don't stay firmly in place. Pegs are made from different wood than the main body of the violin, so the pegs expand and contract at different rates with natural heat and humidity changes. Before you peg out, here are the common problems violinists have with pegs, and some handy suggestions for overcoming them:

- ✔ **The peg won't stay in place once you reach the pitch.** Solution: As you near the desired pitch, hold firmly around the neck of the violin, and then push the peg in toward the pegbox as you turn —it's like putting a cork back in a bottle! Figure 2-10 illustrates how to push the peg in place.

- ✔ **The peg won't move.** Solution: Gently pull the peg outward (as though you're unscrewing it) from the pegbox (as shown in Figure 2-11) as you turn. The peg usually loosens. Loosening the tension of the string usually releases the friction before you tune up again.

✔ **The peg is generally hard to turn.** Solution: Commercial compounds are available that coat pegs with a smooth substance. The compound is commonly sold in a small stick, like a tube of lipstick, and it used to be labeled "Peg Dope" before too many shipments got held up in customs! (But many violinists still call it "peg dope" anyway.) You can apply the compound to the two circular tracks on the peg where it comes into contact with the peg hole, and the peg will then turn smoothly. Figure 2-12 shows you where the circular tracks are. You need to undo the string and then remove the peg completely in order to apply the compound. Try turning the peg a few times in the peg holes before restringing the violin to be sure that you're happy with the feel. If you don't have "peg dope," scribbling on the peg at the same circular tracks with a soft pencil also helps it turn more smoothly.

If a peg is really stuck, don't force it. Take your violin to a professional repair-person. Forcing a peg into the peg hole can damage the scroll or break the peg. Also, if your violin gets a small crack or needs any repair, don't get Uncle Arthur's crazy glue out of the garage. Take your violin to a reputable shop or repair specialist, where a qualified "doctor" can take care of your instrument and restore it to health.

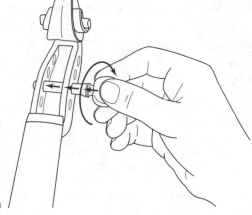

Figure 2-10:
Pushing the peg in place.

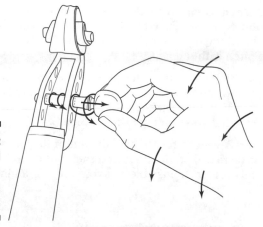

Figure 2-11:
Turning and pulling a stubborn peg.

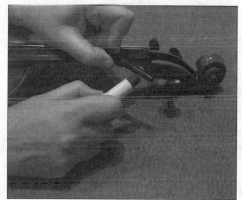

Figure 2-12:
Applying "peg dope."

Fine tuner problems

Fine tuners are generally easier to deal with than pegs because they're mechanical devices made of metal, fixed into their grooves and not subject to such variations in weather as are wooden pegs. You can overcome fine tuner problems more easily than peg problems:

✔ **The fine tuner is stiff to turn.** Solution: Apply a little graphite by scribbling with a soft pencil on the thread of the screw. You can also apply a little dry soap (as in an old cake of soap that's never seen water) to the thread of the screw (see Figure 2-13). This solution works well unless the thread of the screw is cross-grained, in which case you may need to take the violin to the shop to have the fine tuner replaced (fortunately, not an expensive endeavor!).

✔ **The fine tuner is turned so far down that the end of the screw is scratching the violin.** Solution: Unscrew the fine tuner as far as it will go (without falling out and rolling under the baseboards!), and then tune the string close to pitch with the peg.

Checking on the condition of the fine tuners once a week, making sure they aren't screwed down too far, is good for preventing any gouges to the top of your violin. Also, you can keep the fine tuners in the middle of their turning range so that you don't get them stuck.

✔ **The fine tuner is unscrewed so far that it falls out of its groove.** Solution: Find the little rascal on the floor and then put it back in gently, keeping the screw as upright as possible to avoid cross-graining the mechanism.

Figure 2-13:
Using a soft pencil to help the fine tuners turn smoothly.

Chapter 3

Holding Up Well

• •

• •

*V*iolins are beautiful instruments, but they can be tricky to hold, due to the force of gravity! You can see from old paintings and photographs that the violin hold has changed and evolved a lot over the years. Quite a few variations of holds exist, but everyone wants the same thing: to be comfortable and have ease of movement. In this chapter, I look at how you can find a violin hold that works for you.

Understanding the Importance of a Good Violin Hold

A good violin hold makes your playing job much easier. Taking care to make your violin as balanced as possible when you start playing is worth the effort — and so is checking on its balance from time to time as you progress. If you hold your violin the right way, you play well and in tune, your fingers move with ease, and your shoulders are fairly relaxed.

Keep both your shoulders at the same level and move your arms with as little tension as possible when holding a violin, to ensure that you don't experience any muscle problems or pain.

You can sit or stand to play your violin. Traditionally, violinists stand to practice or play solos, and they sit to play chamber music or while in orchestra. However, you can practice sitting down, too, as long as you maintain a balanced and comfortable posture.

When standing

I recommend that you first try the standing position without your violin. If guitarists can play the air guitar, why can't violinists play the "air violin"? Here's how:

1. **Stand comfortably, looking straight ahead, with your weight balanced equally on both feet, which are about shoulder-width apart.**

2. **Hold an imaginary tray in front of you with both hands.**

3. **Keep your elbow bent at about the same "tray" angle throughout this move. Swing your left hand up and over to the left, until it is a bit further out than your shoulder and just under shoulder height.**

   The outer side of your left palm and pinky finger are facing toward you. Keep your hand somewhat cupped and relaxed.

4. **Roll your right hand over so that your palm is facing down, something like holding lightly onto the handlebar of a bicycle.**

5. **Swing your "bow" arm freely toward your "violin." Swing back and forth a few times to get a general feel for the activity.**

   You can even waggle your left-hand fingers for a more realistic effect!

Playing the air violin gives you a sense of the freedom of movement you look for when you play your real violin.

Keeping your knees flexible, not firmly locked into position, when you're playing allows your whole body to absorb all the waves of movement.

Okay, you're ready to try the real thing. Remember that in all these preliminary steps, the violin remains basically parallel to the floor while your face looks forward. This stance feels pretty weird, but it helps you to arrive well in position. See Figure 3-1 for a demonstration; you also can watch it on the CD-ROM. One way to bring the violin into playing position is to do the following (Check out Chapter 2 if you're unclear about the names of any of the parts of the violin.):

1. **Pick up the violin from its case or a table top, with the scroll end to your left.**

   To do this, hold the neck of the violin on the upturned palm of your left hand, with your fingers curved gently around the violin's neck and your thumb across the strings.

   Hold the top end of the violin's body with your right hand. Your thumb is resting gently on the chinrest, your index finger is along the ribs, and your other fingers are resting on the back of the instrument.

2. **Continue cradling the neck of the violin with your left hand, and then, keeping your right hand as described in Step 1, hold the violin in front of your middle, like a tray. (See Figure 3-1a.)**

   Refer to Step 2 of the "air violin" method.

3. **With both hands in place, lift the violin up and a bit toward the left, keeping it on a horizontal plane.**

4. **As you move your violin upward, turn the violin in a clockwise motion, bringing the tailpiece button toward the center-left side of your neck and, at the same time, extending your left arm to move the scroll away from you, close to its final destination.**

5. **Slide your right hand lightly away from you — along the curve of the violin's ribs on the E-string side — while you bring the violin toward your playing position, and then let your right hand come to rest in any comfortable spot on the side of the violin, a few inches to the right of your chinrest.**

   If you think of straight ahead as being 0 degrees, violinists usually aim their scrolls between 50 and 70 degrees out to the left, depending on the shape of their shoulders and jaw, and their general physique. Comfort and ease of movement determine the ideal angle for each player.

   At this point, the violin is placed over the length of your extended left arm, and the tailpiece button is about at the height of your left jaw, just like in Figure 3-1b.

6. **Bring the violin gently toward you, and then rest the back edge of the violin (under the chinrest and tailpiece area) on your left collarbone.**

   The ribs of the violin, just to the left of the tailpiece button, touch your neck below your left jaw. When the violin is in place, its tailpiece button is quite near the center of your throat. The E-string side of the violin probably sits slightly lower than the G-string side, the exact alignment depending on your collarbone and shoulder anatomy.

   As you prepare to bring the violin into playing position, the line along your left forearm from elbow to knuckles is fairly straight.

7. **Notice that when the violin is close to your neck and resting on your collarbone, the violin's neck slides into the *U* shape between your thumb and index finger, and the fingers of your lightly rounded hand hover over the strings to make a preliminary left-hand shape.**

   The details of your left hand placement are described in Chapter 5 — your left hand eventually sits about an inch lower in relation to the violin's neck, and you make a little space between the *U* of your thumb and the underside of the violin's neck. But allowing the violin to sit in the *U* as a preliminary move helps to shape the hand and to hold the violin comfortably as you get started.

8. **Turn your head on a horizontal axis, and then look along the fingerboard toward the scroll of the violin.**

9. **Gently lower the left side of your jaw onto the chinrest, as shown in Figure 3-1c.**

Done! Your right hand can continue to support the body of the violin until you feel ready to let go and support the instrument with your left side alone.

When sitting

Just like your parents asked you not to slouch at the dinner table, I'm asking you not to slouch when you play sitting down. Keeping a balanced posture leads to a good playing experience. Both comfort and functionality are at their best when you sit on a chair that has a flat seat and you keep your hips and shoulders well aligned.

Figure 3-1: Holding the violin; swinging it up into playing position.

The quickest and easiest way to play in a seated position is to begin in resting position, which I describe here and show you on the CD-ROM:

1. **Sit on the front half of the seat, and keep both feet flat on the ground.**

2. **Make sure that your back is comfortably straight and your shoulders and hips are aligned.**

3. **Hold your violin with its back toward you, the scroll pointing toward the ceiling and the button end of the violin resting on your left leg near the knee, as shown in Figure 3-2a.**

   Imagine your left hand is holding on to a glass of cool juice — but instead, hold the violin's neck (thumb side up) lightly near the scroll end.

4. **Swing the violin up into playing position easily, as shown in Figure 3-2b.**

Your right hand can help with steadying and supporting the violin as you lift it into playing position.

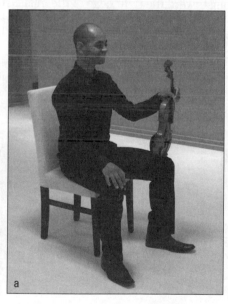

Figure 3-2:
Sitting
position
with violin in
resting
position; in
playing
position.

a

b

Reading from a Music Stand

You might feel pretty silly just standing (or sitting) there, holding your violin. But when you have a music stand, you look like you know what you're doing — even though you likely can't play a note of music yet (don't worry, I won't tell anyone).

In both standing and sitting positions, the height of the music stand's shelf is most comfortably set for practice at close to the same height as the player's shoulders (or a tad lower) for good sightlines. In concert performances, the stand is set lower than it is during practice so that the audience has a good view of the violinist — but by the time you're ready to perform, you have a good sense of what's on the page.

A readily adjustable music stand, such as a Manhasset or Wenger stand, is a good investment for use as your home stand. A light metal folding stand is useful when transporting it to gigs, going to friends' houses to play, or taking it to orchestra rehearsals. Even extra-tall folding stands are available, useful to those who are taller than about 5 foot 10 inches.

The best way to read and play at the same time is to stand or sit so that the violin's scroll is pointing toward the outer edge of the left page of music.

This stance enables you to bow freely and to look comfortably at the music without twisting your head. You may need to stand or sit with your feet (and consequently, your body) facing toward the right edge of the music stand, so that your body remains well aligned while playing. Figure 3-3a shows the correct position while sitting, and Figure 3-3b shows the correct position while standing.

If you stand or sit with your body facing the music stand squarely, the frog of the bow can easily bump the stand as you bow, and you need to put your head at an uncomfortable angle to see the music.

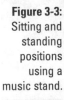

Figure 3-3: Sitting and standing positions using a music stand.

Finding a Good Fit: Chinrests and Shoulder Rests

In the old days, violin players didn't use chinrests or shoulder rests. But playing was a simpler process back then. Violinists didn't try a bunch of tricky techniques with their left hands, so it was okay to hold the violin casually. With the arrival of such amazing acrobats as Paganini, violin technique regularly called for a lot more movement, and so players began to look for ways to support their instrument while keeping their arms free. Whether Paganini himself used a chinrest isn't certain, but almost all violinists (and violists) use one nowadays. Most players use a shoulder rest, too.

Finding the right chinrest and shoulder rest is a very individual process, rather like finding a comfortable pair of shoes. The good news is that, although violins come equipped with a chinrest that's already attached, chinrests are easy to put on and take off. Most violin stores give you a choice of chinrests when you buy your violin.

Don't be afraid to ask to try a few different chinrests if the one that comes with the violin you're interested in buying feels uncomfortable. Specialist violin stores are used to helping violinists choose the right chinrest, and they're happy to have a comfortable and satisfied customer.

Chinrests

Keeping your chin and jaw clear of the top of the violin means less damping of sound and less damage to the varnish from the heat and sweat of your chin. (You can see patches of lighter or darker wood on the tops of old violins where the players' chins used to rest. Modern violin makers sometimes imitate this look when building new instruments so that the violins look "antiqued.")

Chinrest history

The first chinrest was a kind of simple wooden block, placed over the violin's tailpiece. But soon after, a small crescent-shaped model, fitted on top of the violin to the left of the tailpiece, became the most popular chinrest. This design gives the player something to steady the instrument and keeps the chin off the top of the violin.

The chinrests in use today evolved from a model invented by the German violin virtuoso, composer, and conductor Louis Spohr in about 1820. Spohr was one smart cookie and a very innovative musician. In addition to the chinrest, he is responsible for inventing the system, still in use today, of marking musical scores with letters in alphabetical order to indicate the beginning of each new section in a piece of music, very helpful for finding your place during rehearsals. He was also one of the very first conductors to use a baton for better clarity and visibility of the beat.

Leading violinist-composers of the mid-1800s such as Viotti and Baillot also promoted the use of chinrests. Their music is characterized by very free movements of the left hand, techniques that became easier with the advent of the chinrest.

Today's chinrests come in a range of shapes and sizes, to suit just about everyone. A plastic chinrest can retail at less than $10, and a top-of-the-line handmade wooden chinrest can cost more than $100. Expect to pay between $6 and $40 for a chinrest that will work for you and your violin.

The elements that are important in a chinrest are height, shape, and angle — all variables in the designs of the many chinrest models you can see at a well-stocked violin store. You can find models made of plastic or wood, such as ebony and rosewood, plus several other options. Professional violinists often match the wood of the chinrest to the wood of the tailpiece, but at the beginning, a black plastic chinrest that matches the ebony of the fingerboard looks quite fine. Make a modest investment until you become used to holding the violin and develop specific preferences about your chinrest.

Choosing a chinrest

The number and choice of available chinrests will clue you in to how individual their fittings can be! If your chinrest doesn't feel comfortable, playing the violin won't be the joy you'd anticipated. In this section, I show you the four main types of chinrests, and I suggest who might be suited to each type.

When choosing a chinrest, be sure to look for a gently rounded edge on the cupped part where you place your jaw!

Here are the available styles of chinrests, shown in Figure 3-4:

- **Tekka:** These models are installed just to the left of the violin's tailpiece, and they're the kind many young students have on their violins. Tekka could be described as a middle-of-the-road chinrest, though you probably don't want to leave your chinrest in the middle of the road! This style of chinrest is certainly worth a try.

- **Vermeer:** These models are shaped so that they go halfway across the violin's tailpiece, allowing the player's head to balance more centrally on the instrument. Vermeer models can be useful to violinists with shorter arms, because the violin sits a little farther to the left side, making it easier to bow all the way to the tip. However, the height of these chinrests is also greater because they have to clear the tailpiece. If you have shorter arms and a longer neck, these models may work for you.

- **Flesch:** These chinrests are installed directly in the middle of the violin, across the tailpiece. As with the Vermeer model, you will be comfortable on this kind of chinrest only if you have a fairly long neck. Some Flesch chinrests have a raised middle ridge, which seems to work well for violinists with narrower chins. Tall, willowy violinists often find Flesch-style chinrests useful because, in addition to their height, they have the added advantage of balancing the violin more centrally, which makes it seem lighter.

✔ *Guarneri:* These chinrests are made in what's perhaps the most generally comfortable style. This model has the chinrest just to the left of the tailpiece, but it also features a bar that runs across to the right side of the tailpiece. Violinists can hold the violin fairly freely and allow their heads some latitude — the cup is not deep, and the bar across the tailpiece is also comfortable to rest on. Violinists with fairly square or fleshy jaws, or who don't hold their violins very snugly, like these rests.

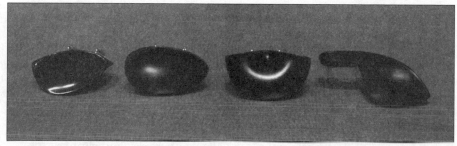

Figure 3-4:
Four kinds
of chinrests:
Tekka,
Vermeer,
Flesch, and
Guarneri.

Chinrests are available in different heights. The cup for your chin can also vary greatly in size. Finding the right height means getting a chinrest that fits the length of your neck when the violin is resting on your collarbone and in playing position. I don't advise getting a chinrest that fills the space completely, because you will be stuck in one position, but you shouldn't have to clamp down, either. As long as you have a chinrest that is reasonably comfortable to start with, you can always change to one you like better as your playing evolves.

Shoulder rests

Telephones have 'em, camcorders have 'em, and violins have 'em too. I'm talking about shoulder rests, which have been around for about 150 years.

A *shoulder rest* is a bracket or cushion that fits on to the back of the violin and helps the player to support the instrument. The violin needs support because there is a bit of space between the back of the violin and the shoulder and pectoral area.

You can support your violin just fine on your collarbone, with a little help from your left hand. But for many players, the slippery wood and the playing movements of the left hand make the violin feel somewhat unsteady. I'd like to be able to tell you that included in all the useful parts that make up the violin (refer to Chapter 2) is an invisible shelf that supports the violin perfectly on your shoulder as you play. Oh well. Until violin makers tune in to my wild imagination, violinists the world over have to deal with shoulder rests. Fortunately, shoulder rests help to fill the space between your shoulder and the violin, and thus make playing feel comfortable and easy.

REMEMBER

Although violins come ready-fitted with a chinrest, you buy your shoulder rest separately.

Choosing a shoulder rest

As with chinrests, you can choose from lots of shoulder rest models, so here's a closer look at what's involved. Ideally, a shoulder rest should do the following things:

- Function rather like a lever. When you use a shoulder rest, if you press down lightly on the chinrest with your head, the scroll end of the violin should move up slightly. The extra lightness eases the movements of your left hand.

- Fill the space between your shoulder and the back of the violin. Filling this space combats the effects of gravity and slipperiness.

- Damp the sound as little as possible. Sound quality suffers when your shoulder rest contacts the body of the violin over a large area.

- Leave plenty of freedom of movement for your neck and arms.

Shoulder rests fall into two broad categories: bracket-type and cushion-type models (Figure 3-5 shows you an example of each). Any good rest is adjustable in height and in position, or is available in different heights so that it can fit many different body types.

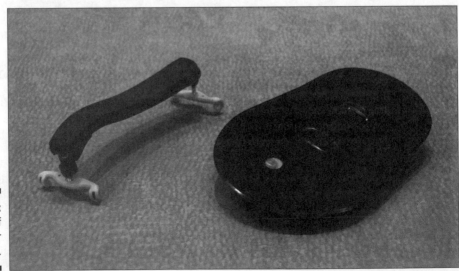

Figure 3-5: Two types of shoulder rests.

To get the right shoulder rest, try on quite a few at the store to find out which one is the most comfortable for you. Most shoulder rests retail between $15 and $25, so if you want to try a different one after you've been playing for a while, you won't be faced with a major expense.

Watch the demo on your CD-ROM, which illustrates how to set up, put on, and adjust the fit of the main types of shoulder rests.

Fixing Common Problems with the Violin Hold

If gravity didn't exist, I wouldn't have to give you all this information about problems with the violin hold. Violins would just float around, and you would be able to play lightly on a lovely Stradivarius as it wafted by. However, the reality is that you do have to support your violin in the most practical and comfortable way possible, and sometimes this can be tricky.

Keeping the scroll afloat

The most common problem violinists encounter when first coming to grips with the violin is that the scroll gravitates too much toward the center of the body (because players instinctively want to see what their hands are doing) and then starts to sink down a little as they play.

Keeping the scroll out a little to the left of your shoulder makes it easy for your bow to travel on track. A useful way to practice putting your scroll in position is by holding the violin as usual, picking up the bow, and then placing the middle of the bow on the A and D strings together, as shown in Figure 3-6. At this stage, both your elbows are about the same distance out from the side seam of your shirt or sweater, giving you a sense of the balance that exists between the two sides.

Watching the horizontal angle

Another common problem is that holding the violin at a completely horizontal angle isn't favorable to comfortable playing, and comfort is very important. For most players, the right side of the violin sits between 10 and 30 degrees lower than the left side. You can tell if the angle of the violin is about right for you by setting your bow, near the tip, on the E string. Your right arm should be relaxed and fairly perpendicular, and your right hand not too far from your side. See Figure 3-7 for an example of a good horizontal angle. The angle of your shoulders also plays a role, so you have to steer a middle path between what is comfortable and what is necessary when setting up.

The angle at which you hold your violin depends on your body type. If you're a lightly built person, you may hold your violin at a slightly steeper angle than a person of substance does.

Figure 3-6:
Keep your arms balanced.

Keeping your elbow under

When you first begin playing the violin, you may find it tempting to stick your left elbow quite far out to the left side. Remember, just keep your elbow more or less under the main body of the violin for now. (I give that elbow more marching orders in Chapter 6.) When your elbow is under the violin, your upper arm is pretty relaxed, which saves your energy for the task "at hand." If you look downward through the "waist" of the violin on the E-string side, you can see a glimpse of your sleeve, which tells you that your arm position is correct, as shown in Figure 3-8.

Figure 3-7:
The
horizontal
angle.

Gripping too much with the shoulder

Initially, your left shoulder may want to pull upward quite strongly to support
the violin. (And if at first you don't notice that your shoulder's too high, you'll
probably know after a few minutes — ouch!) Negotiate most diplomatically
with your shoulder, and ask it to cease and desist from tensing up. The violin
may feel unfamiliar, but it is a light object and doesn't need heavy-duty
hydraulics to hold it up. If your shoulder tenses up, take the violin down for a

few seconds, give your left arm a few free swings, and then try to set up the violin hold again. Stay aware of keeping your shoulders as relaxed as possible while balancing the instrument between your shoulder area and your left hand.

Figure 3-8:
The correct elbow position.

Part II
Getting Started: The Basics

The 5th Wave   By Rich Tennant

"Try this bow. The horsehairs came from a
Triple Crown winner, so you may tend to
rush the tempo a bit."

In this part . . .

*W*hen you find out the basics of tuning and holding your violin, I bet you can't wait to play it for real. Even if you're itching to put everything together, take the time to get each basic step right before you move on — you'll be thrilled at the lovely sounds you can make. Chapter 4 is all about your right hand, showing you how to handle the bow before you get your left hand to shape up (but not ship out) in Chapter 5. In the last chapter of this section, Chapter 6, you put both hands officially together to play some real songs. You're up and running!

Chapter 4

Taking a Bow

. . . .

In This Chapter

▶ Getting to know your bow

▶ Caring for your bow

▶ Holding your bow properly

▶ Putting your bow to the strings

▶ Bowing a few tunes

▶ Comparing two bowing styles

. . . .

The violin bow may look simple, but it's actually quite a complex piece of equipment. Bows have come a long way from the original bow-and-arrow shape they began with in ancient times. Both Robin Hood and William Tell would be mighty impressed!

Take a look in any music shop, and you might be surprised at how many types and makes of bows are available to buy. Most violinists consider French bows to be the most precious and refined *(mais oui!)*, although some famous players prefer English or German bows. Funnily enough, the most beautiful violins, violas, and cellos are made in Italy, but the country isn't renowned for its bows.

Anyway, all you need for now is a sturdy and functional bow that doesn't cost a whole lot of money. The bow that comes with your violin could be just the thing (for more information about renting or buying a bow, see Chapter 16).

In this chapter, you find out all about getting started with the bow — from making sure it's in tip-top shape to drawing out those first sounds from your violin.

Looking at the Bow

Would you like to meet the violin's literal right-hand man? Let me introduce you to the bow. This unassuming stick is actually a remarkable piece of engineering, and it's responsible for making your violin sound its best. You can refer to Figure 4-1 as I tell you about all the bow's wonderful little complexities.

- **Eye:** The circular inlay on each side of the *frog*. Eyes usually have a mother-of-pearl center with a silver ring around it.

- **Ferrule:** This is a metal band (but luckily not heavy metal!) that's usually made of nickel or silver, and it surrounds the frog where the horsehair is attached. The ferrule's job is to keep the bow's horsehair evenly aligned for a consistent sound. The bow maker slips the ferrule off when *rehairing* the bow (see Chapter 17).

- **Frog:** Usually made of ebony, the frog forms the end of the bow and houses the screw mechanism, which you use to tighten and loosen the horsehair every time you play your violin. You hold the bow at the frog. (The frog's name actually has nothing to do with amphibians. The word most likely comes from the Portuguese word *froco*, which was the name of a gizmo that clipped a sword onto a belt.)

- **Horsehair:** The ribbon of white hair that strokes the strings to make sounds. Horsehair seems to draw the best sound out of violin strings, because it combines the qualities that make a violin string sing: flexibility, evenness, and a slightly fibrous surface that activates the vibration of the string as you pull the bow. The horsehair used comes from Mongolia, Siberia, Argentina, Australia, or Canada. Mongolian stallion tail seems to be the most prized.

- **Lapping (or winding):** Made from metal thread or synthetic materials, lapping is wrapped snugly around the stick near the frog to protect the bow from wear and tear — and a player's sweat.

- **Point:** The top end of the bow; it's shaped like a letter *V* to be aerodynamic!

- **Screw:** The octagonal metal piece fitted into the end of the stick near the frog; the screw you use to tighten and loosen the horsehair extends along inside the stick over the frog area.

- **Stick:** The long piece of wood from which the bow is carved. Bows are available with circular- or octagonal-shaped sticks, and although some players have strong preferences, a good bow of either shape plays well. All bows retain the octagonal shape at the frog, for ease of holding.

  Bows aren't quite as climate-sensitive as violins, but the wood does expand and contract according to humidity.

- **Thumb leather:** This surrounds the stick where the thumb holds the bow, both for the comfort of the player and for protecting the wood of the stick.

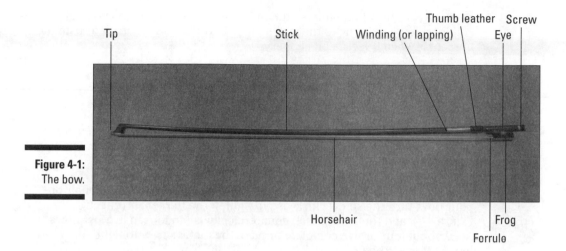

Figure 4-1:
The bow.

Tip　Stick　Winding (or lapping)　Thumb leather　Screw　Eye

Horsehair　Frog　Ferrule

Preparing the Bow

The violin may get all the attention, but the bow is nothing to sneeze at. (Unless you're allergic to rosin, in which case you can actually buy hypoallergenic rosin! See the section "Using rosin on the bow," later in this chapter, for more about rosin.)

The bow is made from some pretty special stuff. Bows have traditionally been made of a strong and springy rainforest wood called *pernambuco*, a wood that comes from the Pernambuco (surprise!) region of Brazil. This special wood is a relative of mahogany.

Because no one wants to chop down all the rainforests so that we can keep making bows, other woods are often being substituted nowadays, including brazilwood, snakewood, and even some composite materials. The ribbon of horsehair used on violin bows comes from the tails of special white Russian horses. You can't say neigh to that!

Your bow requires attentive care because it's made of such rare materials. To keep your bow in tip-top playing condition, you need to do three things:

✓ Tighten the horsehair before playing.

✓ Loosen the horsehair before you put the violin and bow back in the case.

✓ Rosin the horsehair from time to time.

Keeping your bow in tip-top condition is pretty easy, so long as you tighten it and loosen it according to the instructions in the next section, and rosin the horsehair when it feels a bit slippery.

Tightening and loosening the horsehair

Tighten the horsehair before you play, and then loosen it again when you're done. These measures preserve the elasticity of the bow's wood and prevent the ribbon of horsehair from stretching too far.

You can follow these moves on the CD-ROM: To maintain the horsehair on your bow, turn the screw clockwise to tighten the horsehair (check out Figure 4-2), and then (surprise!) counterclockwise to loosen it. Most bows need about four or five complete turns of the metal screw to tighten or loosen the horsehair.

You can tell that your bow is at about the right tension (as shown in Figure 4-3) by inserting the very tip of your pinky finger between the stick and the horsehair at the narrowest point near the middle of the bow. Your fingertip just about fits into the space.

Figure 4-2:
Tightening
the bow.

Figure 4-3:
The right
tension for
playing.

Using rosin on the bow

Rosin is a slightly sticky substance you apply to the bow's horsehair so that your bow doesn't slide all over the place when you set it on the strings. Rosin comes from the sap of various pine trees. By the time you buy it, it has been processed into a small, hard, golden or black cake, round or rectangular in shape, that fits into the palm of your hand. The rosin cake comes either with a cloth backing or mounted into a wooden block, and it's packaged in a neat and enticing little box or velvet pouch.

You probably have a cake of rosin in your violin case, but if not, you can go to a store or view a string catalog online. You may notice a lot of different makes of rosin and a fairly wide variation in prices. Luckily, there's no need to buy anything fancy when you begin. "Student grade" rosin, around $3 to $5, does a good job on your bow.

For violinists who are sensitive or allergic to rosin, hypoallergenic brands exist that don't create any powder or give off any pine scent — the two main allergens in regular rosin.

Keep your rosin wrapped up in its little box or pouch when it's not in use so that the cake doesn't chip, break (which happens quite easily), or come into contact with the case, violin, or anything else you don't want to get covered with sticky rosin powder or fragments.

If you play for about half an hour every day, you'll need to rosin your bow about once a week. Here's how (you can also watch this on the CD-ROM):

1. **Tighten the bow hair as you do for playing.**

2. **Unpack your cake of rosin and hold it in your hand, with the cloth backing or wooden block resting on the palm of your hand.**

   Take care to handle the cake by the cloth or wood and not by the rosin itself. If you touch the rosin, you'll end up with sticky hands and you'll get oily residue from your skin (or plum sauce from your lunch) on the rosin.

3. **Rub the bow hair firmly back and forth on the rosin, about three times up and down (see Figure 4-4).**

   You can rub the cake of rosin back and forth on the bow, or you can rub the bow back and forth on the rosin, whichever works for you.

Figure 4-4:
Putting rosin on the bow hair.

You may need to score the top of a shiny new cake of rosin a few times with a knife to roughen the surface slightly before any of the rosin will rub off on the bow.

Your bow needs rosin when it feels slippery as you play. However, if you see a lot of whitish powder on the strings and on the top of the violin where you bow, there's too much rosin on the bow, and you certainly won't need more for several days!

After playing, use a soft cloth to wipe off the top of the violin, preventing the rosin from sticking to the varnish.

Getting a Grip on Your Bow Hold

How you hold the bow has a real impact on the sound you coax out of your violin. If you look at videos of famous violinists, you see quite a few variations of bow holds. All violinists look for the same thing, though: the right combination of firmness and flexibility.

I've come up with two bow-hold techniques for you to start with. You can use whichever method works best for you, for the next week or two, until you become more familiar with holding the bow. Try out both methods to see which style suits you best.

- **The famous diva method:** This method is rather relaxed and gives you a general feel for how little tension you need to hold the bow.
- **The hidden treasures method:** This method is a bit more precise, familiarizing you with the exact placement of the fingers on the bow stick.

The famous diva method

Yes, you're learning to play the violin, but for the moment, I want you to imagine that you're a world-renowned singer about to deliver your best and longest top note in a Carnegie Hall recital. You're looking cool, calm, and collected. Your right forearm from the elbow to the wrist is resting on a flat surface (the palm of your hand is facing down), which could be the top of your Steinway grand piano, but it's more likely to be a kitchen counter or a shelf!

Now, take a look at the following steps — they walk you through from your starting point and help you to position your hand for a relaxed bow hold. Figure 4-5 shows what a true diva looks like; you can also follow along with the CD-ROM after you work slowly through my instructions.

1. **Stand elegantly by a grand piano (if your grand piano is at the shop, any flat surface that is about at the level of your elbow will do).**

2. **Drape your right forearm over the top surface, letting your hand hang over the edge, facing down, as shown in Figure 4-5a.**

   This is your hand's natural, relaxed shape. In this state, your fingers gently curve inward.

3. **Take the bow horizontally in your left hand, with the bow's tip facing left and the frog facing right, and then pass it to your right hand, frog first (refer to "Looking at the Bow" to get to know the parts of the bow).**

4. **Place your naturally curved thumb into its spot just next to the frog, place your middle finger opposite your thumb, and then your other fingers find their places with ease.**

5. **Rest the tip of your pinky finger on top of the stick.**

   Your right hand holds the bow quite lightly, maintaining the bow's horizontal level as it takes hold. Check out Figure 4-5b for an example.

6. **Release your left hand from the stick, take a step or two away from your piano, gently straighten your wrist so that the back of your hand aligns with your forearm, and then rotate the stick to a vertical position, with the tip pointing toward the ceiling.**

   Figure 4-5c shows you what this last step looks like. In addition to giving you a chance to admire your lovely bow hold, holding the bow vertically is comfortable for violinists when not playing, because it feels light.

The hidden treasures method

Avast, me hearties! Although violins aren't the kind of thing you find in *Pirates of the Caribbean,* a sure-fire way of starting to hold your bow correctly involves marking three *X* spots on your right hand — which makes it look rather like a hidden-treasure map. And when you hold the bow correctly, those *X* spots are . . . *hidden.* Take a felt-tip pen and mark an "X" on the following parts of your right hand (see Figure 4-6):

- On the flesh of the tip of your thumb, about ¼ inch behind the nail and over to the index-finger side

- On the underside of your index finger, toward the thumb side, about midway between the top and middle joints

- In the very middle of the tip of your little (or pinky) finger

After you've marked the three *X* spots, draw a line across the joint crease at the base of each fingertip on the underside of your middle and ring fingers.

Now you're ready to take your bow in your right hand. With your left hand, hold the bow vertically about a quarter of the way up the stick, with the tip pointing toward the ceiling and the wooden stick to the right side. Use the *X*-marked spots as a guide to where your fingers and thumb contact the stick and frog of the bow, following the steps below. When all the "hidden treasure" *X* spots on your right hand are hidden by touching the bow stick, as indicated in Figure 4-6, you indeed have something to treasure: a good bow hold.

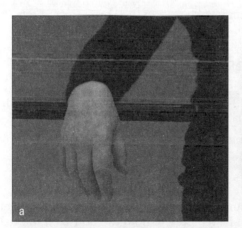

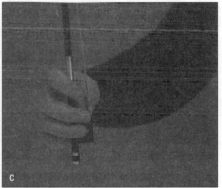

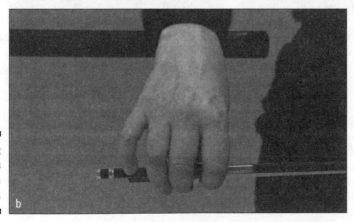

Figure 4-5:
The famous diva method.

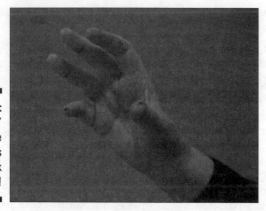

Figure 4-6:
Mark an "X"
on these
spots, or it's
the plank
for ye!

Here's what goes where, and in what order (I show you these moves on your CD-ROM too):

- ✔ Your thumb bends gently and parks in the corner just above the frog, where the wood of the bow meets the ebony of the frog.

- ✔ Your middle finger sits approximately opposite your thumb; the wood of the bow separates them.

- ✔ Your ring finger is placed next to your middle finger, with just a little space between them. The tip of your ring finger sits near to (or on top of, depending on the size of your hand) the eye of the frog.

- ✔ Your little finger sits nicely curved on the top facet of the octagonal end of the wooden bow stick.

- ✔ Your index finger rests a little on its side on top of the stick.

Although the hidden treasure method is great for getting your fingers in just the right places, you might be tempted to hold the bow a bit too tensely. Remember to keep your fingers relaxed.

Keeping the bow tightened and ready across the shelf of a music stand in front of you, frog end to the right and horsehair down, makes it convenient to pick up the bow when you're all set to play.

Conquering common problems with the bow hold

Holding an unusual object that's tricky to balance can certainly feel very strange at first. Your fingers might stiffen up, or your hands might hold the bow too tightly. Here are some tricks to help you:

✔ **If your fingers stiffen:** Some violin players find it useful to imagine that they're holding the handlebar of a bicycle, to keep their right hand rounded.

✔ **If you're holding too tightly:** Violinists who feel they are holding the bow too tightly can imagine that they're holding a baby bird, so that their right hand remains light.

✔ **If your arm tightens up:** Be aware of keeping your shoulders pretty relaxed. A quick and light shrug releases any tension.

No matter which method you choose for setting up your bow hold, maintain a fairly straight line from your elbow, along your forearm, and through your wrist to the back of your hand when you first pick up your bow.

Setting the Bow on the Strings

When you know how to care for and hold your bow, you're ready to set it across the strings of your violin. (I bet you were wondering when we'd get to this part!) Follow these steps to get your bow on the strings:

1. **Place your bow (stick on top) across the shelf of your music stand, with the frog extending slightly over the right end of the stand.**

2. **Get your violin ready in playing position (refer to Chapter 3).**

3. **Lift the bow from the stand, using your preferred bow-hold method, but this time keeping the bow more or less horizontal.**

4. **Place the bow hair, at about the midpoint of the bow, on the E string, which is the one on the far right as you're looking along the violin from the playing position.**

   Figure 4-7 shows you a violinist's-eye view of the bridge and strings.

After you land your bow on the E string, on a track about halfway between the bridge and the top of the fingerboard, draw the bow for small distances to and fro (or to the left and to the right) across the string.

You get a pleasing sound if you play smoothly and use 2 or 3 inches of bow, with the bow traveling parallel to the bridge.

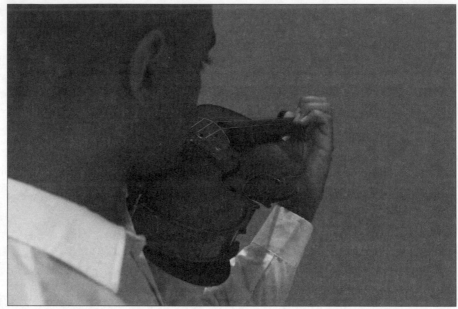

Figure 4-7:
Violinist's-
eye view of
the bridge
and strings.

Bowing on different strings

To bow on different strings, you follow the same steps as for the E string. And then you do a little rock 'n' roll! Think of your bow as a seesaw (or a teeter-totter to some). If you raise your right hand (and the frog of the bow), the bow rolls over the strings, and the tip of the bow lowers accordingly. Your arm's level naturally floats up a little as you roll your bow over to the A string, and again for the D and G strings (and, of course, it floats down a little as you return past the D and A strings to the E-string level).

At first, you can roll the bow over the strings silently by moving your right hand up and down, without drawing the bow. After you have a sense of the different hand levels needed to land the bow on each string, you can rock (or roll) over to the A string to try some small strokes — just like the bowing on the E string. The same technique works for finding the D string and the G string.

At first, until you know which string is which and how the bow should be set on each one, you may find it helpful to set your bow gently on the E string and then roll it over to the string you need.

Diagnosing strange sounds with Dr. Violin

Hi, I'm Dr. Violin, an expert on diagnosing all kinds of violin problems. Today, I'll be answering readers' most frequently asked questions about strange sounds that sometimes happen when bowing.

Q: What do I do if I make a crunchy sound when I play?

A: Use a bit less weight and a bit more speed as you draw the bow stroke.

Q: Why do I make only thin, gauzy sounds?

A: You're probably bowing too close to the fingerboard.

Q: What if I make a screeching sound?

A: Try bowing a little farther away from the bridge!

Thank you; I'll send you my bill.

Here's a useful rhyme to remember the order of the strings until they become familiar to you:

E is first; right hand is low.
A is next; up we go!
Rolling on, we get to D.
Last on the left is good ol' G.
(There are many better poets than poor little me!)

Understanding bowing signs

With your bow already on the strings, you're well on your way to playing a few songs. Before you begin, you need to know two movements and signs:

- **Down-bow:** (⊓) In a down-bow, your hand draws away from the violin as you pull the bow, starting from the frog end, toward the tip.

- **Up-bow:** (∨) In an up-bow, your hand moves toward the violin as you push the bow, starting from the tip, toward the frog.

Figure 4-8 is a short chart you can use to practice your new bowing symbols and their associated movements. Strive for as little variation in sound as possible between your down-bow and up-bow movements. Make each bow stroke equal in the first two examples, and then, in the last two examples, use more bow for the bowing symbols followed by a line.

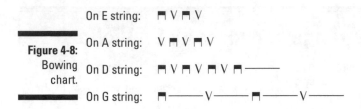

On E string: ⊓ V ⊓ V

On A string: V ⊓ V ⊓ V

On D string: ⊓ V ⊓ V ⊓ V ⊓———

On G string: ⊓——— V——— ⊓——— V———

Figure 4-8:
Bowing
chart.

Playing Your First Concert!

If you're all set with your violin and bow in hand and have a pretty good idea of what you're doing, you're ready to start playing! On the CD-ROM are some songs you can play, as an accompanist or in harmony, using your open strings (no fingers on the strings yet) with short strokes. You can read the charts to figure out what you're going to play. The name of the open string you bow on is written right inside each note head. Have fun!

TRACK 2

Theme from Dvorak's "New World" Symphony

Play along with this lovely theme using your two lowest strings. In preparation to play, put your bow on the G string, setting the bow at about its mid-point. Starting with a down-bow, you remain mostly on G, but occasionally you need to roll over to the D string for a couple of notes. If you make sure your arm's level changes with the bow's level, you sound fine. Use about 6 to 8 inches of bow for this song.

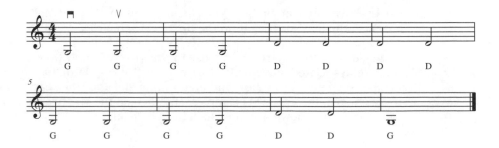

TRACK 3

Jingle Bells

Begin by setting your bow silently on the E string, and then roll the bow across to the A string. Play a down-bow on the A string, for the first note, and then play an up-bow for the second note. Do the same pair of bowings for the next three sets of As. Roll the bow over to the D string for the pair of Ds, which also get one down-bow followed by one up-bow, and then roll back to A for the same pair of bowings. Lastly, sink your whole arm and bow over to your E string for the end of the first section. You can play the second section in almost the same way as the first section, because everything's the same except for the ending bit, where the two Es happen before the final As.

The CD-ROM recording of "Jingle Bells" also includes a staccato version of the song, which I discuss in the next section.

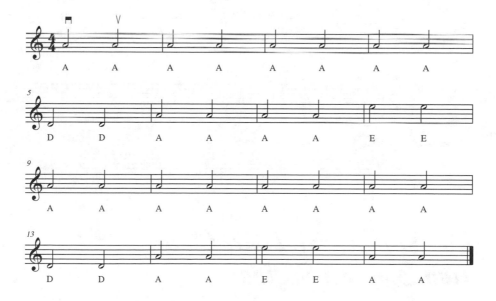

TRACK 4

I've Been Workin' on the Railroad

You may well feel as if you've been working on the railroad after all this practicing, but this old song is a big favorite *and* offers you the chance to bow on three strings with lots of string-level changes. Set your bow one more time on the A string in readiness to start the song with a down-bow. Roll the bow smoothly to the next string whenever you change over, making sure the bow travels parallel to the bridge for a great sound.

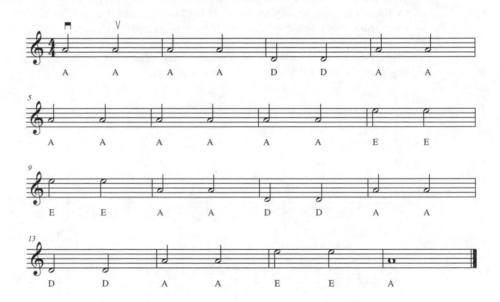

Mr. Smooth and Mr. Clean: Two Bowing Styles

By watching some professional violinists, you may get the crazy idea that bowing is really easy and doesn't involve a lot of technique — that you can simply zigzag across the strings and produce music. But a quick reality check tells you that idea's not true. Your right hand has to be as skilled as your left; in fact, you need to know two basic ways to bow just to get started on your violin. In Chapter 13, I look at some fancier options.

The most basic and common bowing style is called *détaché*. Despite its name (which comes from the French word *détacher*, meaning to disconnect or separate), détaché is actually a smooth bowing style. Instead of bowing only up or only down, you simply change the bow's direction for each note. Détaché bowing strokes can use as much or as little of the bow as you want, but they are often bowed using about a third of the bow around the middle of the stick.

Little did you know that all along, ever since you set your bow on the string and drew out those first sounds, you were playing in détaché style!

Most bowings have French names, because French violinists were brilliant at inventing bowing styles. They had to be, to figure out lots of ways to use those beautiful bows that were crafted in France! However, just to be contrary, the second basic bow stroke you need has an Italian name.

Staccato bowing is quite like détaché, except it's a firmer style that bites the string a bit more. Staccato bowing makes the notes sound crisp, with a short separation between each sound.

To begin a staccato stroke, you add a little hand weight to the bow, pushing the string down slightly. Draw the bow quickly on the string for a short distance, say 1 to 2 inches, slightly releasing the weight as you begin the bow stroke. Stop the bow lightly on the string after each note.

You can use some of the songs in the "Playing Your First Concert!" section, earlier in this chapter, to practice the détaché and staccato styles. Try the theme from Dvorak's "From the New World" Symphony using the détaché style and "Jingle Bells" using staccato bow strokes. You can hear me play "Jingle Bells" in staccato on Track 3, after I play the song smoothly.

Chapter 5

Getting the Left Hand Right

- -

In This Chapter

▶ Shaping up the left hand and fingers for playing

▶ Putting your fingers on the strings

▶ Getting the measure of your fingerboard

▶ Listing the ingredients for pizzicato

▶ Playing your first songs using fingers

- -

*V*iolins make beautiful-sounding music — after you master a few tricky playing techniques. When you balance the instrument well in playing position and set up your left hand so that your fingers move comfortably to land in the right spots, you can enjoy your music and sound good! In this chapter, you find out exactly how to set up your left hand and where to place your fingers on the strings so that everything works smoothly — and so that you prevent arm strain and fatigue. You also start training your fingers to work together as a team.

Shaping Up Your Arm and Fingers

Every instrument has its own playing position, and each of those positions has its comfortable (and less comfortable!) aspects. Violinists are lucky in one way: the left shoulder acts as a natural shelf on which to rest the violin. But the violin's playing position gets a bit tricky for your left hand, because you have to turn your forearm around quite a bit for your fingers to reach their notes. By doing so, you're using muscles I bet you didn't even know you had, muscles you've got to build up for strength and flexibility. In this section, I outline a simple exercise to keep your left arm and fingers in top shape, and I tell you how to achieve a comfortable playing position.

Southpaws feeling left behind?

It may be tempting for some left-handers to think about switching their violin holds to their right hands — even though very few violinists switch-hit. "Left-handed" violins are made differently from regular violins, and they're relatively rare.

If you're struggling with the idea that everyone plays the violin the same way, regardless of handedness, remember that violin playing is a two-handed operation. Lefties have a slight advantage in fingering, righties in bowing. And of course, ambidextrous violinists are laughing.

If, for some physical reason beyond handedness, you need to hold the violin in your right hand and the bow in your left (for example, you lost one of your left-hand fingers in an accident), it's possible to turn a regular violin around, but a qualified violin repair person needs to make the modifications. Both the outside and the inside of the instrument require careful work for the violin to sound, well, *right*.

Getting your arm in shape

Try this little rotation exercise, which is very helpful in developing the range of motion you need when you play — you may not use this movement a lot in other everyday activities. Figure 5-1 shows you how the exercise looks when you follow these three steps:

1. **Sit at a table.**

2. **Rest your left elbow on the table in front of your left side, with your forearm more or less perpendicular to the elbow and your hand floating directly above your elbow.**

3. **Leading off from your pinky side, rotate your forearm gently to its full extent in either direction.**

Figure 5-1:
Drop and give me ten . . . arm rotations, that is.

Rotating your forearm until your left palm faces almost all the way to the left side is the position that most closely resembles your actual playing position. Doing this exercise about five times in each direction, without forcing your range of motion, is a good daily dose in your first few weeks of playing.

When you've rotated your forearm into violin position, try wiggling your fingers as if you're actually playing — it may be air violin, but you're nearly there!

Taking your fingers to tap dancing class

Fingers need to move quite independently when you play different notes. Unless you've done these movements on the piano or while typing, your finger muscles probably haven't met anything quite like this before!

Try this little exercise to teach your fingers the right moves. Swing the violin up into playing position. Instead of lining up your left hand alongside the violin's neck, ready to land your fingers on the strings, just place your left palm flat against the violin's ribs next to the right side of the fingerboard. Your knuckles are aligned with the top plate of the violin, and your thumb rests underneath the violin's body, touching the back of the instrument. Your left-hand fingers are curved gently so that your fingertips land perpendicularly on the top of the violin.

Keeping your palm still, tap each fingertip, one at a time, on the top of the violin in a distinct rhythm, such as "Pa-ga-ni-ni, Pa-ga-ni-ni," or "A-bra-ham Lin-coln," or your full name. I demonstrate this exercise on the CD-ROM.

If this seems easy, try tapping your fingers, 1 through 4, in a different order. How about 1-2-1-2, 2-3-2-3, 3-4-3-4 and then such combinations as 1-3-1-4 or 3-1-4-2 for a challenge?

Making a hand frame that works

When you're actually playing the violin, you're most comfortable when your left hand forms and holds a well lined-up frame, as shown in Figure 5-2. Here's how to do it (you can also watch this on your CD-ROM):

1. **Stand up, and hold your violin across your waist just like a guitar, with the violin's neck cradled in your left hand.**

   Your left hand encircles the neck quite close to the scroll end, and your right hand supports the ribs under the top end of the instrument.

2. **Keep your left palm facing up and your fingers curved gently around the neck of the violin.**

   The side of the ebony fingerboard leans lightly on the left side of your palm at the crease where your index finger joins to your palm. The base joints of your other fingers remain very close by the side of the fingerboard, without actually touching the wood.

3. **Place your left-hand fingertips very lightly on the fingerboard, between the D string and the A string.**

   This position is the correct alignment for your fingers.

4. **Swing the violin up into playing position with a little help from your right hand, which supports and steadies the violin by holding gently under its upper ribs (refer to Chapter 3 for more about swinging the violin into playing position).**

   As you swing up, keep your left-hand fingertips on the violin's fingerboard in the same position described in Step 3. Don't force your knuckles to be completely parallel to the violin neck, just keep your attention on your fingertips, and you will arrive in a good position.

For best results when getting into playing position, swing the violin up to a level that's a bit higher than its final resting level, so that you place the violin on your collarbone from above. Landing the violin from above helps make holding it feel quite light.

Figure 5-2:
Getting your fingers into line on their first day of school.

In all of these steps, the inner side of your thumb pad rests gently on the neck of the violin, more or less opposite your index finger. Keep your thumb fairly straight and relaxed, with its tip just peeking over the top of the fingerboard while its base forms a U shape under the neck of the violin. Figure 5-3 shows you how your left hand looks when it's in the correct position.

You know your left hand is in the correct playing position when enough space exists between the lowest curve of your thumb's U shape and the neck of the violin for a little mouse to sneak through (eek!).

Keeping your thumb loose on the violin's neck

As your fingers start to tap on the fingerboard, your thumb naturally wants to grip tighter to support each finger. Boy, does your thumb have the wrong idea! You need to save your hand's energy to use it where it's needed: in your fingers. Right from the start, keep your thumb's grip light and airy. To ensure this happens, take your thumb off the violin's neck intermittently so that it doesn't have a chance to grip tightly. When you play on open strings, it's the perfect moment to loosen your thumb.

Figure 5-3:
Left hand
position.

Keeping the area between the base of your thumb and the palm of your hand in a U shape is also U-seful for keeping a relaxed hand frame.

Putting Your Fingers on the Strings

Another milestone in learning to play the violin is the moment you get to use your fingers to make notes on the strings, rather than using open strings only (refer to Chapter 4 to see how to bow on open strings). In this section, I show you how to be sure your fingers are properly shaped, explain the way fingers are numbered for playing the violin, and tell you how to lift and place your fingers to get the right notes.

Getting groovy fingertips

You might think that when you press down on them, the strings should run straight across each fingertip, parallel to your nails. But when you position your left hand the way I describe in "Making a hand frame that works," earlier in this chapter, each string actually runs along your first three fingertips slightly diagonally. The little finger is the only one where the string runs more or less straight across.

Checking that your fingers are shaping up properly is easy. Just look at the *grooves,* which are the tiny lines imprinted on your fingertips from pressing briefly, but firmly, on the strings. To check that your fingers are in the correct position, hold your violin like a guitar (refer to "Making a hand frame that works"), but this time, line your fingertips up on the A string. Swing the violin up to playing position, and then press your fingertips down firmly on the A string for a couple of seconds. Lift your fingertips off the string, and then look at them to see if the grooves are in the right places. Figure 5-4 shows you how properly positioned grooves look.

Since all hands are slightly different, the precise locations of the grooves that the strings make on your fingertips may vary slightly. Figure 5-4 shows you what to look for.

When you're actually playing the violin, you press your fingers just enough to push the string down onto the fingerboard, a very small distance. So, when checking your finger grooves, don't press down too hard, or you'll hurt your fingers.

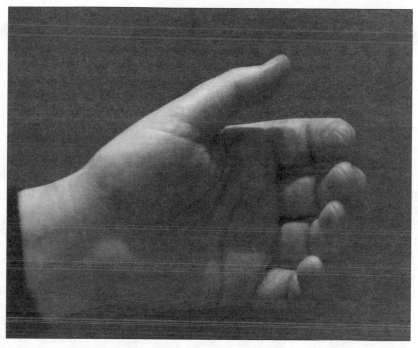

Figure 5-4:
How groovy
are you?

Counting your fingers

If you've ever taken piano lessons and remember the way your teacher numbered each of your fingers, forget those numbers — you're a violinist now! Pianists call their thumb "number 1," and they live their whole lives under the illusion that they have five fingers. We violinists know that the thumb's not a real finger, just the opposition (opposing thumbs being the distinguishing characteristic that makes *homo* more *sapiens* than other species). So, as shown in Figure 5-5, violinists number their fingers like this:

- ✔ **Finger 1:** Index finger
- ✔ **Finger 2:** Middle finger
- ✔ **Finger 3:** Ring finger
- ✔ **Finger 4:** (Yes, you've guessed it!) Little finger

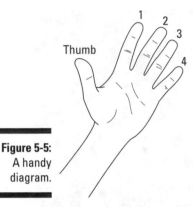

Figure 5-5:
A handy
diagram.

Each finger has a number, just as every person has a name — so that you can identify which finger is which! Later on, when you play fancier pieces, you may sometimes see a finger number, called a *fingering,* written over a note here and there on your music. Those fingerings help you to play the music smoothly. For now, all you need to do is to get acquainted with each finger and its number so that you can find your way through the songs in this chapter.

Knowing which finger to use for what note

For the exercises in this chapter, all you need to do is follow the finger numbers that I show you for each song, because each finger always plays on the same note each time. In Chapter 7, I show you how the finger numbers correspond to the letter names for each note, and how you can use your fingers to play even more notes.

Lifting and placing your fingers

All four fingers make their main moves from the base knuckle, where your finger joins your hand. Most of the up-and-down movements work this way. At this stage, your fingers retain their slightly rounded shape, and each fingertip drops (or lifts) quite quickly and decisively to make its note.

Keep this slightly rounded shape, whether your fingertip is placed on the string or your finger is just hovering, waiting to play. To place each fingertip on the string, simply "throw" the whole rounded finger shape forward.

Getting It Taped

When you're used to playing, your fingers know instinctively where to land on the strings to get the right notes. But at first, they may need some pilot training. Don't worry; most violinists' hands are a little tentative when feeling their way around the fingerboard for the first time. After all, your view of the fingerboard when you're in playing position is telescopic (which is kind of weird), and violins don't have frets to guide you like guitars do.

Believe it or not, all you need are a couple of useful props — a tape measure and some stick-on dots — and you're on your way toward mastering your fingering. You can use these props to create *fingerboard guides,* which are marked-off spots on the fingerboard where your fingers land. Just think of these marked spots as training wheels for your fingers.

You can find the stick-on dots at office supply stores. Or, if you prefer, you can cut narrow strips of tape and place them across the fingerboard. What you use is up to you — some like tape, others stick with dots. You can find suitable fingerboard tape at violin stores, online, and at art or architect supply stores — even at garages that custom decorate cars — and the tape comes in an array of colors. Choose a color that will show up well on the ebony fingerboard and look cheerful on your violin! Tape comes in various widths; for your violin's fingerboard, pick ³⁄₁₆- or ¼-inch tape.

If you don't have a background in music, or if placing your fingers on the fingerboard feels very unfamiliar, marking the spots helps you to get going. Following these steps will help you figure out where to put your fingers and allow you to feel the correct spaces between your fingers. This section is a little bit technical, but it's well worth your time.

Never stick tape or any type of sticker on the body of your violin. The adhesive can permanently damage the varnish.

To get started with marking off the spots where your fingers land, measure the A string to get tailor-made accuracy for your violin. (The same spots will work on other strings as well, you'll be pleased to know!)

Start off by measuring the vibrating length (refer to Chapter 2) of the A string. It's about 13 inches (33 centimeters) on most full-sized violins, so that's the length I use for these steps:

1. **Use a tape measure to establish the length of the A string from the nut end of the fingerboard to the bridge (refer to Chapter 2 to locate the nut).**

   You're measuring the vibrating length of the open string along the fingerboard (see Figure 5-6). For this example, I assume it's the average length: 13 inches, or 33 centimeters.

Figure 5-6:
Measuring
the vibrating
length of the
A string.

2. **Measure ⅑ of the A string's length along the fingerboard (about 1⅙ inches, or 3⅔ centimeters, for this example), as shown in Figure 5-7.**

   As in Step 1, start from the nut end. You're measuring to find the first spot to mark on the fingerboard.

3. **Use a soft lead pencil to mark the spot on the fingerboard between the D and A strings, in the center of your fingerboard.**

4. **Place a stick-on dot or a narrow strip of tape over the pencil mark (see Figure 5-7).**

   This spot is where you put finger 1.

5. **Measure ¼ of the vibrating length of the A string (about 3¼ inches, or 8¼ centimeters, for this example), starting from the nut end, and then repeat Steps 3 and 4 to mark the spot.**

   This spot is where you put finger 3.

6. **Take up your tape measure, as in Step 2, and measure ⅓ of the vibrating length of the A string (about 4⅓ inches, or 11 centimeters, for this example), starting from the nut end, and then repeat Steps 3 and 4 to mark the spot.**

   This spot is where you put finger 4.

If you use tape to mark your fingerboard guides, cut a length of tape that is long enough for the ends to meet when you stick the tape across the fingerboard and around the violin's neck. In other words, the tape's length should slightly exceed the circumference of the violin's neck. (Connecting the two ends of the tape makes the fingerboard guide more stable and less likely to slip around as you play.) To attach the tape, put your violin safely on a table. Slip the tape between the strings and the top of the fingerboard, sliding it toward your pencil mark and then pressing it down when it is properly aligned. Make sure the tape goes straight across the fingerboard, no diagonals.

Notice that I don't tell you to put on a marker for finger 2, but with good reason. Finger 2 is quite the party animal, spending some time nestled close to finger 3 and then going close to finger 1 for other notes. So finger 2 doesn't get its own marker.

The guides don't have to stay on your fingerboard for longer than you need them. Three to six months is a useful period of time to use the stickers or tape. Later on, you may want to use the occasional guide to target a tricky new note. You can place guides on the fingerboard as you need them, for as long as you need them. Luckily, the stick-on dots come in large packets, with plenty left over for occasional use. You may even get your office organized while learning to play the violin!

If glue from the stick-on dot or tape stays on the fingerboard after you've removed your fingerboard guides, just take a facecloth and carefully rub the residual glue from the fingerboard — it comes off easily.

Figure 5-7:
Marking the spot for finger 1.

Preparing Your Pizzicato

ON THE CD

Pizzicato sounds as if it's something delicious to order in an Italian restaurant, but it's actually a technique that can make your violin sound a bit like a harp or a guitar — you pluck the strings. In Chapter 2, you pluck your strings a little to hear pitches for tuning. In this chapter, you use the pizzicato technique to allow you to concentrate on placing your left-hand fingers on their spots without having to think about using the bow at the same time. All you need to do is to leave your bow safely in your case and follow these simple steps, which I show you in Figure 5-8 and demonstrate on the CD-ROM:

1. **Set up comfortably in playing position.**

2. **Make a fist with your right hand, with the tip of your thumb cuddling the middle joints of your first and second fingers.**

3. **Hold your fist over the strings just above the top inch or two of the fingerboard, with your knuckles pointing toward the ceiling.**

4. **Extend your thumb and index finger so that they are fairly straight.**

5. **Park the pad of your thumb along the E-string side of the fingerboard.**

   The tip of your thumb points almost straight down toward the table of the violin, and your index finger is ready over the strings.

6. **Put the pad of your index finger on the left side of any string — try the G string, for example — and then pluck the string by making a little circular pulling motion with your index finger.**

   Bend your finger's middle joint to pull the string a little toward you, and then let the string ping back as your finger continues its circle around for the next pizzicato.

Exploring the fingerboard guides through pizzicato

I'm sure you're keen to get started using your new finger placements, so here are two songs for you to practice on. Right now, you are targeting fingers 1 and 3 only, so you can get a feel for using the fingerboard guides. You can follow the music for these songs and play pizzicato along with your CD-ROM. Just refer to the music chart below. The chart uses the real locations of the notes on five lines. But to help you along if you aren't familiar with reading music (see Chapter 7), I give a finger number for each note inside the note head and let you know which string to play on in brackets just under the music. "0" means open string, no fingers on the string.

On your CD-ROM, I play these songs with my bow so that the notes are easy to hear and play along with, using your pizzicato.

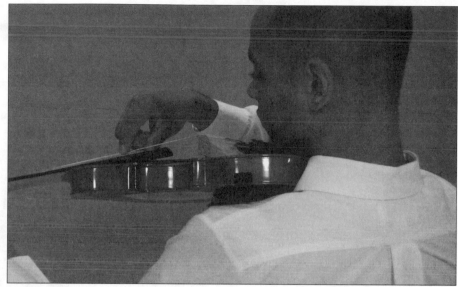

Figure 5-8:
Shaping up
for pizzicato.

TRACK 5

Asian Mood

This song uses an Eastern-sounding scale (you find out all about how to play scales in Chapters 10 and 11). In the very first bit, try keeping finger 1 on the A string while finger 3 plays, because you're coming right back to finger 1 again. Things go smoothly if you watch carefully when you land your fingers on the D string to make sure you're aiming them at the right spots.

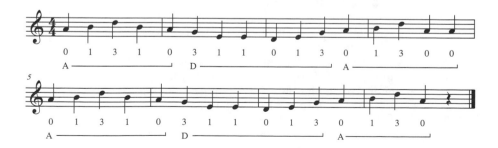

Octave Ping-Pong

I composed this *bagatelle* (a short, light musical piece) to help you practice something very important: getting finger 3 on target. If you can land finger 3 accurately, chances are good that the rest of your fingers will be on target too! Because you are landing finger 3 on the note A on the E string, you'll be able to hear that A matching the sound of your open A string. And of course, the same thing applies when you land finger 3 on other strings: The notes match their corresponding open strings. You can feel the ping-pong effect in the movement of finger 3. Just let your finger bounce onto the string to play and rebound off again when it isn't playing.

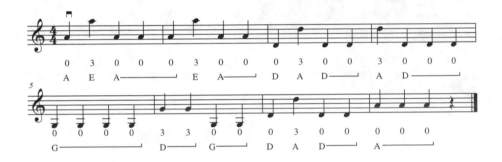

Three's Company: Putting Finger 2 to Work

In this last section, I give you a few more notes to help you to get to know your instrument. After you feel confident using fingers 1 and 3 (which I show you how to do in "Putting Your Fingers on the Strings"), it's time to find the right place for finger 2, which is a busy little digit. As I mention in "Getting It Taped," earlier in this chapter, finger 2 often needs to play really close to finger 3 *or* really close to finger 1 to make its notes.

When finger 2 goes to work, it uses the other fingers as guides. So if it needs to play a note that's close to 3, it touches or stays very close to finger 3. But if it's to play a note that's close to finger 1, it touches (or stays close to) finger 1.

The closeness of your fingers on the fingerboard depends on the size of your hand and the width of your fingers. The spaces between the notes are consistent, but the position of your fingers feels different according to your hand's individual characteristics.

Figure 5-9 shows you what your fingers look like when finger 2 is next to finger 3 and when it is next to finger 1. Try placing your fingers on the A or D string in each of these ways (violinists refer to these placements as *finger patterns*).

To get a feel for the space in which finger 2 travels on a string, place fingers 1 and 3 on the D string and then slide the tip of finger 2 on the string in a "polishing" motion between 1 and 3. This motion allows finger 2 to practice moving between fingers 1 and 3, and it also encourages flexibility in the finger, which is useful in finding its way.

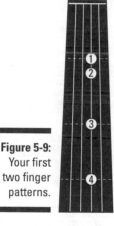

Figure 5-9:
Your first
two finger
patterns.

Further on in this book, I show you many different finger patterns, but with these first two patterns, you can play lots of great songs already. For the two songs in this section, finger 2 nestles up to finger 3.

You can start by playing these notes pizzicato, but you may be very keen to try bowing them after your fingers can find their way. For these songs, you can use your bow and fingers simultaneously, which might feel a little strange at first. In Chapter 6, I give you lots of tips on how to get both hands working together. But for these songs, start on a down-bow, use comfortable amounts of bow — not too much — and enjoy! You'll notice that most of the notes on the chart are black. These are your regular notes. Just a few notes are white. These notes last a bit longer, just like in the song you know and love, so allow more bow on these, to hold on to them. On the last note of "Jingle Bells," you can hold on as long as you like, just for fun.

TRACK 7

Jingle Bells

This song also appears in Chapter 4, but for this version, you use your left-hand fingers to play the melody. Start by setting finger 2 on your D string to play the first note, which is an F♯. After all those F♯s, play your open A string and then pop finger 2 off the D string right away so that you can play the open D string. Continue with finger 1, and then use 2 for the long note. Finger 3 needs to be very close when you land it after finger 2. The rest of the song is plain sailing, jingling!

TRACK 8

Shortenin' Bread

Before you play, start by setting up fingers 1 and 3 on their spots on the A string. Each time this first bit of the song comes back, you can make things work really well by landing fingers 1 and 3 at the same time so that finger 1 is ready on the string when you lift finger 3 off. Just a couple of other places to watch for: At the asterisk (*), land finger 2 on the D string and then release finger 1 from the A string so that it's free to land on the D string right after you've played finger 2. At the double asterisk (**), notice that you need to play finger 3 on the A string just that one time!

Chapter 6

All Together Now

*I*n this chapter, you put it all together and begin to coordinate your hands to bow out sounds while fingering the notes. Then, after you have the moves sorted out, I tell you how to play some songs that call for bowing and fingering simultaneously.

Using Your Hands Together

Bowing and fingering together can be quite a handful (or two!) at first. It's like that old game where you try to pat your stomach and rub your head at the same time — or is it the other way around? The hands work together, but they do different things, and those things don't always happen at the same time. The violinist's fingers have to get ready for the next note before the bow arrives to sound that note. The bow has to move to different strings and play different note lengths. At the same time, the bow also has to vary the volume *and* shape the musical phrases. Both hands are really busy making sounds happen on the violin.

Starting to use both hands

Getting started with both violin and bow comfortably in hand takes just a bit of organization. Here's a useful way to get yourself in order until it becomes second nature:

1. **Get the bow out of the case, tighten the horsehair for playing, and then place the bow (stick on top, ribbon of horsehair down) across the ledge of your music stand, with the frog of the bow extending slightly over the end of the stand.**

   (Refer to Chapter 4 for bow basics.)

2. **Take your violin out of the case and swing it up into playing position.**

   (Refer to Chapter 3 to know how to hold your violin.)

3. **Pick up the bow with your bow hold in place (refer to Chapter 4).**

   Hold the bow vertically, with its tip pointing up to the ceiling, until you're ready to place it on the strings.

To start in the best bowing position, place the middle section of your bow on the E string and then roll the bow over the strings until you reach the string you want to play.

Developing fitness for hands together

Doing the exercises in this section is like going to the gym for the first time: You may feel rather clumsy when you start out, because your hands have never done these movements before — or you haven't attempted them for a long time. Don't be afraid to make mistakes; you get better with practice.

Before you start the actual songs, these basic preparation workouts get your fingers and bow working together. The music charts tell you which string to play, and the number tells you which finger to put on the string. For example, "0" means play the open string, "1" means put finger 1 on the string, and so on (refer to Chapter 5 for a list of finger numbers). Figure 6-1 shows you which part of the bow to use for the workouts.

Figure 6-1:
Use this part of the bow for workouts.

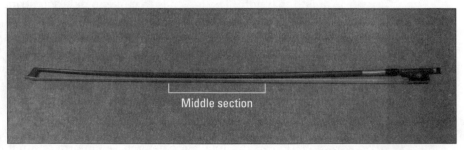

Middle section

Try doing exercises at a comfortable, slowish tempo at first. Relax and have fun with them. If you tense up, you push your coordination into overload and you may get frustrated. Later, you can use your exercises as a warm-up, trying them on different strings and using different finger patterns.

Two special symbols help you to move smoothly as you first play these workouts:

- When you see the asterisk (*), stop the bow gently on the string. Take plenty of time to place the next fingertip on the string before you begin bowing the new note.

- When you see the double asterisk (**), stop the bow gently on the string. Take your time to lift the finger that just played off the finger-board before you start bowing the next note.

After you have the moves in good order, try the exercise without the stops, along with your CD-ROM.

Marching your fingers in an orderly fashion

In these exercises, your fingers may feel like soldiers on the march as they land purposefully on the strings, one after another. Try marching on the A string in the first finger pattern, with finger 2 close to finger 3. Figure 6-2 shows you exactly where to place your fingertips on the A string; Figure 6-3 shows you which fingers to use; and the CD-ROM lets you hear how the exercise sounds.

Figure 6-2:
Finger pattern on the A string.

Note: As your fingers ascend the string, as shown in Figure 6-3, leave the finger that just played resting lightly on the string while the new finger plays — this keeps your fingers waiting on the string for you when it's time for them to march back down.

How do I know if I've got it right?

So much is going on at once when you get both hands working together that knowing what to watch out for can be a bit of a conundrum. Here's a useful checklist to help you get things working right (and left!):

- Is finger 1 landing correctly on its fingerboard guide? (Refer to Chapter 5.)

- Is my left wrist nicely aligned with my forearm and the back of my hand, with no bends along the way? (Refer to Chapter 5.)

- Does my bow run fairly straight on a track parallel to the bridge, about halfway between the bridge and the top of the fingerboard? (Refer to Chapter 4.)

- When fingering the notes, am I playing on my fingertips between the nail and the pad of the finger? (Refer to Chapter 5.)

- Does my violin remain in a comfortable playing position, with the scroll out to the left side at about a 50- to 70-degree angle, as I try everything together? (Refer to Chapter 3.)

If you ask yourself these questions and concentrate on one aspect at a time, you're off to a great start.

TRACK 9, 0:00

Figure 6-3: Hup, two, three, four! Marching up the hill (and down again).

Hopping your fingers around

You remain on the A string for this workout.

As you may have guessed, you don't need to leave any fingers on the string in this exercise (see Figure 6-4). In fact, each finger lands and lifts independently, only touching the string when it's called for. You can listen to how the exercise sounds on the CD-ROM.

Figure 6-4:
Leapin'
lizards! Your
fingers are
hopping
away.

TRACK 9, 0:42

```
0   0   2   0   0   0   3   0   0   0   4   0   0   1   0
A
```

Crossing Over to a Different String

After you get the hang of playing notes on one string at a time, you start to become interested in being more adventurous on your violin. So you need to know how to cross over to a different string. Using a few simple techniques for both hands, you can accomplish a smooth transition between strings, which is what I talk about in this section.

Crossing strings with the bow

Imagine you are a bird and that the upper parts of your arms are wings. Go on, give a little flap, or do your best imitation of a chicken dance! What does a bird impersonation have to do with playing the violin, you ask? Well, when you cross over to another string with your bow, your upper arm changes levels, just like a bird flapping its wings.

Warning: Do not try this exercise on public transit!

To work on your arm-level skills, first set up your violin and bow in playing position and then land the middle of the bow on the E string (see "Starting to use both hands," earlier in this chapter). Make a few free-ranging rock 'n' roll moves (refer to Chapter 4). As you roll the bow to and fro across the strings, you feel a gentle wave that travels all the way from the tip of the bow, through the bow to the frog, and then along your whole arm to your shoulder — almost as though you're rolling a table tennis ball back and forth along the top of your bow stick, without letting it fall off at either end. To keep that imaginary ball moving, your right arm waves up and down, too. Keep your wrist a bit flexible so that it floats lightly up and down with the movement. Observe the bow's path carefully, making sure the stick moves more or less parallel to the violin's bridge.

Picturing yourself as an elegant bird with a large wingspan, such as a swan, helps to give you the right smoothness as you practice rolling your bow from one string to another.

When you have a sense of the scope of the rolling movement, the next step is to go more steadily so that you can feel the specific level of each string.

Two neighboring strings

First, try rolling the bow silently (without pulling it to make a sound) from the E string to the A string and then back again to E, letting your arm's level float up and down with the general level of the bow. The movement is not big, but keeping the same relation between bow and string at each level helps the bow sound equally good on each string — and keeping your bow arm moving freely is what we're about here! See the movement illustrated on the CD-ROM for more clarification.

After you can roll from E to A and back, it's time to try the same rolling motion between different pairs of strings. Starting with the bow on the A string, roll back and forth between A and D levels, letting your arm's level float up and down with the bow. Then try rolling the bow between the D and G strings.

Playing the violin requires your arm to float to a *higher* level to play a *lower*-sounding string. Now, how weird is that?

Two non-neighboring strings

You can expand the bow-rolling motion so that your bow crosses over to strings that are not next door to each other. The movement is illustrated on the CD-ROM, so you can see it in action.

Land your bow on the E string again, and then roll silently over to the D string. Simply roll over the A string without lifting the bow at all, and then stop the movement when your bow reaches the D string. Rolling back to the E string involves exactly the same process, just as if you're putting the bow into reverse. The whole movement has a slightly greater arc than it does when you roll to a neighboring string.

When crossing with your bow to a non-neighboring string, keep your focus on the place where the bow contacts the string, letting your arm's level float up and down as needed. Depending on the curvature of the bridge and the length of your arm, the level of your elbow will change by up to about 6 inches. Stand in front of a mirror to watch the point of your elbow doing this rolling movement, so that you have a sense of what it looks like.

Use the same rolling motion for the next pair of strings. Set your bow on the A string to start. After you're balanced well on the A string, roll over to the G string, passing silently over the D string as you go. This action is the same as crossing from the E string to the D string, but if you watch your elbow's level in the mirror, you'll see that it begins and ends at slightly higher levels than when you use the E and D strings.

I've saved the biggest (and most fun) string crossing for the very last: E string to G string. After setting your bow on the E string, roll the bow all the way over A and D until it comes to rest on the G string. That's quite a big arc! Going back and forth between the E string and the G string will let your arm feel the full range of bowing levels.

Avoid rolling so far with the bow that the horsehair touches the edge of the violin when you cross over between your E and G strings. All you need to do is to go as far as you need to *just* touch the E string or the G string — in this case, more is not better!

Seven wonderful levels

Okay, I'm doing some math in this part. The violin has four strings, so placing the bow on each individual string involves finding one of four possible arm levels.

Additionally, because you can place the bow on two strings at the same time — when the bow is resting on E and A, A and D, or D and G — three in-between bow levels exist. So in fact, you need to know seven levels.

Go on, try it out! Just resting the bow silently on each level gives you an idea of how it feels to have your arm adjust to the seven different levels. When you have a sense of where the levels are, you're ready to try bowing on the open strings.

Four ways to exercise your options

In this section, I give you four useful exercises to put your string-crossing skills into action. The exercises shown in Figure 6-5 give you a workout involving changing to higher strings (you can also listen to these exercises being played on the CD-ROM).

When you first try the moves, you can stop the bow gently after the last note of the measure, and then roll your arm and bow to the next level. Later, when you develop your skills further, and you play along with the CD-ROM, you won't need to take extra time for this. But as you practice how to do the movements, moving calmly is just what the doctor ordered!

Both exercises start with the bow set on the G string, about halfway between the frog and the middle of the bow, and they begin with a down-bow (refer to Chapter 4 for bowing signs). Use the whole middle portion of the bow for these exercises, to give the string crossings a smooth and spacious feel. See how the exercises look, with extra pauses so the string crosses are clear, on the CD-ROM. The second exercise shown in Figure 6-5 gives you a chance to change strings on up-bows too.

Figure 6-5:
Exercises
for changing
to higher
strings.

The exercise shown in Figure 6-6 helps you practice changing to lower strings. Start with your bow ready on the E string, about halfway between the frog and the middle of the bow. Play this exercise in the same way as the exercises in Figure 6-5, with one big difference: Each time you change to a lower-sounding string, your arm and bow levels float *up* a notch. You're traveling along the same path, but in the opposite direction. Watch the CD-ROM to see the exercise being played, with extra pauses so each string crossing is clear; I even throw in a 3/4 version on the video, Figure 6-6b, for extra practice.

When changing strings, think of leading the way with your *elbow* as your arm's level drops, and with your *hand* as your arm's level rises.

Figure 6-6:
Exercises
for changing
to lower
strings.

Crossing strings with the fingers

Crossing to different strings with your left-hand fingers is a bit like steering a boat, because your left arm works like a rudder to bring your fingers over the relevant string. The movement, called *arm steering,* or *elbow steering,* is very subtle and keeps your left hand working well when you need to cross strings.

Figures 6-7, 6-8, and 6-9 show you some examples of string-crossing movements for your left hand. At first, just use your violin for these exercises, no bow necessary. When your finger movements feel smooth, you can go back through the exercises, adding the bow to the proceedings.

For Figure 6-7, which shows you how arm steering works, get into playing position and then follow these steps, using finger 4. Because finger 4 is your shortest finger, you can be sure that when finger 4 reaches the correct spot on any string by moving your elbow to the right, your other three fingers can easily reach their notes too. And of course, a slight swing of the elbow to the left brings your hand back across the D, A, and E strings.

Here are the moves, step-by-step, which I demonstrate on the CD-ROM:

1. **Get your hand ready in playing position, with your fingers nicely rounded and ready to land on the E string.**

    2. **Tap finger 4 four times on the E string.**

        Check that the alignment from your elbow through to the back of your hand is fairly straight.

    3. **Swing your left elbow about an inch to the right.**

        You're steering your hand over the A string.

    4. **Try tapping finger 4 four times on the A string.**

    5. **Swing your elbow another inch or so to the right, and then tap finger 4 four times on the D string.**

    6. **Swing your elbow one last time, another inch or so to the right, and then tap finger 4 (you guessed it, four times) on the G string.**

Note: When you return to this workout later to try it with your bow, you don't need to tap finger 4 four times on each string. Finger 4 can settle down and stay quietly on the string until the bow finishes the four bow strokes. But the first time you do the exercise, when you're practicing without the bow, tapping gives you a feel for the elastic action of the finger and allows you to practice landing on target.

Figure 6-7:
A four-ay
into crossing
strings using
fingers.

Doing the exercises shown in Figure 6-8 makes you feel as if you have a table tennis ball on each fingertip. Just tap finger 1 on the G string and then lift it as if it has bounced off the fingerboard and hopped onto the D string. Use the most basic finger pattern for these workouts, with fingers 1 and 3 on their tapes or dots, finger 2 close to 3, and finger 4 in its regular position, a healthy step above 3. I tap my way through this exercise on the CD-ROM so you can see the moves, and bow it on the audio so you can play along.

You use a very springy finger action when you aren't bowing, because this type of exercise is for working your finger muscles. When you play the same exercises with the bow, each finger remains on the string until you bow the next note, at which moment your finger releases from the string.

For the exercises in Figure 6-9, the finger action is a lot like walking, so imagine each of your fingers as being a little foot. While you're playing finger 2, lift finger 1 slightly and walk it to the next string. Pop finger 2 off the "old" string only when finger 1 is safely in place on the next string — just like you lift your foot to take another step only when your other foot is safely on *terra firma!* Your elbow swing adjusts gently as the new finger plays on the new string. Check out the CD-ROM to see fingers walking along — this is a tap exercise only on the video, but you're welcome to bow it later on.

Figure 6-8: Crossing strings with the fingers.

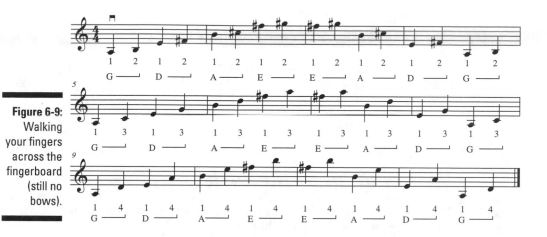

Figure 6-9:
Walking
your fingers
across the
fingerboard
(still no
bows).

Coordinating fingers and bows in string crossings

One important fact that violinists must know is that, when playing any piece of music, their next finger to play has to be ready with the next note by the time the bow finishes playing the previous note. The bow has to wait for the finger to be ready all the time — and usually it's pretty considerate. But having your next finger good and ready to play makes the bow's job much easier, and of course, your music will sound better, too.

Getting the next finger ready is a bit like changing gears in a stick-shift car: You feel a moment of neutral readiness as you go from one setting to the next. So if your next note involves *lifting* a finger, you need to plan to lift the finger promptly to above its spot on the string so that it's ready to play again at any time. If your next note involves *landing* a finger on the string, you just hover over the spot a bit ahead of playing time (usually when the previous finger is playing) and then drop the fingertip at the right moment.

It often feels as if your two hands are doing drastically different moves on the violin. But crossing strings is one important activity where your hands and arms are in excellent sympathy with one another. To get the gist of this comfortable fact, set your bow on the E string and then land finger 4 on E, too. This is a silent exercise, so just roll the bow over to the A string at the same time as you hop finger 4 to the A string. Now, isn't that nice? Your elbows move in the same direction to make the necessary level changes. You can do the same moves all the way across all the strings and back again.

Playing Music with Both Hands

Doing all the exercises and warm-ups in this chapter must have whetted your appetite for playing some real music. This last section prepares you to meet your musical work with aplomb. When you find your way up and down the notes on each string while bowing at the same time, everything starts to cooperate smoothly.

Warming up to the task

These warm-ups allow you to try out all your fingers and give your hands a fitness session in working together.

Try these exercises without using the bow at first; just let your left-hand fingers walk calmly through their steps on each string. Notice that in addition to my system of naming strings and giving finger numbers, I provide the formal musical notation, too. You can get used to looking at the notation, even if you aren't yet actually deciphering the details.

In the exercise shown in Figure 6-10, your fingers climb up the A string. First, watch and listen to the exercise being played on the CD-ROM to get the right idea.

TRACK 11, 0:00

Figure 6-10:
Climbing up
the A string.

You can also try climbing up the D string, as shown in Figure 6-11. You can hear the exercise on the CD-ROM.

TRACK 11, 0:10

Figure 6-11:
Climbing up
the D string.

Now climb up and down the G string, as I show in Figure 6-12 and play on the CD-ROM, both on video and in audio. Keep fingers 1, 2, and 3 sitting on the string after you play their notes, so they're waiting patiently when you climb back down.

Figure 6-12:
Climbing up and down on the G string.

And last, but not least, Figure 6-13 shows you how to perform the same steps on the E string. Check out how it sounds on the CD-ROM.

Figure 6-13:
Climbing up and down on the E string.

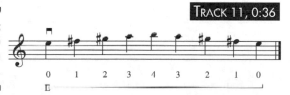

Because the fingering charts resemble actual musical notation, you can start to get used to the look of notes even before you read them in any detail. Familiarizing yourself with the look of notes is very helpful for beginning to read music, which I cover in Chapter 7.

Topping the charts: Three simple songs

You probably know these classic tunes, but if not, you can find them on the CD-ROM. Listen to the songs (and later, play along) before you play them by yourself. The songs appear in progressive order, so getting comfortable with "Hot Cross Buns" is a good idea before you start "Frère Jacques."

TRACK 12

Hot Cross Buns

You can play this song entirely on the D string. Start with your bow set on the D string, halfway between the frog and the middle of the bow, as shown in Figure 6-1. Prepare fingers 1 and 2 on the D string before you begin to play. After bowing open D, place fingers 1 and 2 on the string again for the second 2-1-D. After 1-1-1-1, leave finger 1 on the string while you play finger 2 for the last time, so that 1 is waiting for you when you play the last "Hot Cross Buns." Use about twice as much bow on the longer notes (the ones that have white note heads) as you do on the shorter notes.

TRACK 13

Frère Jacques

This one's as easy as one, two, three — you can play a song that uses three strings! "Frère Jacques" starts on the open A string, so you don't need any left-hand prep to begin that first down-bow. Just leave finger 1 on the A string while you play finger 2 in the first two A-1-2-As, and then pop off both fingers at the same time to return to open A. At 2-3-E, just land finger 2 alone for the first note, add finger 3, and then pop off both fingers when you play open E — this is how violinists play pop music!

When you get to the next bit, old Frère Jacques is in a bit of a hurry, so you have to bow in short, smooth strokes to keep up with him. To be able to make this bow movement happen, let those fingers dance on tiptoes and have the next one ready to land. Here, you can play one finger at a time, not leaving any fingers sitting around on the fingerboard. The last bit is very fun: Just send finger 1 over to the D string for one note. You can swing your left elbow forward a little bit under the violin to help finger 1 reach the D string.

Expanding Your Bow Strokes

After you put both hands to work together, you can take on a new challenge — and that means new music, too. In this section, I guide you through expanding your bow stroke until you can use most of the bow's length to sing out your sounds, and I introduce you to the "Pachelbel Canon."

Using more bow, gradually

After getting your violin hold and bow hold ready (which I describe in "Starting to use both hands," earlier in this chapter), set the middle of your bow on the open A string. Start with short, smooth strokes (just an inch or two in each direction, at first) at a very relaxed speed, or *tempo* to us musicians. (For more about tempo, see Chapter 9.) Gradually start using a little more bow on each stroke, and then a little more, till you are using most of the bow.

Don't force it: If things feel out of control, just back up to your previous amount of bow for a few strokes and then try again. Probably you can use all but the last 3 or 4 inches of bow at either end. Keeping the bow on track, parallel to the bridge, yields a clear and pleasing tone.

Preparing to play Pachelbel

This section offers some instructions for playing the first part of the famous "Pachelbel Canon," which uses long, flowing bow strokes.

Follow along with the musical chart (at the end of this chapter) and the CD-ROM, where I give you some hints about how best to keep your fingers on their toes as you play.

1. **Place finger 1 on the E string, and begin your first down-bow near the frog.**

2. **Lift finger 1 to play the open E when you reach the end of your down-bow, and then bow the E with a long up-bow.**

3. **Land finger 3 on the A string for the next note, and then roll your bow over to the A string, allowing your right elbow's level to adjust accordingly.**

4. **Play the down-bow on finger 3.**

5. **Place finger 2 gently in its spot, close to finger 3 on the A string, while 3 is playing.**

6. **Lift finger 3—finger 2 is waiting and ready for the smooth bow change to the up-bow.**

7. **Do the same thing as in Steps 5 and 6, but with fingers 1 and 2 this time.**

   Finger 1 may naturally sneak onto the string before you lift 2 so that the changeover to the down-bow is super smooth.

After that, the rest of this song is pretty easy. You play open A and then land 1, 2, and 3 in order, with no fancy footwork from your fingers — or your feet (remember to keep them on the ground!). You can hold the last note as long as you wish, for a final effect.

As with the exercises earlier in this chapter, you can practice the moves for each hand separately before playing the whole piece. Putting your hands to work together is easy after each hand has practiced its part.

 TRACK 14

Pachelbel Canon

Part III
Reading Music for the Violin

In this part . . .

You may know how to read music, just from years of seeing it during school music classes, or perhaps at choir practice. Or you may not know what any of those dots and lines mean. Don't worry. In this part, I walk you through all the aspects of reading notes and rhythms on your violin so that you can read with confidence to decipher for yourself the notes of music you want to play. Chapter 7 shows you how to read the notes on the five lines. Then in Chapter 8, you look at rhythm and counting skills, and in Chapter 9, you see how all of that information lines up in bars. Are you feeling thirsty for knowledge? Let's go!

Chapter 7

Translating Five Lines onto Four Strings

- -

In This Chapter

▶ Understanding the basics of music written on five lines

▶ Lining up the notes and the strings

▶ Becoming acquainted with the sharps, flats, and naturals

▶ Reading and playing music

▶ Playing loudly and softly

- -

The five-line system is packed with musical information. When you can recognize the symbols (not to be confused with cymbals!), you have everything the composer could tell you about how the music should sound.

In this chapter, I decipher this five-line system so that you can play some great new songs.

Lining Up the Music

Music has been written on five lines for the past 500 years, but luckily, it wasn't evolving at the speed of a line a century! Collectively, these five lines on which music is written are called a *staff*. Each line and each space in between the lines corresponds to a note, which represents a specific pitch (refer to Chapter 2 for my pitch on pitches), or musical sound. The staff system works rather like a map, which shows you the location of different towns, cities, rivers, and so on — every note has a place where it belongs. Although five lines may not seem like enough for all the notes you can hear in music, they are just about the right number to cover two very important considerations:

> ✒ Enabling the eyes to distinguish one note from another without getting in a muddle
>
> ✒ Providing enough places for all the notes an instrument might be able to play in its *range,* which goes from its lowest possible note to its very highest note

In Figure 7-1, I show you what a note written on a line looks like, versus a note written in a space between two lines, so that you have a chance to see them very clearly before they appear all over a staff.

Figure 7-1:
Notes on a
line and in a
space.

Don't jump off the clef

Learning to read music is like learning another language. As I begin to explain in this chapter, each and every element you see on the staff serves a purpose and tells you how to play a piece — you're cultivating a new vocabulary for music. That lovely swirly symbol at the beginning of the staff, called a *treble clef,* isn't just there for decoration. The clef lets the violinist know, right off the bat (or bow, so to speak), the pitches of notes. When you're reading from the treble clef, the same note is always in the same spot, which is quite a relief! (Take a look at Figure 7-2 to see the treble clef.)

Figure 7-2:
The treble
clef.

The treble clef is also called a *G-clef.* Notice that the curl in the middle of the treble clef winds around the second bottom line of the staff, indicating that this spot is where the note G belongs (see "Every Good Boy Deserves Fudge," a bit later in this chapter). The treble clef also resembles a cursive letter G — which is no accident. The shape of each clef actually comes from the shape of the letter of the note it indicates on its staff.

Different clefs for different folks

The most-used notes of each instrument's range occur in the middle of the clef it uses. That's why violins and flutes, which are higher-sounding instruments, use the treble clef. Here are two other clefs you may see:

✔ **Alto clef:** The alto clef is also called a *C-clef,* and it bears a resemblance to the letter C. At the center of the clef is the middle line, which is also *middle C* (I show you middle C on the keyboard in Figure 2-6). Easy to remember: *middle* line, *middle* C! Viola players read music written in the alto clef.

✔ **Bass clef:** The bass clef is an *F-clef,* and its characteristic two dots are actually remnants of the horizontal bars of the letter F.

These dots surround the fourth line from the bottom of the staff, showing the location of the note F. You won't be surprised to hear that double bass players read music written in the bass clef, and actually, so do cellists.

This F, indicated by the two dots of the bass clef, is actually one note lower than your G string, so you can't play it on your violin — but at least you know it's there. Just to be special, the double bass sounds one octave lower than the written note, because there isn't a double bass clef.

Violin music is always written in the treble clef. Getting to know the other clefs, which I discuss in the sidebar "Different clefs for different folks," is useful for following musical *scores,* where all the instrumental parts are printed together.

Before you start actually playing the violin from written or printed notes, you need to crack the note system. Figure 7-3 introduces you to notes that fit on the five lines of the treble clef. Looking at this figure, you'll easily see the notes progressing up the musical "ladder," step-by-step.

Figure 7-3:
Notes on
the staff.

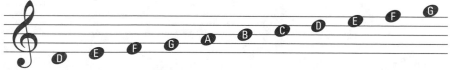

Every Good Boy Deserves Fudge (and so do girls!)

Knowing the note names makes it possible for you to read any music you want to play. If you start referring to notes by their names, explaining songs to other musicians when you start playing together is much easier (so you don't have to ask them to "play that really high note — you know the one I mean?").

Lining up the staff

The first staff line appeared around the tenth century. Music scribes (who were usually monks) traced a horizontal red line, representing the note F, above the text to help singers gauge their pitches. This line must have been pretty helpful, because next they added a second, yellow line, which represented the note C. Eventually, around the year 1200, scribes added two further lines over these, both in black ink. The four-line staff is still used today for the *Gregorian Chant,* the liturgical chant of the Catholic Church, which is a single melody. When music started having several different parts going at once, rather than one single tune, the five-line staff became more popular, until it took over as the system of choice. It was so effective that it prevails today for almost all instruments.

A time-honored way exists to remember where the note names belong on the staff when reading from the treble clef. Notes written on lines (with the line passing across the center of the note head) have their own special phrase to remind beginners how the system works. Starting from the lowest line, which is the note E, and working up line by line, people say "Every Good Boy Deserves Fudge." (Being of the female persuasion, I encourage you to develop your own mnemonic. For instance, *Every Girl Brings Delicious Fudge!*) Anyway, all boys and girls who use these phrases end up knowing that the lowest line of the staff is for the note E for Every, the second line up is G for Good, next comes B for Boy, D for Deserves, and then F for Fudge on the top line.

Reading the notes written in the spaces (with the staff lines passing above and below the note head, making a note "sandwich") is just as easy: If you remember the phrase "face in the space," you have the four notes, F-A-C-E. Figure 7-4 illustrates these little tricks.

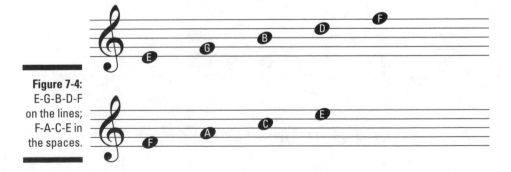

Figure 7-4:
E-G-B-D-F
on the lines;
F-A-C-E in
the spaces.

Climbing on the ledger lines

Many notes in an instrument's range happen within the scope of the five lines of the staff. But if a composer or arranger needs to write a note that is higher or lower than what those five lines can handle, it's time to add an extra little line called a *ledger line*. A ledger line is just a little wider than the note head, and a note can sit across, above, or below the ledger line.

Figure 7-5 shows you the ledger lines used to play the notes you name and read in this chapter. Experienced players regularly read notes on three or more ledger lines, but in this section, I show you the ledger line notes that you need to begin reading your violin notes.

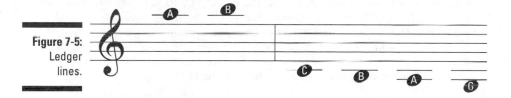

Figure 7-5:
Ledger
lines.

Ledger lines are spaced in the same way as regular staff lines, so your eyes can measure the distance between notes with good accuracy. The line-and-space system works the same way as with the five-line staff.

Music by the score: A brief history of music printing

Soon after the invention of moveable letter type, around 1450, printers realized that they could adapt the same idea to printing music. At first, the five lines were printed out on paper and the musical notes were then written by hand. But soon, a second impression was added on top of the five lines to print the notes too. It was a good idea and a huge step forward, but aligning the two impressions correctly was hard and made for some crazy-looking notes! *Block printing* ultimately superseded this process (which served very well until computers arrived on the scene a few years ago).

In block printing, the printer prepares a whole page of music at once, with the five lines, the notes, and any other signs in place. At first, the music was carved on wood blocks, but this method led to fairly unclear impressions. By the 1580s, engraved metal plates gave a better impression, literally. Sometimes, the composers themselves engraved their own plates for pieces — even the great Johann Sebastian Bach may have done this.

Some printers made attempts to typeset musical notation with musical typewriters and such. Typesetting music on computers became feasible only in the mid-1980s, thanks to some groundbreaking work by Professor Leland Smith, a distinguished member of the music faculty at Stanford University.

Naming Your Notes, String by String

You weren't allowed to do much name calling — I hope — when you were in grade school, but calling your notes by their names is a good thing to do (they're not easily offended, trust me). After you take all those note names and put them together with the notes (refer to Chapter 6), you'll be set up and ready to go!

I use the finger number system to show you how to play a few well-known songs earlier in this book. But when the music becomes more complex, with more variation in rhythms, dynamics, and pitches, you need to have a system that can easily represent all of these elements at once on the page.

Violins have 17 possible notes (plus their sharps and flats, which I discuss later, but for now they don't affect what you're actually doing) that can be played in what's called *first position*. This position means you play the notes using the left-hand setup I show you in Chapter 5, without sliding the left hand farther up the neck of the violin. The next section tells you what the notes are called and how to play them on your violin.

I know 17 notes seem like a lot, but they're really no problem. I go string-by-string, telling you about each note's letter name and the finger number you need to use for that note. Starting with the A string, I show you the process in a way that's similar to starting the alphabet. After getting to know the notes on the A string, transferring the same process to other note sequences is a breeze.

17 notes to know

I divide these 17 notes into four sets of five notes, with one set belonging on each string. Figure 7-6 shows you how those notes fit on the four strings, and it tells you the name for each note as well as the finger number you use to make that note sound (refer to Chapter 5 for information about the violin finger-numbering system).

The mathematicians among you are probably puzzled at 17 notes being divided into four sets of five notes, but a good reason exists for this conundrum: Each time you play finger 4 on any string, it plays the same pitch as the next-higher open string. So the notes produced by finger 4 on the G, D, and A strings don't count as extra pitches because they match the next-higher open string. Therefore, $(5 \times 4) - 3 = 17$. How's that for official-looking proof!

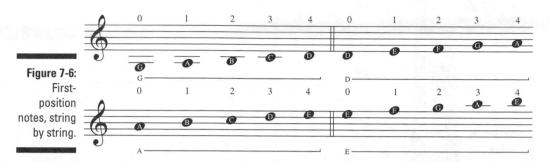

Figure 7-6:
First-
position
notes, string
by string.

Just to make remembering the 17 notes more of a challenge, you use different finger patterns on the different strings (only the D and A strings use the
same finger pattern).

A string

Because violinists always tune the A string first, and because the names of
notes on the A string correspond closely with the alphabet, starting with the
A string gives you a good idea of how naming the notes works — it's as easy
as ABC . . . DE!

To get to know the notes you play on the A string, look at them by name first:
A, B, C, D, and E. Playing these notes involves keeping finger 2 close to finger
1, as shown in Figure 7-7.

Figure 7-8 helps you to put your fingers on the right notes on the A string.
Your first and third fingers will be on their tapes (refer to Chapter 5 for more
about fingerboard tapes).

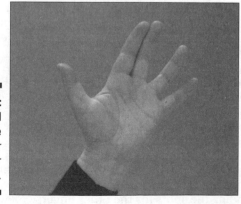

Figure 7-7:
Hand
showing the
finger
pattern for
the A string.

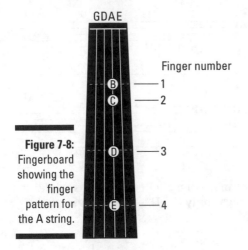

Figure 7-8:
Fingerboard
showing the
finger
pattern for
the A string.

E string

The E string is a very different kettle of fish from the A string, especially because it has nothing to do with fish, even when you play your scales! Most E strings are made of a single piece of wire, rather like the ones on cheese cutters, making it the brightest and clearest-sounding string of all the violin's strings. By playing on the E string after the A string (refer to the "A string" section), you complete your musical alphabet with these notes: E-F-G-A-B. Because the musical alphabet goes only as far as the letter G, you reach the letter A (one *octave* above your A string) again on the next note, and then, presto, the note after that note A is . . . B.

The distance in pitch from one note to the next note with the same name is called an *octave*. The "oct" bit of the word "octave" refers to the fact that the new A is the *eighth* note up from the old A, just as an octagon is an eight-sided figure. You can hear how alike the two As sound, but your new top A is obviously higher in pitch. To get the idea of an octave, sing the "somewhere" from "Somewhere over the Rainbow" next time you're in the shower.

The E-string finger pattern is a little different from the one on the A string. No two fingers are close together when you play the notes on the E string. Looking at the finger pattern in Figure 7-9 gives you the right idea.

You won't be surprised to discover that the correct finger placements on the E string are also a bit different from those used for the A string's notes. Although this instruction may seem strange, putting finger 4 on its spot first and then placing fingers 3, 2, and 1, in that order, helps your hand set up comfortably. Finger 1 is on a different placement from the finger 1 you play on the A string, so by first finding the spots for the other fingers, you help finger 1 reach its "low" spot. Finger 1 sits between the tape and the nut at the end of the fingerboard on the E string (see Figure 7-10).

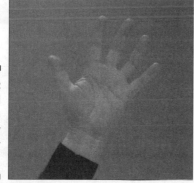

Figure 7-9: Hand showing the finger pattern for the E string.

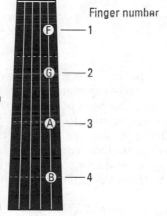

Figure 7-10: Fingerboard showing the finger pattern for the E string.

D string

The D string is a warm and gentle string, but just like some warm and gentle people, it can sound powerful when necessary. Your finger pattern for this string is just the pattern for the A string, with finger 2 close to finger 1 (refer to Figure 7-7).

Transferring the finger pattern onto the D string is pretty easy. Fingers 1 and 3 are on their respective tapes (and you have to respect respective tapes), and finger 2 is close to finger 1. Your resulting notes are D-E-F-G-A. Figure 7-11 shows how those fingers play on the violin.

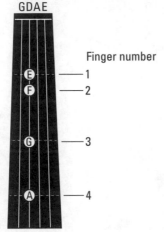

Figure 7-11:
Fingerboard
showing
the finger
pattern for
the D string.

G string

The G string is used for many thongs — oops, I mean songs — where the composer and the player want to impress an intense experience on the audience. The G string is the violin's thickest, deepest, and most powerful string. In fact, Paganini loved the G string so much that he's reputed to have filed down his other strings just before a concert, so that they were hanging by a thread. As the concert progressed, one string and then another would break, leaving Paganini with just the G string left to play on, and he would astound the audience with his musical feats. Rock stars today have nothing on Paganini!

The finger pattern on the G string involves keeping finger 2 and finger 3 close together, just like the picture in Figure 7-12.

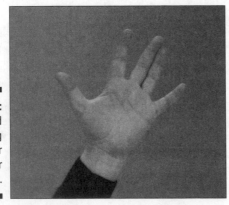

Figure 7-12:
Hand
showing
the finger
pattern for
the G string.

Figure 7-13 shows you where your fingers play on the fingerboard to get the notes G-A-B-C-D in place.

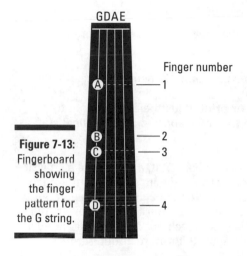

Figure 7-13: Fingerboard showing the finger pattern for the G string.

Meeting the Sharps, Flats, and Naturals

As I show you throughout this book, musical notation is full of some pretty funny-looking symbols. In this section, I show you what three of those symbols mean: sharps, flats, and naturals. *Sharps* look like number signs; *flats* resemble the lowercase letter *b;* and naturals don't actually resemble anything else, but after seeing them in this section, you can recognize them when they happen in the music you want to play.

Looking at sharps, flats, and naturals

Sometimes a composer wishes to modify a note's pitch slightly in order to make it sound just a bit higher or lower. The note is still called by the same name, but it's a different version of that note. It's a bit like when you buy a car: Your next-door neighbor to one side may have the same model as you do, but with a sunroof, and the person on your other side may have the same model again, but with a tinted windshield. They're all the same car, but each is slightly different than the other. It's the same concept with notes — same name, different version of the note. And because musicians aren't also mind readers who know what the composer wants without being told, three little signs exist to tell you.

Basic notes may make their appearances with the following symbols:

- ✔ *Sharp* (♯): Makes a note a *half step,* or *semitone,* higher.
- ✔ *Flat* (♭): Makes a note a half step, or semitone, lower.
- ✔ *Natural* (♮): Cancels any sharp or flat that was marked earlier on a particular note.

I tell you about half steps in the very next section, "Playing sharps and flats."

A sharp, flat, or natural sign is written or printed just before the note to which it applies, on the same line or in the same space on the musical staff as the note head.

Accidental is the musical name for any extra sharp, flat, and natural sign written next to a note on the staff. An accidental also affects subsequent appearances of that note, either until a different accidental occurs to cancel it out or until the *bar line* comes along to, well, *bar* its effect. Bar lines divide written music into sections, so basically, you have to watch out for a particular accidental just until the next bar line (see Chapter 9 for more about bar lines).

Although the symbol appears before the note, when talking or writing about music, players say it the other way around: "B flat," "F sharp," and so on.

Playing sharps and flats

So what do you do when you see a sharp or flat sign in front of a note you want to play? If you see a sharp, you play that note with your finger a *half step* higher than where it plays when it isn't affected by a symbol. You may not know the fancy names for the *intervals* (the distance between two notes), but you meet the smallest interval, the half step, many times in this book, whenever you put two fingers close together. You can find an example of a half step if you refer to the "A string" section of this chapter: Finger 1 (playing the note B) and finger 2 (playing the note C) are a half step apart. The distance isn't very far at all.

So if you see a sharp written in front of the note C that finger 2 plays on the A string, then finger 2 extends a little and lands a half step higher, to find itself close to where finger 3 plays to make C sharp.

If you see a flat written in front of the note B that finger 2 plays on the G string, then finger 2 curves a little and lands a half step lower, to find itself close to where finger 1 is playing.

I show you how to play a sharp or flat with finger 2, but of course, you can make the same kind of move up or down a half step with any of your fingers.

Another name you should know for "half step" is *semitone* (a term used traditionally in England), which appears frequently in references to the interval. A
whole step (or *whole tone*) is the name for the interval that happens when your
fingers have a regular space between them to go from one note to the next.

You meet many more sharps and flats in Chapter 10, where you find out
about scales.

Charting Your Way with the Fingers On

I show you how to crack the code of notes earlier in this chapter in the section
"Every Good Boy Deserves Fudge (and so do girls!)." But here comes the fun
bit: You actually get to play music reading from the notes! Give this song a try,
and find out how easily you can read a song when it's written on five lines.

At this point, you can take a step forward with your music reading by saying
each note name before you play the song. Saying the names out loud helps
you to establish the connections between what you see on the page, the name
of each note, and the finger your brain sends to play the note on the string.

P.S.: It's okay to pencil in finger numbers and note names under each note. A
pencil (with an eraser for later when you know this stuff well) is a musician's
best friend.

 TRACK 15

Boil the Cabbage Down

Here's a funny old country song you can get your teeth (and fingers) into! Set
up fingers 1 and 2 on the A string before you start. Fingers can remain lightly
on the string until you need to lift a finger to play the next note. You probably
don't need a "bow-by-bow" account, but you do need to start your first down-
bow a little below the middle of the bow, and to use about twice as much bow
for the half notes (the ones that aren't inked in) so that they last, well, twice
as long. *Bon appetit!*

Playing Loud and Soft — Dynamite Dynamics!

The last bit of essential info in this chapter shows you how to get some variations of volume into your music — a lot like adjusting the controls on your sound system when you listen to your favorite performers.

You may have noticed some letters and symbols underneath the notes of the song in the previous song, "Boil the Cabbage Down." Those characters aren't there just because I think they look cool — they actually mean something. When composers write music, they have the whole piece in mind, not only the melodies and harmonies but also the shouts and whispers, known as the *dynamics*.

As with a lot of musical language, we're using Italian here. *Forte* means "strongly" in Italian, which musicians translate as "loud." *Piano* means "gently," which we call "soft."

Some terms relating to dynamics (musical loudness and softness, not thermodynamics!) are based on these two Italian terms. Table 7-1 lists the terms and their corresponding symbols. To use your new skills, try playing the songs in the previous section, but this time creating some different dynamics.

Table 7-1	Musical Dynamics	
Symbol	**Name**	**Meaning**
pp	*pianissimo*	very quiet
p	*piano*	quiet
mp	*mezzopiano*	medium quiet
mf	*mezzoforte*	medium loud
f	*forte*	loud
ff	*fortissimo*	very loud
$<$	*crescendo (cresc.)*	getting louder
$>$	*diminuendo (dim.),* or *decrescendo*	getting quieter

Here are the three main ingredients to controlling your violin's sound:

- ✔ **Speed:** With speed, the faster you move the bow, the more the strings move and the more the volume increases. And of course, slowing down the bow reduces the volume.

- ✔ **Weight:** Adjusting the weight of the bow on the string (by pushing a little more or a little less) also affects the sound. Sometimes, in a slow piece of music, playing faster bows isn't an option, because you use up the whole bow before the end of the note. In that situation, you push down a little with your hand on the bow to get a stronger sound.

- ✔ **Contact point (sounding point):** The *contact point* is what string players call the place on the string where the bow is playing. You can control subtle changes in the contact point — by bowing closer to or farther away from the bridge — to change the volume of sound your violin produces. Figure 7-14 shows you the three main points of contact for the bow.

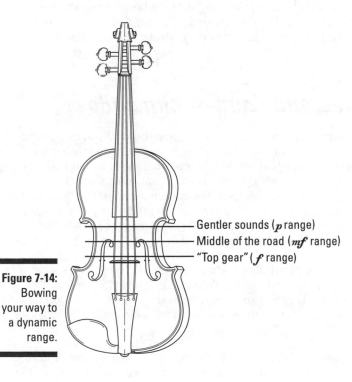

Gentler sounds (*p* range)
Middle of the road (*mf* range)
"Top gear" (*f* range)

Figure 7-14:
Bowing
your way to
a dynamic
range.

Making loud sounds

Playing with a strong sound means you have to add some weight onto the string with your bow. Because the strings have more tension at their greatest height — as they climb over the bridge toward the tailpiece — you can also bow a bit nearer to the bridge than usual to get more resistance from the strings, creating more volume.

If possible, increase the speed of the bow a little when you want to make loud sounds. Without this extra element, bowing too close to the bridge or adding too much weight to your bow can make the notes sound crunchy!

Making soft sounds

Soft sounds result from lightening the weight of the bow on the strings and letting the bow travel nearer the fingerboard, where the string tension is more relaxed. Slowing down the speed of each stroke also lets you create softer sounds.

Adding crescendo and diminuendo

Playing louder or softer means gradually changing the way you're bowing by adding all the "loud-sound" or "soft-sound" ingredients. At first, changing what you're doing can make you feel like you're on a roller coaster, and you may get some pretty strange sounds. But think about how many times Alexander Fleming got strange results in his experiments before he actually discovered penicillin! If your bow slips around too much, or you press too hard and get a crunch, you're also discovering the range of possibilities of your sound, and that's all good and useful.

Try the following exercise to find out what a *crescendo* (when the sound gets gradually louder) feels and sounds like. You can listen to the exercise being played on the CD-ROM. Try the exercise in reverse to feel what a *diminuendo* (when the sound gets gradually softer) is like. You can refer to Table 7-1 for guidance too.

Throughout this exercise, keep the bow moving along in a steady rhythm. If you don't have a metronome, you can groove to the second hand on a clock. Allow two or three second-hand clicks for each note. Spend several bow strokes (four to eight) on each dynamic level in order to gain a sense of the sound and feel of each level.

1. **Bow very lightly on the D string for your first down-bow, playing on a sounding point just over the top of the fingerboard.**

   Use just an inch or two of bow for each stroke. This step produces a *pianissimo (pp)* level of sound, which is very soft.

2. **Start to guide the bow a tad toward the bridge; about ¼ inch closer will be just right.**

   Increase the amount of bow you are using slightly, and add a little weight to the bow as you play. This step gives you one more level of power, called *piano (p),* which is quiet.

3. **Bow the string close to the midpoint between the fingerboard and the bridge.**

   Use about half of the bow, and apply fairly firm pressure. You're now playing *mezzopiano (mp),* which is medium quiet.

4. **Go to the midpoint between the fingerboard and the bridge.**

   This contact point is the classic middle-of-the-road place for a solid *mezzoforte (mf)* tone, which is medium loud. For this tone, use most of the bow — don't hold back your hand's weight on the bow at all.

5. **Drive the bow a little closer to the bridge.**

   Increase the speed of the bow so that you're using all of the bow for each stroke. This step gives you a *forte (f),* or loud, tone.

6. **Play at a strong point of contact quite close to the bridge.**

   Use a very firm bowing action and plenty of bow to get the strongest sound, *fortissimo (ff),* which is very loud.

These are beginning guidelines to getting a range of sounds. Professional violinists can draw a variety of sounds and "colors" from their instruments by using more subtle and varied mixtures of tone ingredients. Starting on these techniques sets you on the right path.

▶ TRACK 16

Ode to Joy

Yes, you guessed it — you need to set up fingers 1 and 2 on the D string before you begin playing "Ode to Joy." (To give finger 4 a workout, try playing 4 on D instead of playing the open A string here.)

Begin bowing about midway between the frog and the middle, just as you do with the other songs in this chapter. Because the first two bars are marked *p*, try setting your bow on the string a little nearer the top of the fingerboard to begin your first down-bow. Use little weight (pressure) and a slow stroke, just an inch or two of bow. When you reach measure 3, you see the crescendo sign, so begin to grow your bow strokes a little more for each note, gradually steering the bow to the middle-of-the-road contact point. The final half note uses about two-thirds of the bow.

The first note of measure 5 starts as an up-bow. Maintain the *mf* level that you reached at the end of the first section by keeping a consistent weight and speed of bowing. Then, at measure 7, start growing your sound again. Increase the amount of bow gradually, a bit more for each note, and steer a little closer to the bridge. Now you're using most of the bow. Adding weight with your hand onto the bow stick brings you to a triumphant and strong *f* ending.

Chapter 8

Here's Counting on You: A Guide to Rhythm

*Y*ou may not be particularly aware of it, but rhythm is a big part of your everyday life. It's relatively easy to take examples of activities you already know and do and then apply them to playing your violin. Before you were born, your heart was already beating rhythmically. Then when you started walking and running, you had two more everyday activities that can be counted pretty steadily. So you're an old pro at counting! In this chapter, I take those skills and apply them to counting note values in music.

Musical *notation,* as we call our system of writing down sounds, is packed with a whole bunch of very important information, all at once. In this chapter, I deal with one aspect of notation, the note's *duration* — the term given to describing how long that note lasts. You discover what the different note values look like, and how to count them. Luckily, you learned how to count in grade school (or earlier), so all you have to do when counting music is know how to keep a steady pace. Hup, two, three, four, off we go!

Anatomy of a Musical Note

You'll be pleased to know that the anatomy of a musical note is not nearly as complicated as the anatomy of a violin (refer to Chapter 2). However, each individual part of a note does signify something important to a musician (notes are functional little guys, aren't they?).

A musical note has four main parts, which you can see in Figure 8-1. Here is what you need to know about their names and functions:

✔ **Note head:** Whether it is filled in with ink or looks like just an empty duck egg, a note head's location on a particular line or space of the staff indicates the pitch of the note. The note head also indicates the duration of a note, depending on its look and on the presence (or absence) of a stem.

✔ **Stem:** All notes except whole notes have a stem, which looks like a stick attached to the side of the note. Stems can point up or down from the note.

✔ **Tail:** Tails look rather like little flags flying on top of the stem of a note. If there is one tail, your note is worth an eighth; two tails make it a sixteenth note; and three tails make it a thirty-second note. When the stem is pointing down, the tail looks like a little foot dancing along at the end of the stem.

✔ **Beam:** A beam may remind you of a kitchen ceiling in one of those charming old farmhouses. Beams go all the way across the tops of the stems of two or more notes that occur within the same beat. Now when you see beams, the system is the same as with tails: One beam means it's an eighth note; two beams mean you're dealing with sixteenth notes; and so on.

When you look at a page of music, you see a dizzying array of notes before your eyes! The next few sections show you what the different note values look like, what they represent, and how they work together in music.

Figure 8-1:
Violinists,
take note.

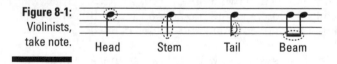

Head   Stem   Tail   Beam

Adding Up the Value of Notes

Think back to when you were in grade school. Remember the little desks, the cubbyhole for your lunchbox, and the way you couldn't wait to get outside for recess? Well, another memory you may have (and don't tell me you blocked it out) is of the time you first started learning fractions. This class probably involved Ms. Crabtree drawing a "pie" on the board and then subdividing it into halves, quarters, and eighths. The lesson may have given you a hankering for a slice *à la mode,* but at the same time, it also prepared you to know musical notes. Some notes are long, some notes are very short, and some have a kind of in-between length. In this section, I show you what these notes are and how to keep the beat according to the notes written on the staff.

Whole notes

A *whole note* is a note in its most basic form: It's made up of just the head of the note, with no stem or tail. A whole note is oval-shaped and hollow (it's not inked in), and it looks kind of like an eye, peering at you from the staff — perhaps to make sure that you're practicing enough? See Figure 8-2 for an illustration.

The whole note has a value of 4 beats, so playing it is like having an entire pie to yourself — except it won't give you a bellyache. When you see a whole note, it means the note will last for 4 counts, or *beats,* as they are called in musical rhythm terms.

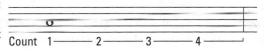

Figure 8-2:
Whole
notes last
for 4 beats.

To really get the feel of a whole note, try this: Tap your foot in a steady rhythm four times (1, 2, 3, 4), and as you do so, hum like Winnie-the-Pooh. Your hum should last four taps; that's how long a whole note is. In fact, you keep on humming right up to the point where the next (fifth) tap would begin.

Here's a trick to help you remember what a whole note is: It looks like a hole, and it lasts a whole lot of time!

Using whole notes, you can play two important sections (let's call them *phrases,* which is the-musical-word-for-a-section-of-music-that-you-could-sing-easily-before-you-need-to-draw-breath — phew!) of the "Pachelbel Canon." Figure 8-3 is the music, and you can listen to it being played on the CD-ROM.

Figure 8-3:
First two
phrases
of the
"Pachelbel
Canon" in
whole
notes.

It's fine to play in whole notes for a little while, but soon you crave a little variety so that you don't get hypnotized! Luckily, so did Pachelbel, so he went on into other note values in the next section of his Canon.

Half notes

The next note value you want to meet is the half note. A *half note* lasts half as long as a whole note (surprise!): two counts. Going back to that pie, you wouldn't get the whole thing all to yourself; you'd share it with your best friend! It sounds as if a half note isn't worth as much as a whole note, but that's true only in terms of how much *time* it's worth. In terms of music, the time it lasts can be just the right amount.

Half notes look a lot like whole notes, except each half note has its own stem. The stem is attached to the right side of the note head when it points up, making the note look like the letter *d,* and to the left side of the note head when it points down, making it look like a letter *p* (see Figure 8-4).

The stem points up or down depending on the note's position on the staff. The idea behind this system is to keep the stems from sticking out too far above or below the five lines, in case they get tangled up with stems from another staff — and we can't have those kinds of entanglements happening, now can we? The stem of any note on the middle line of the staff can go up or down, depending on the context.

With the same foot-tapping action that you used for whole notes, tap twice for a half note (humming optional). You can also try those first two phrases of "Pachelbel Canon," only this time in half notes, as shown in Figure 8-5 and as played on the CD-ROM.

Figure 8-4:
Half notes in
action.

TRACK 17, 1:01

Figure 8-5:
First two
phrases of
"Pachelbel
Canon" in
half notes.

Quarter notes

Quarter notes are the most basic beat in music. Their name derives from the fact that they last a *quarter* as long as whole notes — one count each — and not because they cost 25 cents each! Your original apple pie is now divided into four slices. Quarter notes are instantly recognizable because their note heads are completely inked in, which makes them easy to read on the staff, and they have stems, just like half notes. Now when you tap your foot, each quarter note begins at the sound of the tap.

To really get the feel of quarter notes, which are the note values you find a whole lot in music, try this little exercise: Pace steadily around the room (but try not to feel stressed as you pace; this is supposed to be fun). As you pace, count each step like this: "1, 2, 3, 4, 1, 2, 3, 4." The count happens as you land your foot on the floor. After you pace and count a few times (don't make yourself dizzy), you can write your steps down as quarter notes, just like the ones you see in Figure 8-6.

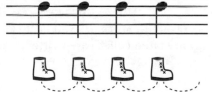

Figure 8-6:
Pacing in
quarter
notes.

After you know how to recognize and count quarter notes, you want to play them, right? Follow the exercise in Figure 8-7 (you find this on the CD-ROM too). I give you a few hints to help you along.

Start with your bow ready on the D string, just below the mid-point. Play evenly, using the middle portion of the bow. Imagine your arm is the pendulum of an old-fashioned grandfather clock, and tick away as you add the new finger at the start of each group of four quarters. Play the last note on the open A string, using a slower bow stroke, and keep counting the same quarter note values while you play the whole note: "1, 2, 3, 4, stop."

TRACK 17, 1:37

Figure 8-7:
Close
quarters.

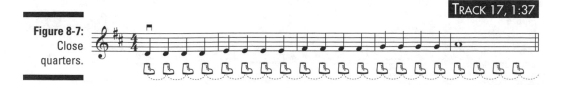

Eighth notes

The next note value you have to meet in this chapter is the eighth note. That old apple pie is getting cut up into smaller slices now — eight of them altogether! In fact, *eighth notes* are thought of as having two eighths living inside a quarter note. Think of taking the pie that has been cut into quarters and then taking each slice and cutting it in two again. Figure 8-8 illustrates eighth notes. So going back to the pacing, this time you say "1, 2, 3, 4" for the first four paces, to establish the beats. Then you add in the word "and" between each count, so you say "1-and, 2-and, 3-and, 4-and." That "and" puts the eighth notes in place between the quarter note beats, just where they belong.

Figure 8-8:
Eighth
notes.

Sometimes you see a whole bunch of eighth notes in a row, as in Figure 8-9. When two or more *eighths* (as they are often called) are written, they are usually beamed together.

Figure 8-9:
Beam up
the eighth
notes,
Scotty!

In Figure 8-10, I give you an eighth note exercise (although I throw in some quarter notes to mix things up a little) for you to count and tap along with your CD-ROM.

Figure 8-10:
An exercise
with eighth
and quarter
notes.

TRACK 17, 2:00

Say: "1   2   3   4   1 and 2 and 3 and 4 and 1   2   3 and 4 and 1 and 2 and 3   4 "

Sixteenth notes

Now the original pie is starting to get a bit squashed up from being divided into some pretty small pieces. For the 16 slices that you need here, taking the quarter notes and dividing each one into four works best. So you can still pace (fairly majestically — Queen Victoria would be amused), counting "1, 2, 3, 4" for a bit. Then add the *sixteenth note* words inside each count like this: "1-ee-and-a, 2-ee-and-a, 3-ee-and-a, 4-ee-and-a." You get a face muscle workout at the same time as you figure out note values!

Some musicians use words for rhythms, a helpful and fun alternative. Sixteenths can be called "Londonderry," "Manitoba," and so on — four resonant and rhythmic syllables!

Sixteenth notes work just like eighths for tails and beams, only sixteenths have two little flags at the end of each stem. Figure 8-11 shows you how those sixteenths might appear all alone, and together with other sixteenths, in the course of a piece of music.

After you know how to count sixteenth notes and you know what they look like, Figure 8-12 is a little exercise to play along with your CD-ROM.

Figure 8-11: Three ways sixteenth notes pop up in music.

16ths alone   16ths in groups   16ths with 8ths   Dotted 8ths with 16ths

Figure 8-12: An exercise with sweet sixteenth notes.

TRACK 17, 2:20

Triplets

As its name suggests, three *triplets* are in a quarter beat. Although triplets look a lot like eighth notes, you can tell the difference when you see them, because they are grouped in threes and have an italic number *3* above or below the beam. (See what triplets look like in Figure 8-13.) Going back to that same quarter note pacing you use in this section to keep things steady, each pace gets three subdivisions. Unlike building developments, these sub-divisions don't take up vast amounts of farmland — but you do need to fit all three inside the quarter note value. Saying "tri-po-let," or, if you have a sweet tooth, "lol-li-pop" on each beat will divide it up nicely into triplets.

When you get the basic flow of triplets, try playing this exercise (Figure 8-14). Triplets and quarter notes are alongside each other in music, and you get to move smoothly in and out of the rhythms. I show you this one on the CD-ROM too.

Notable moments in music notation

Here's a potted history of notation, with a time-line to show you how things evolved.

✔ **Before the first century:** A more specific timeframe is hard to pinpoint, but people used phonetic systems of notation thousands of years ago. The Hindus, the Chinese, the Arabs, and the Ancient Greeks all used similar systems of musical notation, although the details varied. They all wrote music down by using letter names and other symbols. The systems were quite log-ical and exact, but they lacked an extra set of signs to indicate the time values of notes.

✔ **Ninth century:** The next important system became fully evolved around the ninth cen-tury, and the "notes" were called *neumes.* Neumes, which were adapted from Greek inflection accents and punctuation, looked rather like ants marching toward spilled ice cream. Neumes were helpful only if you already knew more or less how the song was supposed to sound. Neumes could indicate the approximate pitches and dura-tions of notes, but they showed mostly note groupings and subtle emphases of musical phrases, which were important to singers at that time.

✔ **Thirteenth century:** A more exact system gradually took over from neumes. *Mensural notation* looked somewhat like our modern system. The system first appeared around 1250, and was the first to define notes in terms of proportion (one whole note = two half notes, one dotted half note = three quarter notes, and so on). The look of the actual notes was significantly different from the ones in use today. Notes were mostly square in shape — which is probably because square and diamond shapes were easier to write with a quill pen. By this time, clefs, sharps, and flats had also come into regular use.

✔ **Seventeenth century to today:** *Staff notation* was a natural development from all these ingredients, accommodating the need for high and low notes, 24 keys, loud and soft playing, and different meters and speeds — all the features we now expect to have communicated in a few signs! The staff nota-tion system is so adaptable and adjustable that composers still use it today (although the system sometimes can't accommodate highly experimental forms of music, for which additional symbols are evolving).

Figure 8-13:
Triplets.

The italic "*3*" lets you know they're triplets

Figure 8-14:
An exercise with triplets and quarters.

TRACK 17, 2:40

Adding Dots (No Need to Cross the Ts)

What do you do if a quarter note is too short for you but a half note is too long? Don't worry; you don't have to cover yet another set of notes — a little dot'll do you.

When a dot appears beside a note, believe it or not, it's usually not a fruit fly or an ink spot. The dot means that the value of the note increases by half of its regular duration. Dot's about all you need to know!

Don't worry, I don't go through every note to show you what they look like followed by a dot — I'm sure you can picture them. Besides, you won't bump into a dotted sixteenth note that often. The upcoming sections describe the dotted notes you see quite frequently.

Dotted half notes

If you see a half note with a dot next to the right side of its head, it means the note is worth its usual 2 beats, plus a half of that — which, as you realize, is 1 additional beat. So in total, the note is worth 3 beats. See Figure 8-15 for a little practice in counting dotted half notes. Depending on its position in the measure, count 1, 2, 3 or 2, 3, 4 for a dotted half note. I also play it on the CD-ROM, if you want to hear it all together before you try it.

Figure 8-15:
Dotted half notes in real life.

TRACK 18, 0:00

Moderato

mf

Dotted quarter notes

If you see a quarter note with a dot next to the right side of its head, it means the note is worth its usual 1 beat, plus half of that, which is an eighth note. So in total, dotted quarter notes are equal to 1½ beats. Dotted quarter notes always leave an eighth note over, which needs to be fitted in before the next quarter note.

Probably the best and easiest way to count dotted quarter notes is to pace around the room in quarter notes. (Hope your carpet isn't getting worn out!) Count the usual steady 1, 2, 3, 4 as you step along. After a few paces, count "1, 2-and, 3, 4," fitting the "and" between the second and third pace. (You're right if you figure out that you turn the second beat into two eighth notes.)

The next step, because I'm all about stepping out the beats, is to do the same stepping and counting, with one small but vital difference: Leave out saying beat 2. So you count and step the same way, but when you get to beat 2, just step and don't say the number. You get a dotted quarter note on the first beat, and it looks like the rhythm in Figure 8-16 and sounds like the rhythm on the CD-ROM.

Of course, dotted quarter notes can appear in all kinds of musical situations. In Figure 8-17, I show you a real piece of music with some dotted quarter notes included. You can listen to it on your CD-ROM and play along with the demo I provide.

Figure 8-16: Dotted quarter notes.

TRACK 18, 0:19

1   2   and   3   4   1   2   and   3   4

Figure 8-17: "Dot's all for now, folks!"

TRACK 18, 0:31

Moderato

mf

Taking a Rest

Rests are valuable little signs that prove that silence can be golden. Sometimes the music doesn't sound for a beat or two — or four. Luckily, it's not up to you to guess when that's supposed to happen; the composer lets you know by writing a rest, to signify a pause. You'll be happy to know that I don't present you with a whole new system of counting. When you get to know the various notes, familiarizing yourself with the corresponding rests is a snap.

The value of each rest corresponds to the value of a note with the same name. Figure 8-18 shows you what rests look like, and the notes they correspond with.

- **Whole rest:** This rest corresponds with the whole note, so it's worth 4 beats. It looks a bit like an upside-down hat (you know, the kind street musicians use to collect donations from passersby).

- **Half rest:** This rest corresponds to the half note, and it's worth 2 beats. Imagine that street musician going home, emptying out the coins, and putting the hat on a table with the brim down.

- **Quarter rest:** A quarter rest is worth 1 beat, and it looks a lot like those seagulls you used to draw on pictures in art class!

- **Eighth rest:** An eighth rest corresponds in value to an eighth note; it looks a lot like a number 7 on the staff.

- **Sixteenth rest:** The shortest rest in the chart is equivalent to the sixteenth note. This rest has a long name and a short value. The sixteenth rest looks a lot like the eighth rest, but with an extra tail added to make it look like the tail of a sixteenth note.

Rests usually appear in the middle bit of the five lines, unless they need to be moved higher or lower because another note's already in the middle position on the staff — but that kind of thing happens much more in piano music, so don't worry!

Figure 8-18: Everybody needs a rest.

| Whole rest (= o) | Half rest (= 𝅗𝅥) | Quarter rest (= ♩) | Eighth rest (= ♪) | Sixteenth rest (= ♬) |

I'd like to recommend that you listen to the CD-ROM to hear the different rests, but for some reason, I can never hear them after they're recorded. How strange . . .

You've Got Rhythm: Pieces to Play!

When you have a whole range of notes and rests at your fingertips, you can play lots of different songs. On the CD-ROM, I show you how to count and play these songs, and you can listen and count your way through them too.

Getting back to your starting place

When playing a piece of music, if one phrase ends on a down-bow and you're going to play a down-bow to start the next phrase also, you need to make what's called a *circular retake* to get back to the right starting place for your second down-bow. Try these retakes using the A string:

1. As you finish the down-bow, imagine your bow is an airplane and the string is a runway, and take off without stopping your momentum.

2. Lift the bow a few inches up from the string, fly back through the air (an up-bow in the air) to the frog, and then make a smooth touchdown for the next down-bow.

Okay, so the retakes aren't exactly circular; they may be a bit sausage-shaped. But hey, we're violinists, not Michelangelo!

For each new song, get a grip on the rhythms first, and then add the left-hand notes afterwards. We may not be pianists, but we can borrow their idea of practicing "hands separately" for getting on top of violin music too. So for your left hand, you can work through the fingering without bowing the notes. Just find your way silently to the right spots at first, and later you can try the song pizzicato to work on the timing (refer to Chapter 5 for more about pizzicato).

 TRACK 19

Little Brown Jug

Here you're mixing quarters, eighths, and even a couple of sixteenths. I give you the rhythms to play on open strings, so that you can concentrate on getting the different note values in place without having to bother with coordinating any busy fingers. You'll be able to hear the tune of the song going on in the piano part as you play along with the recording.

TRACK 20

Boiling the Cabbage Further Down

Set finger 2 on the A string before you begin. You can keep finger 2 sitting on the string while you play finger 3, because you're coming right back to it. Have finger 1 ready just before you lift finger 2, so you don't have a gap between notes. And hold that last half note for 2 full beats. I give you the bowings over the notes of the first measure, then you continue the same way until the last note, which is a long down-bow.

TRACK 21

Nutcracker Sweet

This tune, taken from the March in Tchaikovsky's famous ballet, gives you a chance to count a whole bunch of rests. The left hand is not at all tricky in this piece — you can give your full attention to counting rhythms and rests. Start on open D, and have fingers 1 and 2 poised over their spots, ready to land briskly as you march along. Go back and repeat the first set of two measures as you arrive at the repeat sign (those two dots just before the first double bar line). In this version, you can count very quietly, so that you can hear the music that happens during your rests, until you play again. Once you know how the music goes, you can try counting out the four rest measures like a professional orchestral player: "ONE-2-3-4, TWO-2-3-4, THREE-2-3-4, FOUR-2-3-4," keeping track of the passing measures as you count.

Chapter 9

Getting Ticked Off: A Guide to Meter

ou already know quite a bit about beat patterns from hearing marching bands at parades and different kinds of dance music in movies, to give two typical examples of meters in action. In fact, it was largely dance music that encouraged the development of more regular and systematic meters, because those dancers didn't want to have to keep measuring their meters with yardsticks!

In this chapter, you find out how to count the different time signatures and hear how they give your music more zip.

Measure for Measure

In Chapter 8, I talk about the different types of notes and rests you find on printed music. But those notes aren't free to roam around wherever they please on the staff — every so often, a vertical line pens in the notes. Those lines, known as *bar lines,* don't appear randomly — each one seals off a set number of beats, literally barring them from invading the rest of the music.

Bar lines came into general use around 1600 to make notes easier for the eye to follow on the page (although the bars didn't always have a consistent number of beats in them till quite a bit later). But thank goodness we have them today, because they divide music into easily countable sections. (See how the bar lines keep everything neat and tidy in Figure 9-1.) The section between bar lines, which contains a set number of beats, is called a *measure,* or *bar*.

Figure 9-1:
Keeping the
beats in line.

Bar line   Bar line   Bar line

You may also notice the bar line's friend, the *double bar,* but you probably won't notice it as often. That's because the composer uses it for a different purpose: When the piece of music is finished, the composer writes a double bar, just to let you know you're done (see Figure 9-2). Isn't that considerate? Otherwise, you may just keep playing forever and ever! Double bars can also happen at the end of a section of music, even if it's not the end of the piece.

If a double bar has two dots aligned vertically along its side, in the second and third spaces, you have a *repeat sign*. The composer is telling the player to repeat the section. You may need to repeat sections in music such as hymns, which have many verses, or in dance music, when the same steps come around again. Composers also use repeat signs because repeating a section not only gives you the pleasure of hearing it again but also helps structure the architecture of the movement or piece into a beautiful shape.

You may be wondering, with these repeat signs, how do you know where to go back to? Either go all the way back to the beginning of the piece or go back to the last repeat sign, whichever one you run into first as you go back toward the beginning. You may also see a repeat sign with the dots on the *right* of the double bar, which shows you where the repeated section *begins*. Figure 9-2 shows you the difference between a regular double bar and a repeat sign.

A term musicians use a lot (and you're one now, so you'd better start using it too!) is the word *meter,* which describes a regular musical pattern of beats per measure. Just like the dials on your gas meter, musical meter has different bits that you need to get to know. So whether you're reading music or your gas meter, you have to know what each bit means. But musical meter is much more fun, and you don't have to pay for it!

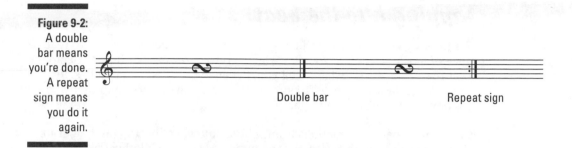

Figure 9-2:
A double
bar means
you're done.
A repeat
sign means
you do it
again.

Double bar   Repeat sign

Keeping Time: Time Signatures

Perhaps it would be convenient if all music was written with the same kind of timing, but it wouldn't be nearly as much fun. You wouldn't get waltzes and tangos, or any of the many different dances and musical movements that you find in the violin's repertoire. Luckily, you already know many songs that use different types of timing, but how do you, as a musician, make sense of it all when you play?

The time in a piece of music is, literally, measured out in fixed portions by the *time signature,* which is made up of two numbers, stacked one on top of the other, at the start of the piece or section and just to the right of the clef (refer to Chapter 7 for more about clefs). Figure 9-3 shows you how the numbers stack up. The time signature tells you two important pieces of information:

- ✔ The top number tells you *how many* beats are in a measure.
- ✔ The bottom number tells you *what kind* of note gets one beat.

Never take your time signature for granted. Sometimes the time signature can change at the start of a new section in the same piece of music.

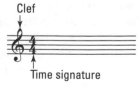

Figure 9-3:
Staff with a
clef and
a 4/4 time
signature.

Clef

Time signature

Tapping into the beat

The time signature is one of the first things you see when you begin to read a piece of music. So before you play, you need to know exactly how to decipher what that little guy is trying to tell you. Because the most usual time signature is 4⁄4 (refer to Figure 9-3), I start with that as an example and then show you how to read other time signatures.

If you remember your fractions from school, knowing how to count a bar in 4⁄4 is pretty easy. In this case, the top number is *4*, which indicates that each bar has 4 beats, and the bottom number is *4*, which indicates that each beat is worth a quarter note. So four quarter notes fill up one measure.

In fact, this time signature is so popular that not only does it appear in lots of songs, but it doesn't even need to use its full name to get recognized — it's also printed as "C" (as shown in Figure 9-4), meaning *common time*.

A 4⁄4 measure can contain any mixture of rhythms, not just quarter notes, so long as they don't add up to more than 4 beats! Figure 9-5 shows some typical rhythms, which you can listen to (and count along with) on the CD-ROM.

Figure 9-4:
C'mon, time
to play!

Common time

Figure 9-5:
Mixing it up
in 4⁄4 time.

TRACK 22, 0:00

Actually, what we see as a letter *C* was originally intended to be a semicircle. A meter with 3 beats per bar was called *perfect time* and was designated with a circle. A meter with 2 or 4 beats per bar was called *imperfect time* and was designated with an incomplete circle. Imperfect time was considered to be very daring in the year 1250!

Conducting yourself well

Before you play each of these different meters on your violin, take some practice runs at conducting (see Figure 9-6). Arm yourself with a pencil or a chopstick as your weapon of choice! The best way to get going is to actually point your "weapon" to the note head you are counting as you go along, keeping the pointer moving steadily as you say the counts (it's the same idea as with a "Follow the bouncing ball!" sing-along).

Figure 9-6:
Four bars of 4/4 for you to forge forth!

The beat indicates the *beginning* of each note.

Bowing out the beat

When you can count steadily, moving your pointer along the musical line as you go, you're ready to try bowing on your violin as you count.

For the purpose of concentrating on those counting skills, just play open strings for now. Figure 9-7 is the same four bars for you to play on your violin. Start with a down-bow, and keep a steady pulse. Say the counts as you play. You can follow along with the CD-ROM.

TRACK 22, 0:19

Figure 9-7:
Playing as you count.

Counting rests

Earlier sections of this chapter focus on counting and playing at the same time — but what about counting and *not* playing at the same time?

Sometimes in music, a beat or two go by where the rhythm continues but the player takes a musical breath, known as a *rest*. You can read about counting rests in Chapter 8, but this chapter puts them into a real musical bar. First, you meet a quarter rest to try out.

Try counting through Figure 9-8 first, and then try playing it on your violin. When you reach a rest, just stop the bow gently on the string for the rest, and then move it again for the next note to sound. Listening to the exercise on the CD-ROM should help you get the hang of it.

Figure 9-8:
Playing,
counting,
and
resting —
oh my!

TRACK 22, 0:38

Emphasizing the right beat

Apart from letting musicians know how many counts are in a bar, the time signature also shows you more about *how* to play the music. Different beats of a bar receive different amounts of emphasis, just as different syllables in a word do. For example, you say FA-ther, and not fa-THER.

In music, the first beat of a bar is called the *downbeat,* because it gets the most emphasis. (In fact, conductors indicate the first beat by moving their batons in a downward motion.) The last beat of a bar usually gets the least weight.

Sometimes songs don't begin on the first beat of a bar. If you have a preliminary beat, it's played as an *upbeat,* or a *pickup.* Just as not all words begin on an accented syllable (we say vio-LIN, not VI-olin), some melodies don't begin with a downbeat. These unaccented first beats are called *pickups,* and they're written as an incomplete measure before the first bar line. (And guess what? Conductors use an upward motion to indicate an upbeat.)

In counting measures, the first complete measure counts as bar 1. For example, the well-known Christmas carol "O Come, All Ye Faithful" begins with a pickup on the word "O." The main emphasis is on the word "come," which works naturally with how you'd actually say the words. If you wrote the song without a pickup, just beginning on the first beat of bar 1, you'd get the wrong accent: O come all YE faithful. Compare the two versions in Figure 9-9.

TRACK 22, 0:57

Figure 9-9:
Two
versions of
"O Come, All
Ye Faithful."

Marvelous metronomes

Around 1812, immortalized by the "1812 Overture" of Tchaikovsky, Amsterdam scientist Dietrich Johannes Winkel (no relative of Rip!) invented a ticking machine with a pendulum that pointed up instead of down — the *metronome*. On the pendulum was a moveable weight. The closer Winkel slid the weight to the bottom of the pendulum, where a fixed weight was located, the faster the machine ticked. The ticks were measured in beats per minute, so if the metronome was set at 60, you got one beat every second, if it was set at 120, you got two beats per second, and so on. Winkel figured out that this invention would make a reliable and evenly paced counting machine.

Unfortunately for him, Winkel's invention was nicked in an act of industrial skulduggery by Johannes Maelzel, who marketed it heavily to such individuals as Beethoven. Beethoven was initially most enthusiastic about the metronome, so he wrote the second movement of his Eighth Symphony to imitate its regular clicks. But Beethoven then quarreled with Maelzel, who was apparently as charming as he was ethical! Maelzel eventually went bankrupt on the metronome, having mismanaged his capital, and then he proceeded to market a fraudulent chess automaton and float other fanciful schemes. Winkel must have been really ticked off!

Most metronomes are now digital, but they still do what they did when they were first invented: They keep a steady beat at a speed the user chooses. Of course, performing music like an automaton isn't something you want to do, but metronomes are really useful for practicing, to keep an accurate rhythm.

Using Metronomes

While playing the violin, you can't always beat time (instead of having time beat you)! That's what metronomes are for — to keep you playing steadily. Metronomes are also useful to composers, for letting conductors and performers know the speed of a piece of music. Of course, many kinds of metronomes are available, so this section tells you what's out there and how to use the different kinds of metronomes.

Mechanical metronomes

Today, many musicians still favor the traditional mechanical metronome because it's almost an icon — a piece of famous, historic equipment for musicians to park on their pianos or coffee tables. Mechanical metronomes look very neat: Despite being old-fashioned, they have the advantage of not needing power sources or batteries to make them work. All you have to do is wind one up.

If you have a traditional metronome that still works, I show you how to get up to speed. Here's what you have to do:

1. **Remove the front cover of the mechanical metronome.**
2. **Wind up the mechanism without forcing the spring.**
3. **Release the top of the pendulum from its clip.**
4. **Listen to the ticking, which begins right away.**

   Occasionally, you may have to give the pendulum a little sideways push for it to begin ticking.

Setting the speed on a mechanical metronome involves lining up the *top* edge of the weight with the speed you want on the number chart that runs alongside the pendulum. Figure 9-10 shows you a mechanical metronome.

Nowadays, you can buy mechanical metronomes built in different shapes and sizes than the original pyramid style shown in Figure 9-10. Mini models, brightly colored versions, and even children's metronomes shaped like animals are available. But all mechanical metronomes function in the same way — you wind them up, and then they tick in a measured beat.

Mechanical metronomes need to sit on a flat, horizontal surface to tick regularly.

Figure 9-10:
Making your way with a mechanical metronome.

Electronic metronomes

Currently the most popular option, electronic metronomes are available in lots of different models. Some metronomes are as small as credit cards, and some are larger models with all kinds of neat functions (except they don't do the dishes!). Some metronomes also double as tuners.

Usually, you see a switch on the side of an electronic metronome that has three settings: off, sound and light, and light only. When you switch on the metronome, you hear a click on each beat and you see a light flash. You can use the flashing light to see the beats when the sound of your music makes it difficult for you to hear the clicks.

The most convenient electronic metronomes have a dial on the front, which allows you to turn quickly to the speed you want.

Electronic metronomes now include more and more features. Winkel (refer to the sidebar "Marvelous metronomes") would be amazed! Figure 9-11 shows two electronic models.

Your best bet is getting a small, rectangular electronic metronome that you can keep in the pocket of your violin case.

Figure 9-11:
Two electronic metronomes.

If your electronic metronome has a dial, you can set the dial to the right speed before you switch on the metronome. Simply turn the dial, rather like setting the dial on a washing machine (but unlike the dial on a washing machine, it's okay to turn it either way on most metronome models). After you switch on the sound, the metronome begins clicking, and then you can play. I give more advice about working with a metronome at the end of this section.

Look for these useful features in a basic electronic metronome:

- Ease of setting the tempo (generally, a dial is quicker but offers fewer settings)
- Good visibility of the flashing light
- Right size to fit in your violin case
- Table stand feature (like on the back of a photo frame)
- Volume control

You may want some fancier features on your electronic metronome:

- Ability to subdivide the beat into two, three, or four sub-beats ("tick, tock, tock")
- AC/DC ability (plug it in, and save on batteries)
- Earphone or microphone jacks
- Simulated pendulum LED (to see time "moving")
- Sound to indicate the first beat of a measure in any standard meter ("*ching,* tick, tick")
- Tuning functions (from a simple A440 tone to a variety of more sophisticated tuning measurements)
- Voice (counts "one, two, three, four" aloud as you play)

Even computer programs can function as metronomes these days. All kinds of musical software are available for those who like their practice time to be a bit more high-tech. Just ask friends who are computer buffs, check out your local music stores, or go online to find out what's available.

Making friends with your metronome

Working with a metronome is part of playing with steady rhythm: It makes the music dance along, and playing with other musicians is easier when everyone moves to the same beat. When musicians are performing, of course the music doesn't just click along like a metronome — it has some ebb and flow, occasional breaths, or places where it slows down or speeds up. But training with a metronome is still something musicians need to do to be sure they know the correct basic moves, and then they let their creativity flow when the music feels right.

So how do you get started? I take you through the first steps of working with an electronic metronome using the song shown in Figure 9-12 as an example.

Figure 9-12:
Clicking
with the
electronic
metronome.

At the top of the music, you see a *metronome marking,* which is the name for the sign that tells you what number to set on your speed dial. "M.M." means "Maelzel Metronome," though it could just as easily stand for "Metronome Marking."

Set your metronome dial to 72, which means the tick for each quarter note happens 72 times each minute, just a little faster than once every second. The *tempo* (which is just a fancy Italian word for the speed of music) is quite Moderate and Manageable, but that's also not what M.M. stands for!

Don't count, clap, or play too loudly when working with a metronome. Bashing out the rhythms is tiring, and it can cover the sound of the metronome's beat.

Notice that the metronome exercise (Track 23) on the CD-ROM gives four clicks before the music begins. Counting a full bar before you begin gives you a sense of the pulse and helps you play in time, not just as a beginner, but whenever you're working on rhythm and counting.

After you count aloud, try clapping the note rhythms as the metronome beats. Clapping with a free, slightly circular motion, as if you're playing the cymbals, keeps you moving well to the beat.

The metronome's click indicates where the beat begins, so when you're practicing counting to the rhythm, line up your clapping as exactly as possible with the clicks.

The next step is to try the bow rhythms on one open string, so that you practice each hand separately, just like pianists do.

When your bowing is in time, you can put down the bow and try your left hand alone, still in time with the metronome. If you're comfortable playing *pizzicato,* which is Italian for plucking the strings, you can hear the notes more clearly. (Chapter 5 explains how to play pizzicato.)

Making Music in 4/4 Meter

If you're thinking you can't possibly count any more, don't worry — counting gets fun in this section. You use your knowledge of meter to play some songs. These songs use the 4/4 meter that you practice in the previous section.

TRACK 24

Old MacDonald

When Old MacDonald bought the farm — literally, I mean — he didn't realize that his song would be a perfect introduction to counting notes and rests in 4/4 meter.

This song begins on note G on the D string, so set up finger 3 ready to play before you begin to bow (refer to Chapter 5 to know how to count your fingers). Start with a down-bow. Most notes in this piece are quarter notes, which you can play near the middle of the bow with a nice, smooth stroke. Because the half notes last for 2 beats, use more bow to sound them out. At the end of measure 4, count "1, 2, 3, stop," and stop your bow lightly on the string on the word "stop." Then you're all ready to begin again in measure 5. A circular retake (refer to Chapter 8) on the rest in measure 8 gets your bow ready to start the eighth notes on a down-bow — and of course, each eighth note uses about half as much bow as a quarter note does.

Pachelbel Canon

This piece is the next bit of our theme song, the "Pachelbel Canon" (which I show you in Chapter 6). This part of the song is a variation that's played in quarter notes. To play this song well, keep finger 1 on the F♯, after you place it, until you play the third F♯ at the end of measure 2.

Leaving a finger on a string is a technique violinists use to make playing smoother. To know when you may benefit from using this technique, ask yourself these questions:

✔ Will I use this finger again very soon?

✔ If my finger stays on the string, will it be in the way of another note?

If the answer to the first question is yes and the answer to the second question is no, then you probably want to leave the finger on.

Counting and Playing in Threes

If you've heard a waltz, you know 3/4 time. Playing in 3/4 time is a lot like playing in 4/4 time, but with one big difference: You get only three quarter notes in a measure. Just as I explain about 4/4 time in "Tapping into the beat," earlier in this chapter, the time signature's top number, *3*, indicates that there are 3 beats in a measure, and the bottom number, *4*, tells you that each beat is worth a quarter note.

Figure 9-13 shows music written in the 3/4 meter for you to count through with your CD-ROM.

Figure 9-13:
Four 3/4 bars to count through.

Count   1   2   3   1   2   3   1   2   3   1   2   3

When you play in 3⁄4, a nifty bow effect occurs due to the uneven number of bows in a bar! The first bar starts with the usual down-bow, and then the second beat receives an up-bow, followed by a down-bow again on the third beat. So far, this is much like other bowings I show you earlier in this book. The different effect occurs on the next bar, which begins with an *up*-bow on the main beat. Because the main beat is emphasized, this up-bow needs to be quite strong. Think "DOWN, 2, 3, UP, 2, 3" to get the feel of the bowing.

Try the exercise in Figure 9-14, and observe the bowings while you count. You can also follow along with the CD-ROM.

Figure 9-14:
Bowing
in 3⁄4 time.

TRACK 26, 0:16

When you're comfortable with bowing in 3⁄4 time, try out the song "Pussycat, Pussycat, Where Have You Been?". If you don't know it, you can listen to it on the CD-ROM first, and then have a go.

 TRACK 27

Pussycat Pussycat, Where Have You Been?

You really see and feel the effect of 3⁄4 meter when you bow this old English song. Start on a down-bow on your open D string, and then bow through the song at one bow per note. Notice that measure 2 begins on an up-bow, and that you get a similar bowing order throughout the song. Hold the dotted half note for three counts in measure 4, and then play the next quarter down-bow and follow on "as it comes," which is violinists' code for playing each note with the next bow direction. When you meet a dotted quarter note, you know what to do — count three quarters and slow down the bow speed (refer to Chapter 8 for more about dotted quarter notes). The last bowing and counting place to observe specially is at measure 12, where you stop your first up-bow lightly on the string just after the second beat, roll the bow over to where finger 1 has just arrived on the D string, and then continue the up-bow movement on the third beat. Just observe that finger 2 is close to finger 1 for C♯ on the A string throughout this song.

Doing (Just About) Everything Else from Fours and Threes

You meet many different time signatures in this book, and this section introduces you to two more, which you may come across quite often: 2/4 and 6/8. Polkas and a lot of fiddle music are written in 2/4 meter.

2/4 time

This time signature doesn't indicate that it's time to buy a case of beer! Rather, the signature indicates something similar to what I explain about 4/4 time: 2/4 works just like 3/4 and 4/4, except each bar has the equivalent of only two quarter notes.

Figure 9-15 gives you an example to try, with 2/4 time in quarters. First, count the beats, and then play the music on your violin. You can listen to the exercise on the CD-ROM as well.

To try out your skills in 2/4, you can play "Twinkle, Twinkle, Little Star," which may be the most famous 2/4 song of 'em all! Follow the music, and play along with your CD-ROM.

Figure 9-15:
Four bars
in 2/4 time.

Count   1   2   1   2   1   2   1   2

TRACK 29

Twinkle, Twinkle, Little Star

After setting your bow fairly near the frog on the open D string, start on a down-bow and play the open D twice. Use about half the length of the bow, from the frog to the middle. All quarter notes use about half a bow in this song. Roll your bow across to the open A string, and play down-bow and up-bow on A. Place finger 1 on A to play the B, and then lift finger 1 so that you can bow the open A again. This time, you play a half note, which lasts twice as long as your quarter note (refer to Chapter 8 for more on counting notes). Because the duration of the note is twice as long, use twice as much bow — nice and logical. So when you play the next finger, which is finger 3 on D, you're bowing an up-bow from the tip to the middle of the bow. All the notes in this bar happen in the upper half of the bow, until you arrive on the open D string at the beginning of the next bar, which is a half note. For this note, you play a whole bow, all the way from the tip to the frog.

After you manage the bow distribution for the first part of the song, you're equipped to figure out the rest of "Twinkle" by yourself. A quarter note uses half of the bow, and a half note uses the entire bow. The very last note is a whole note, worth 4 beats, so it gets a slow whole bow — you don't need to be a mathematician to figure out that this whole bow travels twice as slow as any bow you play for a half note!

6/8 time

I have to confess: I tell a bit of a whopper (with onions) in "Keeping Time: Time Signatures," earlier in this chapter, when I say that the note value indicated by the lower number in a time signature gets one beat or count. Exceptional time signatures occur at quicker speeds, where counting in larger note values is more convenient. These signatures are called *compound time,* which is a fancy name meaning that the basic counting unit is made up of three eighth notes, a kind of compound. The most usual compound time signature is 6/8, where you count in dotted quarter notes.

At first, when you approach 6/8, you enter a different world where the music is counted in eighth-note units, not in the quarter notes I use earlier in this chapter. I look at this meter slowly at first, so that you have time to understand its components and feel how it works. Eventually, when you get up to speed, this signature has a rocking rhythm to it, quite like dancing. Count along with Figure 9-16 to get the feel, and listen to the exercise on the CD-ROM.

In 6/8, if the music is slow, count to six in eighth notes. You say, "ONE-two-three, FOUR-five-six." If the music is fast, count the bar in two dotted quarter notes. For this music, you say, "ONE-and-a, TWO-and-a," at first, but when you get the flow, you can just count "one, two."

TRACK 30, 0:00

Figure 9-16: Counting in 6/8 time.

Now that you have the hang of 6/8 time, you can help the "Irish Washerwoman" hang up her laundry. Figure 9-17 shows you the music for this song, and you can listen to it and play along with your CD-ROM. This piece uses short bow strokes near the middle of the bow, and it moves at quite a jolly tempo. Just to get you up to speed, I do a slow counting version and then a faster dancing version on your CD-ROM.

TRACK 30, 0:25

Allegro

Figure 9-17: A verse of "The Irish Washerwoman."

Getting Up to Speed: What Those Tempo Markings Mean

Composers can tell players a lot about the mood and speed of the music by means of tempo markings. *Tempo* is just the Italian word for "speed," but it sounds very musical! Here is a list of the most usual tempo indications you meet, from slowest to fastest:

- ✔ *Largo:* Downright slow, broad, and expansive.

- ✔ *Lento:* Still good and slow.

- ✔ *Adagio:* Literally means "at ease," and it is a very relaxed tempo.

- ✔ *Andante:* Literally, at walking speed; quite sedate, like a Sunday afternoon stroll.

- ✔ *Moderato:* You guessed it; it's a moderate speed.

- ✔ *Allegretto:* Almost as fast as allegro; it literally means "a little *allegro.*"

- ✔ *Allegro:* A bright and fairly breezy speed.

- ✔ *Presto:* This music goes fast.

- ✔ *Prestissimo:* Pretty crazy, fast tempo!

While I'm on the subject of speed, here are two words that occur frequently in music:

- ✔ *Ritardando (rit.):* Getting slower, like a clockwork machine winding down — often just before the end of a piece. You may also see *rallentando* (rall.), which means the same thing.

- ✔ *Accelerando (accel.):* Getting faster, like a car accelerating; it can occur anywhere that's very exciting in a piece.

Metronomes sometimes have labels on them that give you a range of numbers for *Andante,* and so on, but I recommend you take these with a pinch of salt — and perhaps some relish too! The right tempo of a piece depends on the character of the music and a lot of other factors, so start where you're comfortable with the tempo and then build from there. Labels on metronomes are useful for a general idea, but not necessarily for a specific rule.

Time for Some Songs

I know what you're thinking — you've got rhythm, but where's your music? Well, here it is: four songs with four different time signatures. All the songs in this section are on the CD-ROM too. I also give you a few useful pointers for each song.

◀ | TRACK 31

Theme from Symphony No. 1 by Brahms

This song lets you practice playing in 4/4 time. Begin this luscious melody by setting the middle of your bow on your violin's G string. The first bow is a pickup, so count "one, two, three" steadily, and then play an up-bow on open G on the fourth beat. Use plenty of bow, going most of the way to the frog for the first quarter note. Have your third finger ready to drop on the G string for the note C, which comes next, using a full down-bow. From then on, use the same kind of bowing division for the whole theme, except where you have eighth notes, which need only about 2 inches of bow for each note.

Allegro non troppo

◀ | TRACK 32

Old French Folk Song

The bow works very smoothly in this calm old song, which is great for practicing 3/4 time. Meanwhile, your fingers climb steadily down the scale. If you set up fingers 1, 2, and 3 on the A string before you start to play, you have everything beautifully ready! For the dotted half notes, use a slower bow stroke and count 3 beats aloud, until you can play the right rhythm with confidence.

Molto moderato

TRACK 33

Simple Gifts

Here's a chance to practice 2/4 time and try out a song with a pickup before the main beat. This pickup beat is even divided into two eighth notes. The words of this song go "'Tis a GIFT to be simple," so you make this effect on your violin. 'Tis also a gift that this song's pretty easy to play. Just start on the open D string with two eighth notes played in the lower half of the bow, and away you bow! Use a good, broad stroke for quarter notes, and about half of that stroke for the eighth notes. Your second finger plays close to your first finger on the A string for the C♮.

Allegro

TRACK 34

Oranges and Lemons

This old cry of London is a perfect introduction to playing in 6/8. Begin with finger 1 and finger 3 ready on the A string. Playing at around the middle of your bow, start with a short down-bow on finger 3, which is playing note D, and then lift finger 3 and play finger 1 on note B with an up-bow. Your next note is another D, but keep finger 1 on the string because you're about to use it again. While you bow the second B, the finger 3 that you just lifted off the A string pops across to land on the D string to play the note G. When you're playing the G, let go of all other fingers to prepare for the open A string that follows.

Next, you see two sixteenth notes, which fit into the time of one eighth note. In this context, they get very little bow, just half of what you're using for an eighth note! At the end of the phrase, in bar 2, you see an eighth rest. Just stop your bow lightly on the string and then roll the bow across to the A string just after your third finger has done a little bunny-hop across. The last thing to remember about "Oranges and Lemons" is that you count a dotted quarter note in measure 8. At first, you can count out all three eighth notes, but when your tempo gets up to speed and the music lilts along, that dotted note is worth one compound beat. Now, *orange* you pleased I told you that?

Playing long notes

Violinists have three choices about what to do when playing a longer note:

- Use more bow.

- Slow down the bow stroke.

- Combine both slowing the bow stroke and using more bow.

Deciding what to do takes some experience, and it's usually determined by what works best for the violin's sound and the player's comfort. I go into more detail in Chapter 13, where I discuss fancier bowings.

Part IV
Musicianship and Harmony

The 5th Wave   By Rich Tennant

"In the key of C major, F is the sub dominant, and G is the dominant. You're playing the passive aggressive F# and the arrogant pushy G#."

In this part . . .

Although you may often play the violin solo, someday you may want to play with other musicians too. Playing with others could mean accompanying a friend who's singing or playing the piano, or even jamming along with a group of friends in their garage. Doing so is much easier (and sounds better) if you understand how two or more notes go together to make beautiful music.

In this Part, I show you some fundamentals of sound to help you know how notes fit with each other. In Chapter 10, I show you what a scale is and how to play one yourself. Chapter 11 gives you the key to how notes go together, and Chapter 12 is about getting all these elements to live together in harmony.

Chapter 10

Weighing In on Scales

1 know the word *scales* conjures up images of severe, old-fashioned piano teachers rapping students' knuckles with rulers, but actually, scales are nothing to be frightened of. Getting to know some basic musical scales is pretty easy, and it's a great way to become fluent in the language of music.

A scale's job is to provide you with a path — to show you what notes go together. Understanding scales lets you know what notes you likely have to play in a piece of music, so you don't have to keep guessing at each and every note as you go. You hear scales at work during most pieces of music, so working on your scales really pays off.

In this chapter, I show you how scales are built and teach you how to play them.

Climbing Up and Down

Just about everyone involved in music uses the word *scales* quite frequently, but what exactly is a scale?

Well, in a nutshell, a *scale* is a series of notes that climb up and down, step-by-step, one note at a time. So as the scale goes up, each note sounds a progressively higher pitch, or as the scale goes down, each note is of a progressively lower pitch (Chapter 2 discusses pitch in more detail).

By the way, the word *scale* comes from the Italian word *scala,* which means "ladder" or "staircase." Now if you practice your scales well, you could end up playing at the famous *La Scala* opera house in Milan!

In its most basic form, a scale has eight notes. In fact, when you keep climbing up your scale until you arrive at the next note called by the same letter name as the one you started on, you've completed a whole *octave.* (An octave isn't to be confused with an *oct*opus, or *oct*agon, but it does share the "eight" characteristic, because it has eight elements — in this case, notes.) So each span of eight notes in a row makes an octave.

Musical notes have only seven letter names, which are the first seven letters of the alphabet (as I explain in Chapter 7 about how to read notes):

A B C D E F G

If you keep climbing up the scale to continue to the eighth note, the next note after G is called A again, and it sounds an octave higher than the first A you played. A piece of sage advice: Thyme is not of the essence — take it nice and easy with scales. Don't hurry at the beginning; you'll be comfortable and fluent before too long, with a confident sense of note names, patterns, and your location — both on the musical map and on your violin.

The simplest scale spans one octave, but you can continue through two, three, or even more octaves on scales when you get the pattern going.

Marching through the Major Scales

Major scales are the most basic kind of scale, so I start with these. What makes a major scale major, and not minor? Well, it's all in the pattern of whole steps and half steps, also known as whole tones and semitones (see Chapter 5 for details about these), that follow each other, one by one, to create the scale. The upcoming section shows you how to build a major scale pattern.

On your violin, a half step happens when you play the next finger close by the one that just played, and a whole step (which, logically, consists of the sum of two half steps put together, side by side) happens when you put a regular space between fingers like the one that happens between fingers 1 and 2 in your very first finger pattern (refer to Chapter 5).

Building major scales

Each scale is named after its *key note,* or *tonic,* which is the note where the major (or minor) pattern of notes begins and ends.

A major scale sounds "major" because a *whole step* (or *whole tone*) exists from the first to the second note, and there's another whole step from the second to the third note. (The distance from the first to the third note is even called a *major third,* because you've arrived at the *third* note of a *major* scale.) Figure 10-1 shows you the pattern for a major scale, and how it's put together, using the A major scale as the example.

In music theory, each note in the scale has its own Roman numeral (making it look very serious and important!), which refers to the *degree* (a fancy name for any step of the scale, but you don't get a Ph.D. for knowing that!) of the scale the note is on. I look at this system now because it's useful to *arpeggios,* which come up later in this chapter.

Figure 10-1:
Major scale pattern.

Each degree of the scale also has a name, just to sound extra impressive. Here's the scoop on their names and Roman numerals (and you can see them in action in Figure 10-2):

- ✔ *I, Tonic:* A fancy word for the key note (not to be taken with gin and ice).

- ✔ *II, Supertonic:* A note one note higher than the tonic (and it has nothing to do with Superman).

- ✔ *III, Mediant:* The mediant's halfway between the tonic and the dominant. Don't drive over this with your car, or you'll get the third degree!

- ✔ *IV, Subdominant:* This may sound like a huge sandwich, but it's just one note lower than the dominant.

- ✔ *V, Dominant:* A bossy little number, as I discuss in Chapter 12, where you read about harmony.

- ✔ *VI, Submediant:* No funny stuff here, this degree is halfway between the tonic and the subdominant — if you go down the scale.

- ✔ *VII, Leading note:* So called because it *leads* you to the next tonic, as Mozart's father, Leopold, discovered when he wanted young Wolfgang to get up and practice his scales in the morning. I tell you the story in the sidebar "A shaggy tale about a scale."

Figure 10-2:
Degrees of a scale.

A shaggy tale about a scale

Apparently Mozart's dad, Leopold, who was a fine musician himself and who wrote one of the very first books about playing the violin (which was not called *Violine für Dummköpfe*), was also quite the stage dad. So when Wolfgang wanted to sleep in and not get on with being a genius, Leopold would go to the *Klavier* (as it was called over there) and play a scale — but only as far as the seventh note, the *leading note*. Wolfgang couldn't stand to leave the music just hanging there, so he would leap out of bed to play the top note! And that was that. Better than an alarm clock. However, Leopold had nothing on Paganini's dad, who is reputed to have locked young Niccolò in a room for 17 hours to practice, and no dinner till he was done. . . .

Major scales you need to know

Although music uses a grand total of 12 major scales, you can play a whole lot of great songs using only four kinds of scales, each with its own finger pattern, which I show you in this section. The good news is that because you can use similar finger patterns in different scales, these four patterns equip you to play more than just one scale each. The basic major scales I show you are A major, G major, E major, and F major. From these four patterns, you're able to build two two-octave scales as well — G major and A major — covering pretty much all the notes on your violin (in *first position,* anyway — more about positions in Chapter 14).

As you find out in Chapter 7, a sharp (♯) written in front of a note makes it a half step higher, a flat (♭) makes it a half step lower, and a natural sign (♮) cancels out any sharps or flats that may be lurking around in the vicinity.

A major scale

Scales can happen in all kinds of note values and rhythms, but to keep things simple, I write them in quarter notes.

The A major scale uses the same finger pattern as the one that I show you for the G string in Chapter 7. Hold your left hand up in the air with your palm facing you, and take a look at your finger pattern before you get going on this scale — seeing what your fingers are doing before you turn your hand to play the violin makes playing easier.

Keep your fingernails nicely trimmed and short to make your playing sound and feel good. Too-long nails make for a brittle-sounding tone — and they can damage your strings. Keep a small pair of nail clippers in a pocket of your violin case, because nails have a strange way of suddenly being too long just as you're about to launch into the performance you've been preparing for months!

Good news: Playing the A major scale is pretty straightforward, because all these notes appear in several songs in earlier chapters, only without being constructed into a systematic step-by-step scale.

Practicing scales using whole bows (or most of the bow) allows plenty of time for each note. Also, using lots of bow helps you practice producing a healthy basic sound. Stopping the bow quietly on the string and leaving a little time between notes allows you to prepare the next note without undue pressure and tension. Believe me, the extra bit of time you need to prepare the next note becomes smaller and smaller as you practice, but developing relaxed styles of playing remains with you in all areas of your music making!

Upward mobility

I start by climbing up the A major scale. In Figure 10-3, I show you the music for the A major scale so that you can get practice in knowing your notes *and* their names *and* their look on the page — all in one! When you play this scale, allow a quarter rest between notes, so as to have a little time to get ready for the next step. Follow these instructions to get the full set of info on the moves, and then play along with your CD-ROM.

Playing scales successfully depends on doing the actions in a particular (and favorable) order, which is called *sequencing* the actions. Sequencing feels a bit strange at first, but it makes sense when you remember that the bow can't play a note until the finger is in place. So make sure the finger is ready a little before you bow the note, and that's how you experience the joys of good sequencing! This process is also useful in playing songs: Violinists' notes aren't just there waiting for us, like they are on the piano, so we have to make our notes ourselves.

Follow these steps to climb up the A major scale:

1. **Use a down-bow to play your first note, which is A on the open A string.**

   Start with your bow set on the string near the frog, and then draw a generous down-bow. Stop the bow gently on the string for a second (or three!) while you prepare the next note.

2. **Land finger 1 on its dot while the bow waits, and then play the second note, B, with an up-bow.**

3. **Leave finger 1 sitting on the string, but not pressing, while you put finger 2 on the string a whole step above finger 1.**

   This note is C♯, the third note, which occurs on a down-bow.

4. **Leave fingers 1 and 2 sitting lightly on the string, and land finger 3 close to finger 2 to play the fourth note, D, with an up-bow.**

5. **Relax your right arm level a little to bow the fifth note, the open E string.**

   Lift off all the fingers from the A string right after the E has begun to sound.

6. **Continue on the E string by landing fingers 1, 2, and 3 in exactly the same way as you did when you set off on the A string, following the same sequencing process.**

    You're playing notes six, seven, and eight of your scale: Finger 1 plays F♯, finger 2 plays G♯, and finger 3 plays A for "abracadabra" — you've just climbed your first scale and lived to tell the tale!

TIP

Saying the note names as you play your first scales (at a laid-back speed) helps you to know where you are — and connecting a name with each note will reinforce your music-reading skills. Say each note name just as you begin sounding the note: "A" (play), "B" (play), "C sharp" (play), and so on.

TRACK 35, 0:00

Figure 10-3:
The A major
scale,
ascending.

Downward trends

What goes up must indeed come down! The descent is a little trickier because the next playing finger has to be prepared on the string *before* you lift the previous finger — otherwise, all sorts of strange extra notes may try to invade the scale. So follow these sequences carefully to descend the A major scale as you work with Figure 10-4, and with your CD-ROM:

1. **Play top A again, using a down-bow, and then stop the bow lightly on the string.**

    (My instructions assume you've just ascended the A major scale, and have fingers 1, 2, and 3 sitting on the E string as you prepare to descend.)

2. **Lift finger 3 and play G♯ on an up-bow with finger 2.**

    Finger 2 is waiting on the string.

3. **Lift finger 2 when you have finished bowing G♯, and then play the F♯, on a down-bow using finger 1.**

    Finger 1 is also waiting patiently on the string.

4. **Lift finger 1 smartly at the end of F♯, and then play open E, with an up-bow.**

5. **Land finger 3 on the A string, and then roll your bow over to the A-string level to play the note, D.**

6. **Land finger 2 close underneath finger 3, on C♯, and then lift finger 3 off to play finger 2.**

7. **Finish bowing the C♯, place finger 1 on the string, lift finger 2, and then bow the B.**

8. **Lift finger 1 off the string and bow the open A for an easy finish.**

   There, you climbed back down a scale and didn't fall off — "A major" triumph!

Note: Using the same moves, you can play a D major scale starting on open D, and a G major scale starting on open G: a three-for-one deal!

TRACK 35, 0:21

Figure 10-4:
The A major
scale,
descending.

G major scale, upper octave

You can start the G major scale on open G and build from there, using exactly the same moves that apply in the A major scale (refer to "A major scale"). Now if you continue upward from the top note of the G major scale (you'd be starting that new octave on finger 3 on the D string), you build a second octave of the scale, the *upper octave,* which is higher in pitch. The upper octave uses a slightly different finger pattern, which is the same as the finger pattern for the A string (see Chapter 7), where finger 2 is close to finger 1. Expanding your G major scale to include the upper octave doubles the range of music that you can play.

When you get the correct finger pattern, playing the upper octave of the G major scale (which I show you in Figure 10-5) is pretty straightforward.

REMEMBER

I give you bow-by-bow instructions for the A major scale to get you started with every detail as clear as possible. Now that you're on your way with scales, I don't keep mentioning the bowing directions, because I'm sure you have the idea: Each new note gets its own bow. I just mention any special bowing instructions when a tricky move comes up.

Before you begin, shape up your left hand for this scale by tapping finger 1 on an "imaginary" E on the D string, but don't actually play the note — you're just ensuring that your hand placement is correct. Then land finger 3 on the D string for the starting note, G.

Figure 10-5 is the upper octave of the G major scale. Here's how to climb up the G major scale:

1. **Prepare finger 3 the D string (the note G), then set your bow on the string, ready for your first down-bow.**

2. **Roll the bow gently to the open A string, and then play A with an up-bow.**

3. **Place finger 1 on A to play note B.**

As with the previous scales, leave fingers you have already placed sitting lightly on the fingerboard until you play the next open string. In this case, leave fingers 1, 2, and 3 on the A string until you begin to bow the open E string, and then pop them up lightly so they're ready for their next assignment.

4. **Land finger 2 close to 1, because you've arrived at the half step in the major scale pattern!**

5. **Place finger 3 on the string a whole step away from 2 on the dot or tape.**

   (Refer to Chapter 5 to read about fingerboard tapes.)

6. **Roll the bow over to play the open E string.**

7. **Release fingers 1, 2, and 3 from the A string as soon as the bow starts playing E, and allow them to hover over the E string.**

8. **Play F♯ with finger 1 on your dot or tape.**

9. **Play the top G of this scale using finger 2, close to finger 1: your final half step.**

Follow these steps when you're climbing down the G major scale:

1. **Repeat the top G, this time on a down-bow.**

2. **Lift finger 2 to play F♯ with finger 1, which is waiting on the string for you.**

3. **Lift finger 1 after you play F♯, and then bow E on the open string.**

4. **Take a moment to prepare finger 3, note D, on the A string.**

5. **Roll your bow over to the A string when finger 3 is safely in place, and then play an up-bow on the new note.**

6. **Land finger 2 a whole step away from finger 3 when you've finished bowing note D, and then lift 3 off to bow note C.**

7. **Prepare finger 1 close to 2, lift off 2, and then play note B with finger 1.**

8. **Bow an open A, and while you do so, hover finger 3 above its spot on the D string to play the final G.**

9. **Roll your bow over to the D-string level and land finger 3 on the final G, which you play with a smooth up-bow.**

If you want to make a C major scale, start with finger 3 playing note C on the G string, and then follow the same pattern as you do to play the upper octave of the G major scale.

Figure 10-5:
G major
scale, upper
octave.

TRACK 36, 0:00

G major scale, two octaves

Putting the two octaves of G major together allows you to play all the way across your four strings — almost all the basic notes on your violin. In Figure 10-6, you can try out the whole two-octave scale of G major in all its glory.

When moving from the lower octave to the upper octave of the G major scale, switch your finger 2 placement as you arrive on the A string so that it's close to finger 1. Reverse the process in the descending scale.

As you now realize, finger 2 has two very usual placements: either next to finger 1 or next to finger 3. That's why you don't make a specific tape or dot for finger 2 when you first measure up the fingerboard in Chapter 5. Violinists call finger 2 *low* when it plays close to finger 1 (because it plays a lower note) and *high* when it plays next to finger 3 (yep, because it plays a higher-sounding note). This rhyme helps you to remember how to play the scale of G major with finger 2 on the right spot each time:

2 is high *on G and D;*
2 is low *on A and E.*

I show you the whole two-octave scale on your CD-ROM, and you can check it out in Figure 10-6.

For your first "Fauré" into two-octave scales, I keep things crystal clear. I show you a scale pattern where you finish the lower octave on G (finger 3 on the D string), take a breath, and then play that G again as the starting note of the upper octave. Doing this pattern is just like steering by famous landmarks in a new city — it helps you keep track of where you are and what you're doing.

On the violin, the finger patterns in scales don't happen the same way on all strings, because you don't always use the same finger to play all notes with the same name (keeping violinists' brains alert to a ripe old age!). Saying the note names as you start to learn the scales really helps you to always know where you are.

TRACK 36, 0:22

Figure 10-6:
G major
scale, two
octaves.

E major scale

With the E major scale, you use a finger pattern (which you meet briefly in Chapter 5) where your third and fourth fingers are close together. I show you this pattern in Figure 10-7.

If you have tapes (or dots) on your fingerboard (like the ones I show you how to apply in Chapter 5), finger 1 is on its regular tape. Finger 2 is set close by the finger 3 tape. Now the third finger is the really new placement: It needs to land *between* the tapes for fingers 3 and 4, because it is a *high* 3 placement, meaning it's set a half-step higher than usual to sound the G♯. So in this pattern, nothing lands on the third-finger tape.

After trying the finger pattern in the air, away from your violin, pick up your violin alone, no bow needed, and show your third finger exactly where it should land:

1. **Set fingers 1, 2, 3, and 4 in the first finger pattern, where 1, 3, and 4 are on their tapes, and 2 is close to 3.**

2. **Keep fingers 1, 2, and 4 exactly in their same spots, and slide finger 3 lightly on the string a few times between 2 and 4.**

3. **Notice how the new place for finger 3 is very close to, or even touching, finger 4.**

   If you practice this little ski-slide, you can find the new place for finger 3 with ease.

Playing the E major scale involves very symmetrical finger patterns. I show you this scale using finger 4 instead of open strings so that 4 gets a good workout, and because using finger 4 is very easy here.

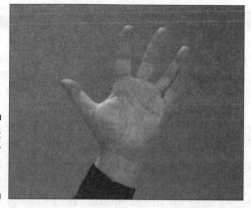

Figure 10-7:
Finger pattern for E major scale.

You can use finger 4 instead of an open string for any scale. Traditionally, students learn their scales using open strings when ascending and finger 4 when descending, because this fingering trains the left hand to stay in shape when lifting fingers off the strings. (Letting the left hand pull back a bit too much when lifting fingers to descend is too easy.) In actual music, you choose whether to use finger 4 or an open string, mostly depending on what sounds best and what is good for keeping the bow up to scratch . . . er . . . I mean up to perfection! But for now, going back over scales you already know and using finger 4 instead of open strings gives you an excellent workout and ups the ante for your skills.

Figure 10-8 gives you the music for the E major scale. Watch it on the CD-ROM, and play it following these steps:

1. **Begin with your first finger on the D string to sound the note E with a down-bow.**

2. **Land finger 2 on F♯, a whole step above E.**

3. **Place finger 3 in its "new" placement, a good space above the second finger, to play the note G♯.**

4. **Use finger 4 placed close to the 3 you just played to sound the next note, A.**

Although you can of course sound the next A by playing an up-bow on the open string, I recommend using the fourth finger to allow all four fingers to be on the D string together in the new finger pattern. Using finger 4 also contributes to shaping up your left hand frame very thoroughly.

5. **Place finger 1 on the A string, and then release all the other fingers from the D string just after you begin to bow note B.**

6. Follow the same steps and patterns as in Steps 1 to 4, but this time, play on the A string until you arrive at the top E, finger 4, using an up-bow.

7. Notice that all four fingers are ready on the string as you begin your descent by playing top E again, but with a down-bow— just lift each finger off decisively as you finish bowing it, until you reach finger 1 on the A string.

8. Prepare finger 4 over the D string a little ahead of time, hovering just above its spot, while finger 1 is playing note B on the A string.

9. Release your pinky's weight slightly on the frog to allow the bow to go over to the D string, and simultaneously place finger 4 on the D string.

10. Have each subsequent finger for the remaining notes ready on the string just before you lift the playing finger, so no gap in sound occurs.

You can stop the bow for a moment between strokes to make sure you have the moves in order.

Using exactly the same finger pattern as you do for the E major scale, but starting with finger 1 on the G string, you can play the lower octave of the A major scale.

Figure 10-8:
E major
scale.

TRACK 37

A major scale, two octaves

Playing the higher and lower A major scales together gives you the full two-octave range. I show you the scale in Figure 10-9, and demonstrate the moves on your CD-ROM.

As with the two-octave scale of G major, the finger pattern used in the A major scale is different between the lower and upper octaves. In this scale, finger 3 must make the adjustment. As you begin the A major scale, finger 3 is close to 4 on the G and D strings, but after you pass the second A — the open A string — finger 3 needs to play close to finger 2.

ON THE CD

Hand exercises

For playing many different finger patterns, you need to get your hands really fit. Violinists do quite a number of stretches to keep their hands and arms moving smoothly, and these hand exercises are just the ticket for practicing your different finger patterns.

Holding fingers 2, 3, and 4 together, draw finger 1 away from the rest of the fingers so that you form the letter *V* between fingers 1 and 2. Your hand should remain pretty much on the same plane when you are moving the fingers, as if it was up against a window pane (you can see how it's done on the CD-ROM). This stretch makes for excellent finger flexibility and independence!

A dash (–) indicates where a *V* is located:

1. 1–234

Try the same idea on these patterns too:

2. 123–4

3. 12–34

4. 1–23–4

You can practice these moves at any time, not just during violin practice. At a red traffic light, waiting for a bus — there are lots of everyday opportunities to get those fingers moving! If your left hand can't manage all the moves when you start out, use your right hand to help by gently holding the "together" fingers . . . together.

TRACK 38

Figure 10-9: A major scale, two octaves.

F major scale

When you first look at the finger pattern for F major, the placement looks new: Your first finger is all the way back, close to the nut at the scroll end of the fingerboard to play B♭ on the A string. You're right — you haven't done this yet, but it's not too tricky. (Refer to Chapter 7 for a brief discussion about the finger pattern.) Finger 1 just moves back a bit from finger 2 (without moving the whole hand back — 1 is a very independent operator) and lands between its usual dot or tape and the end of the fingerboard.

Figure 10-10 shows you the printed notes for the F major scale, which I also demonstrate on your CD-ROM. Playing this scale on your violin calls for a little preparation before you play the first note, so follow these steps:

1. **Imagine playing open D, and then place finger 1 silently on E, a whole step above D, followed by finger 2, close to finger 1, ready to play the key note F.**

2. **Release finger 1 from the D string when finger 2 is safely on F.**

   You're ready to begin the actual scale.

3. **Bow steadily, one bow per note, on F, G, and open A.**

4. **Make sure finger 1 is very close to the nut of the fingerboard in order to sound the B♭.**

5. **Take a whole step to finger 2 on note C.**

6. **Play note D with finger 3.**

7. **Play the open E string.**

   Of course, you release all fingers from the A string in this step.

8. **Use the same low placement of finger 1 on the E string for the final F as in Step 4 for B♭ on A.**

9. **Descend the scale, being sure to prepare your next finger for each note a tad before your bow begins to sound.**

Figure 10-10:
F major
scale.

TRACK 39

Casting Light on Those Minors

Don't let the name fool you — minor scales aren't less important than major scales, and they wouldn't like you to think so. Minor scales are often used for sad or reflective music, so you need these in your collection. These scales may seem a little complicated and mysterious at first, but when you start playing them, they add so much to your musical expression that the extra effort is worthwhile.

The name *minor* derives from the fact that a *minor third* happens at the start of the scale. What happens when you play a minor scale is that the first and second notes are a whole step apart, just like the start of a major scale. The third note is where things are different: It's only a half step higher than the second note, really close by!

Building a minor scale

The big difference between major scales and minor scales is that whilst major scales always follow the same pattern, minor scales come in two slightly different patterns, both of which are commonly in use. The two patterns for minor scales are called *melodic minor* and *harmonic minor*. The pattern is the same for both scales for the first five notes. It's only the sixth and seventh notes (the VI and VII degrees of the scale) that you have to pay attention to.

In the *A melodic minor* scale, shown in Figure 10-11, after the fifth note, the remainder of the scale works the same way as in major scales while you complete the climb up to the top. But things are different with VI and VII when you climb down. After you reach the top note and are poised to begin your descent, the seventh (VII) and the sixth (VI) degrees of the scale (in this case, G sharp and F sharp) each switch to play a half step lower than they did in the ascending pattern, sounding now as G natural and F natural.

Figure 10-11:
The A melodic minor scale pattern.

The *A harmonic minor* scale, shown in Figure 10-12, sounds a little like Middle Eastern music and involves a bit of a stretch between the sixth (VI) and seventh (VII) degrees of the scale. After playing the first five notes of your minor pattern, the sixth note is just a half step above the fifth. The seventh note is just a half step below the top note. If you put both those fingers in place, you notice that you have quite a big space (known as an *augmented second*) between the sixth and seventh degrees of the scale. Very true — that space covers three half steps. Another good reason for practicing those finger stretches explained in the "Hand exercises" sidebar!

Figure 10-12:
The A
harmonic
minor scale
pattern.

Playing A melodic minor scale

Showing you exactly how to play the A minor scales equips you to play well in the most usual minor *key* you meet on the violin (more about keys in Chapter 11) — and to figure out other minor scales you may meet. You also feel and hear how the A minor scales differ from the A major scale, discussed near the beginning of this chapter.

A melodic minor scale uses no less than all three of the finger patterns that you meet in Chapter 7 — all in one scale! You use the A string pattern, with fingers 1 and 2 close together, for the notes on the A string. Then, climbing up on the E string, you borrow the G string pattern, with finger 2 close to finger 3. Finally, climbing down on the E string, you use the actual E string pattern.

Playing the scale gives you a taste of how all its components work together (but if you want to just watch and listen, you can do so with the CD-ROM). Follow these steps to play the A melodic minor scale, shown in Figure 10-13:

1. **Go up the scale, just as you would when playing scales I show you earlier in this chapter.**

2. **Lift off fingers 1 and 2 when you reach the top A, leaving finger 3 all alone on the E string, playing top A.**

   The reason for removing fingers 1 and 2 is that the finger pattern changes on the way down in melodic minor scales. So you won't be using G♯ or F♯ on the way down. If you leave your fingers on their old notes, sliding them to their new notes is very awkward.

3. **Prepare finger 2 a whole step below finger 3, so that it's waiting on the E string just before you lift 3.**

4. **Get finger 1 ready on the E string a whole step below finger 2 while you're bowing the note G with finger 2, so that finger 1 is waiting when you lift off 2.**

5. **Descend the remainder of the scale in a similar way to when you go back down the A major scale.**

   You need to watch out only for the low finger 2 on the C♮.

Figure 10-13:
The A melodic minor scale, ascending and descending.

TRACK 40, 0:00

Playing A harmonic minor scale

Harmonic minor scales are rather exotic-sounding and fun to play. Also, the scales' pattern is the same going up as it is coming back down, which means you can return by way of fingers that are already waiting for you.

You begin the A harmonic minor scale using exactly the same finger pattern that you use to start the A melodic minor scale, the A string pattern (refer to Chapter 7). Then, on the E string, you play a finger pattern that you haven't met before: from your E string pattern, keep all the fingers in their original placements *except* finger 2. Finger 2 slides really close to finger 3, making a bigger stretch between 1 and 2. Take a look at Figure 10-14 to see the extra big space between fingers 1 and 2.

Figure 10-14:
Finger pattern on the E string for the A harmonic minor scale.

The A harmonic minor scale is the last scale you need to play for now. This scale works exactly like the A melodic minor scale for the first five notes. But then comes the exotic bit, where you have F♮ and G♯ going upward, and the same descending the scale.

To play the A harmonic minor scale (see Figure 10-15), follow the same steps as for the A melodic minor scale until you reach the E string (refer to "Playing A melodic minor scale," a bit earlier in this chapter). Listen and watch on the CD-ROM, and then follow these steps:

1. **Play your first finger low on the E string to sound an F♮.**

2. **Make a bit of a stretch with finger 2 to play G♯.**

   This is the first time you have (intentionally!) played an interval of three half steps (a tone and one-half) on your violin. This interval is called an *augmented second* in polite company!

3. **Play finger 3 close to finger 2 for the top A, leaving fingers 1, 2, and 3 on the E string, because you descend using those same notes.**

4. **Follow the same steps for the descending scale as in "A major scale," earlier in this chapter, but play the notes of the A harmonic minor scale.**

Figure 10-15: The A harmonic minor scale.

TRACK 40, 0:22

Meeting Other Scales in Brief

Of course, music has many more scales than the major and minor scales that we traditionally emphasize. I show you some examples of other scales you might meet, but they're still based on the home key of A, so you can give them a nod of recognition when they pop up in your pieces. You don't need to play these scales right now, but by all means, give them a try if you're adventurous, because you have the skills to figure them out. I show each scale, and I play them for you on your CD-ROM.

Natural minor scales

Natural minor scales refer to minor scales with no extra accidentals added. You take the eight notes of a major scale going from the sixth degree to the sixth degree (VI to VI), instead of the first to the first (I to I), and you play just those notes without any additional sharps or flats along the way. You can play the scale in Figure 10-16 to give it try, or give it a listen on the CD-ROM.

Figure 10-16:
Natural
minor
scale of A.

TRACK 41, 0:00

Pentatonic scales

Pentatonic scales have, as their name suggests, only five notes (the *penta* part comes from the Greek word for "five," and *tonic* here just means "notes"). Pentatonic melodies are found in folk music all over the world, but they're most typical of Chinese music. You can build a pentatonic scale like the one in Figure 10-17 using the first, second, third, fifth, and sixth (I, II, III, V, and VI) degrees of a major scale, or using the black keys of a piano, starting on F♯. And you can listen to this scale on the CD-ROM, if you like.

Figure 10-17:
Pentatonic
scale, start-
ing on A.

TRACK 41, 0:22

Chromatic scales

Chromatic scales go up and down all the way by half steps (semitones). Apart from the exotic sound and slithery feel of chromatic scales, you can gain a very useful piece of technique for your left hand: Sliding each finger a half step higher or lower on the string to alter the pitch of the note. I show you how to go about chromatic finger movements so that you can try the scale in Figure 10-18, and you can watch me play it and listen to how it sounds on the CD-ROM.

Keep your left hand still and calm during chromatic scales; let the individual fingertips do the skating actions instead of moving your whole hand for every note. Letting the fingertips do the moving leads to quicker, lighter movements. Just allow the finger joints to bend and stretch freely so that the finger can reach a little further up and down the string — no need to keep fingers perfectly rounded at all times.

Moving each fingertip a half step up or down is most easily done when the surrounding fingers are on their spots, allowing you to feel the movements and distances very clearly. Try these moves on the A or D string, for middle-of-the-road comfort. Set all four fingertips on the string, with finger 2 close to finger 1, and don't bother using the bow on this silent (but not deadly!) exercise.

✔ **For finger 1:** Slide finger 1 from close to finger 2 away toward the ridge at the end of the fingerboard, where the strings disappear en route to the pegbox. Slide to and fro several times to feel the movement and the distance. Then settle finger 1 back on its regular spot.

✔ **For finger 2:** Slide between fingers 1 and 3, finishing close to finger 3.

✔ **For finger 3:** Slide between fingers 2 and 4, finishing close to 2.

✔ **For finger 4:** Slide close to finger 3, and then push your fingertip gently toward the bridge of the violin as far as it can slide comfortably, which may be less than an inch. Finger 4's just inching along!

When you play the scale in Figure 10-18, I show you the fingering that most violinists use: They slide fingers 1 and 2, and then after finger 3, they place finger 4 close by 3. All good for keeping those fingers limber!

TRACK 41, 0:39

Figure 10-18: Chromatic scale, starting on A.

Harping on about Arpeggios

I harp on about arpeggios for a brief moment, to get you started. The technique is just the ticket for making flowing accompaniments and for filling out your sound more richly. The *arpeggio* draws its origins from the Italian word meaning "in the style of a harp." To play an arpeggio, you play the notes of a *chord* one after another (usually pianists and guitarists make chords by playing the first, third, and fifth — I, III, and V — degrees of a scale all together for a juicy sound). I talk more about chords in Chapter 12, but for now, you can play the arpeggios by using the notes in the scales.

Arpeggios are really useful for developing good technique on the violin, because you develop a sense of being able to land a finger on any note you want, not just the next note of a scale. Skipping fingers to get to the next note is great for coordination and agility. Additionally, since arpeggios are made from the notes of a chord or scale, you can use arpeggio patterns to accompany songs and to improvise when you play with friends.

Arpeggios can run for one, two, three, or, even occasionally, four octaves on the violin. But for now, I look at the arpeggios from the one-octave A scales you play earlier in this chapter.

A major arpeggio

The A major arpeggio uses the notes A, C♯, and E. The sound bounces back off the top A, like a ball, and comes back through E and C♯ to the starting A. To play this arpeggio, follow Figure 10-19. You can watch and listen to me play it on the CD-ROM.

1. **Start on the open A string with a down-bow.**

2. **Land finger 2 on C♯ on the A string, close to the fingerboard marker for finger 3, and play an up-bow.**

3. **Roll your bow over to the open E string to play a down-bow on E, releasing finger 2 from the A string as soon as the E starts to sound.**

4. **Land finger 3 on its spot, and play the top A with an up-bow.**

5. **Lift finger 3 off the string at the end of the up-bow, and play down-bow on open E, hovering finger 2 over its C♯, all ready to land on the A string when the down-bow is finished.**

6. **Roll your bow over to the A string to play an up-bow on C♯.**

7. **Finish the arpeggio by playing a down-bow on the last A, your home note.**

Even when fingers land on different strings, you can still get a sense of their whole-step (or whole-tone) and half-step (or semitone) relationships to place them accurately. In A *major* arpeggio, fingers 2 and 3 are in a half-step relationship across the strings, whereas in A *minor* arpeggio, a whole step is between the two fingers. You can try this on all arpeggios, and even in pieces.

Figure 10-19:
A major
arpeggio.

A minor arpeggio

Playing the A minor arpeggio takes only one small step from the A major arpeggio. You follow exactly the same steps as for A major, except your finger 2 on A plays a C♮, very close to the first finger tape, to make the minor key clear. Look at Figure 10-20 for the notes. You can see and hear me play on your CD-ROM.

Figure 10-20:
A minor
arpeggio

TRACK 41, 1:26

Major (And Minor) Achievements

The following songs give you a chance to enjoy the musical benefits of playing in the different scales you meet in this chapter.

Before you play a piece, try playing its scale so that your fingers can find their spots with ease.

TRACK 42

Mozart Clarinet Quintet

Mozart composed this beautiful work in A major for clarinet and string quartet in 1788 for his clarinetist friend, Anton Stadler. (Stadler was not only a brilliant player but also a fellow Freemason!) The theme of this cheerful *finale* (last movement), which leads on into a set of variations, feels like a dance. Play lightly using just a little bow near the middle.

TRACK 43

Aunt Rhody Becomes "A Minor"

I always thought of "Aunt Rhody" as an elderly lady, but here she's becoming "A minor" to help you on your way with the new scales! After you set up your first and second fingers on the A string, with finger 2 close by finger 1, land your bow near the frog and then draw a full down-bow for the first quarter note. Eighth notes will need about half a bow each, so play the first eighth using an up-bow that goes to about the middle of the bow. And then when you switch to finger 1, play a down-bow that goes back to the tip. All the bowings will be very smooth in "Aunt Rhody" to make it sing sadly. For half notes, play a full bow's length, but slow the bow speed to last as long as you need.

Chapter 11

Signing Off on Key Signatures

• •

• •

Key signatures are aptly named — they really do help you unlock a piece of music. Although they may seem a little complicated initially, they actually make reading music easier. In this chapter, I cover what exactly a musical key is and how you can recognize the different types. I also cover some of the most common keys you find as a violinist, and I provide you with tunes so that you can put those keys into the ignition and go!

Unlocking Keys

A *musical key* is a way of talking about a particular group of notes where the most important one, designated as the *tonic (I),* gives the musical key its name. Players refer to each musical key by the name of its tonic so that everyone can understand what's involved. Another name for the tonic is the *key note,* because it's the most important note; it gives a composition a feeling of completeness. (Speaking of key notes, that's where scales start and end. Refer to Chapter 10 to find out more.)

Getting the key to key signatures

A *key signature* is the name for the sharp or flat signs you see immediately after the clef at the beginning of a piece, and then as a reminder at the start of every subsequent staff (refer to Chapter 7 for more on clefs and staffs). At some point in musical history, a bright spark of the Henry Ford variety realized that it wasted a whole lot of time (and ink) to put a sharp or flat in front of a note each time one appeared. Music is just as clear when the necessary sharps or flats appear at the start of every musical line.

Key signatures are a handy system for telling you exactly which notes you need to play in any piece of music. When you're used to key signatures, you can recognize the key of the music right away.

Reading the key signatures for major keys

What key signatures do is take the sharps or flats that occur in any musical key and organize them into a message, right at the start of the piece. This message tells players a lot about the home key of the music and what scale patterns to organize before starting to play.

You never get both sharps and flats in the key signature at the same time.

The sharps and flats are organized into a neat system, so that they occur in the same order each time. The order of sharps is determined by the order that you find in real music. For example, the G major scale uses one sharp (F♯), and the D major scale uses two sharps (F♯ and C♯). You keep adding sharps in the same order till you reach your full complement of seven sharps — if you're rash enough to go as far as that! Here's a brief rundown of the most usual key signatures.

When no sharps and flats are in the key at all, the music is in the key of C major. C major uses the notes C, D, E, F, G, A, B, C, as you can see in Figure 11-1.

Figure 11-1:
Notes in the
key of C
major.

C major (no sharps or flats)

C   D   E   F   G   A   B   C

Having no sharps or flats means that if you go to a piano, you can play all the notes of a C major scale on the white keys. Your fingers never clamber up onto the black notes, which are used for the sharps and flats!

C major is the easiest key for pianists, but for violinists, it's one of the trickier keys, so there's no need to actually play this yet. What *is* useful to know is what "natural" notes are: They're the notes that occur on the white keys of the piano, as well as in the key of C major!

One sharp in the key signature indicates that the music is written in the key of G major, which uses the notes G, A, B, C, D, E, F♯, and G. Figure 11-2 shows you these notes on your violin.

Figure 11-2: Notes in the key of G major.

G major (one sharp)

Going on to two sharps brings you to the key of D major, which uses the notes D, E, F♯, G, A, B, C♯, and D. Figure 11-3 shows you the notes of D major on the violin.

Figure 11-3: Notes in the key of D major.

D major (two sharps)

When a key signature has three sharps, your music is written in the key of A major, which you play quite a bit in this book without necessarily knowing the details. A major uses the notes A, B, C♯, D, E, F♯, G♯, and A. Figure 11-4 lines up the notes in the key of A major for your inspection.

Figure 11-4: Notes in the key of A major.

If you see one flat, you organize yourself to play in the key of F major, which uses the notes F, G, A, B♭, C, D, E, and F. Figure 11-5 shows you the notes you play on your violin.

Figure 11-5: Notes in the key of F major.

F major (one flat)

If one flat isn't enough for you, you can use two. This puts you in the key of B flat major, which uses the notes B♭, C, D, E♭, F, G, A, and B♭. Figure 11-6 shows you the moves for this key signature.

Figure 11-6:
Notes in the
key of B
flat major.

B flat major (two flats)

B♭   C   D   E♭   F   G   A   B♭

Keeping order

If you want to remember the order of the sharps and flats in a key signature, two excellent mnemonic (phew!) devices exist to help you out. The first letter of each word tells you the next sharp or flat in the right order.

For sharp keys, remember

Father **C**harles **G**oes **D**own **A**nd **E**nds **B**attle

. . . and for flat keys, remember

Battle **E**nds **A**nd **D**own **G**oes **C**harles' **F**ather

Figure 11-7 shows you what the key signature would look like with all seven sharps or flats — an impressive sight!

Figure 11-7:
All-dressed
key
signature.

F♯ C♯ G♯ D♯ A♯ E♯ B♯   B♭ E♭ A♭ D♭ G♭ C♭ F♭

Locking In to the Right Key

You try out a lot of keys in this chapter, and all those key signatures may seem a bit complicated, but don't despair. Musicians have a quick system that they use to identify the major keys from looking at their key signatures.

With sharp keys, the *last* sharp is always on the leading note of the major key. So looking at the key signature for A major, the last sharp is G♯, and climbing up one note name from there, you arrive at . . . A. Figure 11-8 shows you how to scope this out.

With flat keys, the clue is the *second-last* flat in the key signature. Looking at E flat major as the example, you see in Figure 11-9 that the key signature shows three flats, B♭, E♭, and A♭. So going back one from the final flat, you arrive at . . . E♭.

This convenient system works for identifying all major keys except F major, because it has only one flat in the key signature. So F major is the only key you need to identify from memory.

Figuring Out Minor Keys

Each major key shares its key signature with a minor key. It's one of those two-for-one deals. The minor key that shares the major key's signature is called the *relative minor,* and the major key that shares the minor key's signature is called the *relative major,* so all's fair and square.

Forming the relative minor

Luckily, finding the relative minor is relatively easy. Taking any major scale, your starting note is the sixth degree (VI) of the scale, and you climb up and down from there. If you do just that, the resulting scale is called the *natural minor* (refer to Chapter 10).

For each of these natural minors, you can make small adjustments to the sixth (VI) and seventh (VII) notes of the scales to make them into the melodic or harmonic minor patterns that are the current norm.

Recognizing minor keys when reading music

Before you "card" all your keys, get to know the look of minor keys by the following time-honored method used by professional musicians:

- ✔ If you see lots of extra *accidentals* on the page (I tell you about those extra sharps, flats, and naturals in Chapter 7), the music could well be in a minor key, because of those pesky melodic and harmonic minor alterations. (Luckily, minor alterations are free!)

- ✔ To get more evidence to support your suspicion, look at the *last note* of the piece. If the key signature is for D major, but the music ends on a B, you're likely in its relative minor key, B minor.

Figure 11-10 shows you a piece in E minor so you can see the general look of a piece in a minor key.

Neither the "look for lots of accidentals" nor the "check the last note" method is perfect, but in combination they can certainly be helpful to knowing what key you're dealing with.

Figure 11-10:
Music in E
minor.

Having the Last Dance

Here's a minor masterpiece for you to try with your new knowledge of key signatures: "Bach's G Minor Gavotte." A *gavotte* was a French dance, very popular in the seventeenth century.

Bach's G Minor Gavotte

This sighing piece is written in the key of G minor. Notice that the time signature lets you know about the two main beats in each bar that give the music its dancing effect. Before you play, tap finger 3 on its spot for the first note, to make sure your hand is in its regular place. Prepare finger 1 for B♭ on the A string by opening a little more space away from finger 2, but don't allow your whole hand to slip down the neck toward the scroll. You can see the telltale "minor key clue" accidentals in the fourth full measure. This is where fingers 1 and 2 have to get moving to place a half step higher than they play anywhere else in this music. To make the music flow, bow very smoothly on the slurs, starting your first up-bow from a little above the middle of the bow to allow plenty of room for all four notes in the slur. In this Gavotte, you make the dynamic effects mostly by expanding and contracting the bow strokes, rather like playing an accordion!

Chapter 12

Better Together: Harmony

. . . .

In This Chapter

▶ Seeing chords in harmony

▶ Winning in the big leagues: Major chords

▶ Digging for minor chords

▶ Playing major and minor broken chords

▶ Meeting the bossy chords: Dominant 7ths

▶ Making sweet music in duets: Harmonizing in 3rds and 6ths

. . . .

*W*hen you can play some of the tunes in this book with confidence, you may get interested in playing together with other musicians. Songs in all musical genres can be written with parts for several instruments. And while these instruments all play different parts, they manage to get in sync with each other and make a song sound whole. Playing with other instruments, apart from being really fun, gives color and depth to music and helps listeners understand more about the mood and structure of a piece of music. In this chapter, I show you how different parts of music go together in a complementary way.

Jazz and pop musicians know just how to keep things sweet and simple with some basic chords that sound good in their songs. You take a leaf out of their book in this chapter, and you find out about the harmonies that go along with your music — and how to build them into your violin world.

Making Sense of Chords and Harmony

You meet chords briefly in Chapter 10 when I talk about scales. Musicians use the word *chord* to describe different notes (typically three or four) that blend together nicely when played at the same time — frequently the same notes that you know from trying arpeggios in Chapter 10. Chords give a special context to each note by telling the listener more about the key (and the character) of the music.

You often hear the word *harmony* used in connection with music — or relationships — and you probably know harmony when you hear it, but what exactly does harmony mean to you as a budding violinist?

The violin usually plays the *melody,* the main tune of a piece of music — the bit you might find yourself humming if the song is really catchy. (Unlike the tuba, for example, which often plays a lot of oompah accompaniments.) *Harmony* is the relationship between a melody and other notes that go with it. In most pieces, harmony is organized into chords, and this section shows you how chords work.

Just to get you started, I show you what chords look like in Figure 12-1. After you get used to the fact that chords look rather like tadpoles climbing up a ladder, you can easily recognize one on a page of music. The first chord, a G major chord, has three notes. Notice that the three notes all occur on the *lines* of the musical staff. The second chord is also a G major chord, but it's a four-note version with an extra G added on top for a fuller sound. The third chord is an A major chord with three notes. In this chord, the notes all occur in the *spaces* of the staff. And the final chord is the four-note version of A major, with an extra A added at the top.

Figure 12-1:
Recognizing
chords.

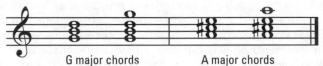

G major chords   A major chords

I show you the chords in their most basic form in Figure 12-1. But composers can take those same pitches and put them in much higher or lower octaves — if they are writing piano music, for example — so the look is much more spread out. But if the notes are vertically aligned, they sound together, meaning you're looking at a chord.

In the Big Leagues: Major Chords

Budding rock stars playing in their parents' garages may not have formal musical training, but they still manage to make music — or something pretty close to it, anyway. Beginners create harmony by very simple means, using chords known as *principal triads*. Principal triads of any key, particularly the one you're playing in at the moment, are the ones that are most important.

You make a triad in the same way that you make an arpeggio (refer to Chapter 10): Combine the starting note, or *root,* with the third and fifth note above it. These three notes played at the same time form a *chord*.

You don't have to be a punk rocker to use these chords, either. Principal triads are also very useful to violinists because they work to accompany just about any folk song, or melodies taken from more popular music.

Finding the principal triads

As I explain earlier in this chapter, a *principal triad* is a three-note chord that musicians use predominantly in any key. Musicians use three principal triads for each key. To find each type of principal triad, locate the tonic (I), subdominant (IV), or dominant (V) note of its scale. (I explain these names and steps of the scale in detail in Chapter 10.)

You build each triad in exactly the same way: From your starting note, the I, IV, or V, you count up to the third note and the fifth note to form the triad. So for a tonic triad built on the first note of a scale (I), you take the tonic as your starting note and add the third and fifth notes above it. Similarly, for the chord built on the subdominant degree (IV), you start on the subdominant and then add the third and fifth notes above that. And the same applies to the dominant triad: Start on the dominant and then add the third and fifth notes above that to get the dominant triad (V).

Musicians measure *intervals* by counting how many notes you pass by in the scale you're using before you actually sound the next note. Musicians count the starting note as *1,* and they keep on counting until they reach the new note.

Here's an example: D to A is a fifth (D-E-F-G-A = 1-2-3-4-5, A is the *fifth* note). Of course, the interval system has all kinds of details, but for now, this info will take you merrily where you need to go — no worries.

Actually, D major makes the best key for violinists to start using their harmonies, because they can play the *root* (the lowest note) of each chord of D major's principal triads, I (D), IV (G), and V (A) on an open string. That's why so many fiddle tunes are in D major! In Figure 12-2, I show you the triads in D major:

A trick that fiddlers use to play the principal harmonies in D major is to bow on two open strings together. You can bow the D and A strings at the same time and imagine the F# in the middle to get a strong impression of the I chord. You can represent a V chord by playing similarly on the A and E strings, and you can represent a IV chord by playing similarly on the G and D strings.

- ✔ *Tonic triad* **(built on I):** Take the tonic (D) with the third and fifth notes (F♯ and A).

- ✔ *Subdominant triad* **(built on IV):** Take the subdominant note (G), and add the third and fifth (B and D) to it.

- ✔ *Dominant triad* **(built on V):** Take the dominant note (A), and add the third and fifth (C♯ and E) to it.

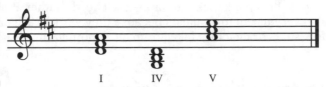

Figure 12-2:
Principal
triads of D
major.

In major keys, the principal triads are also major.

Breaking out in chords

Sometimes violinists play the entire chord at once, but mostly they break up the chord into its component notes to play them in a repeated pattern. (In Chapter 14, I talk about some fancy bowing techniques to play all the notes in a chord at the same time.)

In Figure 12-3, I show you a phrase of Offenbach's famous "Cancan" with the Roman numeral for each chord right underneath that numeral's correspond-ing notes. You can deal with playing the phrase by *arpeggiating* the principal triads, which means playing each note in turn, in other words making them into broken chords. You meet arpeggios in Chapter 10, and here you put those same skills to work in your actual pieces. Just take the chords I show you in Figure 12-3, and play each note, one after the other, as shown in the figure.

You can play the harmonies while the keyboard on your CD-ROM plays the melody. Follow the lower line of the music, and play the notes of the broken chords. Here's how: Using short strokes near the middle of the bow, play each note with vigor. You need finger 2 to be really awake for this song, because it fills in the middle note of each broken chord! Use open strings wherever possible, and just make sure your bow stays well on track when you cross strings, to keep a clear and bright sound. Get ready to play before the music starts (like a tennis player at Wimbledon preparing to return a ball), listen to the first measure of the tune on the CD-ROM, and then begin to play in measure 2. In the last measure, the music calms down (phew!); you play quarters and then a half note to finish up.

Tip: After you get ready to play, count 1, 2, 3, 4 while the first measure is play-ing so that you begin the accompaniment on time and with confidence at the start of the second measure.

Musicians call the kind of pattern, or *figuration,* of the chord that I show you in "Cancan" an *Alberti bass,* named after the minor composer (though he also composed in major keys) Domenico Alberti (1710–1740) of Venice. He used the pattern rather too much in the left-hand parts of his sonatas for keyboard.

TRACK 45

Figure 12-3:
You can-can play harmony with "The Cancan"!

Broken chords aren't a bad thing (they're not like breaking a precious antique Chinese vase in The Ashmolean Museum in Oxford, as an unfortunate tourist did when he fell down the stairs). The term just means you play the notes one at a time, in turn, instead of all together.

Violinists use many different ways of taking the notes of a chord and turning them into arpeggio-like patterns to accompany melodies. But sometimes they can actually play two notes together from a chord to give a full sound to the harmony.

Digging for Minor Chords

If a piece of music happens to be written in a minor key, you can still play it after you turn 18, but you do need some minor chords to go with it. These minor chords use the same notes as minor arpeggios. (I tell you about minor arpeggios in Chapter 10.)

Minor chords work just like major chords, which I discuss in "In the Big Leagues: Major Chords." Just as you can find a major chord by taking the first note (the root), the third note, and the fifth note of a major scale, you can find a minor chord by taking the first, third, and fifth notes of a minor scale. But minor chords sound a little different. (Lots of people feel that minor chords sound a little sad, or nostalgic.)

Not surprising, using a minor scale is a very good way to understand how principal triads work in minor keys. Music uses two kinds of minor scales (refer to Chapter 10), but here, the notes of the *harmonic minor* scale serve as the example because its pattern is more consistent going up and down.

- *Tonic triad* **(I):** Take the tonic (D) with the third and fifth notes (F♯ and A).

- *Subdominant triad* **(IV):** Take the subdominant note (G), and add the third and fifth (B♭ and D) to it.

- *Dominant triad* **(V):** Take the dominant note (A), and add the third and fifth (C♯ and E) to it.

The dominant triad (V) in minor keys is often a major chord, because the leading note is doing just that: leading as close as it dares to the tonic, just a half step (or semitone) above.

Figure 12-4 shows you the principal triads of D minor.

Figure 12-4:
Principal triads of D minor.

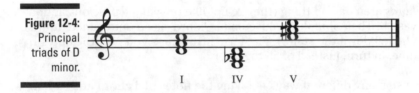

I   IV   V

Making the Most of Major and Minor Chords

Here you get the chance to play both major and minor broken chords to accompany a melody called "Joshua Fit the Battle of Jericho." I label each chord with a convenient shorthand sign that players use to identify major (+) or minor (–) chords. Figure 12-5 shows you the song you play with the names of the chords written underneath so that you can understand more about the harmonies you hear when you play along with your CD-ROM.

To play the broken chords, try them without the CD-ROM at first, so that you can figure out your moves in your own time. Play steady and crisp bow strokes on each quarter, and use open strings whenever possible.

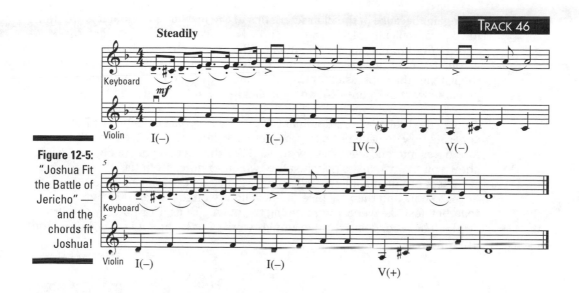

Figure 12-5:
"Joshua Fit
the Battle of
Jericho" —
and the
chords fit
Joshua!

Meet the Bossy Chords: Dominant 7ths

The last chords you meet in this chapter involve four notes, for an even juicier sound. A regular dominant chord is a *triad* (which is a fancy name for a three-note chord) formed on the dominant note (V) of any scale. A *dominant 7th* makes an even richer sound, using the same triad *plus* one more note: the seventh note above the dominant on which the chord begins. You form a dominant 7th chord by adding a seventh interval on top of the third and fifth you already have on a dominant chord. For example, you make the dominant 7th of C major by playing G, B, D, and F.

The *dominant* is the fifth note of the scale, and it gets its name because the dominant is the most important note of the scale after the tonic. In both melody and harmony, this note tends to demand our attention.

Figure 12-6 shows you what dominant 7ths look like when they're built on G, D, and A, the same notes as your open strings. When you look at these dominant 7ths, you see all four notes together, to understand the full chord.

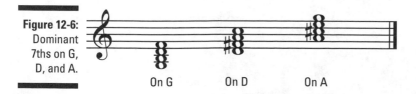

Figure 12-6:
Dominant
7ths on G,
D, and A.

On G   On D   On A

But again, because of the characteristics of the instrument, violinists would have great difficulty playing all four notes at once on most dominant 7th chords. So they usually play dominant 7ths in adapted forms, either arpeggiating the notes, or leaving out one or two of the four notes, but still giving the listener the impression of the full dominant 7th chord. I show you two possible ways in Figure 12-7, and you can listen to them on the CD-ROM.

To play the broken-chord dominant 7th in the first part of Figure 12-7, use a separate bow on each note. (In Chapter 13, I show you how you can fit two to four notes into one smooth bow stroke.) For the second part of Figure 12-7, I show you how violinists play just the two outer notes from the chord to give the effect of a dominant 7th. Place finger 2 on F on the D string before you begin to bow, and then balance the bow lightly on the G and D strings together, just like when you're tuning the open strings. Draw a very smooth stroke. The second and third examples work exactly the same way, but on the other pairs of strings.

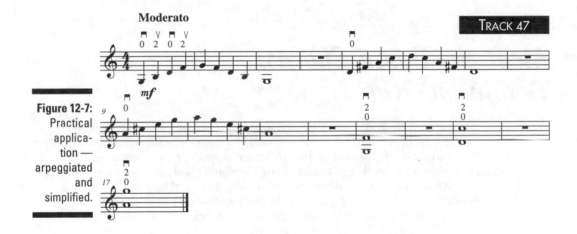

Figure 12-7: Practical application — arpeggiated and simplified.

Before you say goodnight to this section, here's the last bit of Brahms's famous "Lullaby," in Figure 12-8, for you to try with your dominant 7th harmony. Just place finger 2 on the note C (on the A string), and then bow gently on the D and A strings together, so as not to wake anyone! Prepare the fingers and the up-bow on the strings before they have to play, listen calmly to the first couple of bars on the CD-ROM, and then *come in* (as musicians call starting to play) at the third full measure with your dominant 7th.

Tip: I've been waiting for this one: Start that up-bow near — the tip!

Figure 12-8:
The end of "Brahms Lullaby," accompanied by a dominant 7th (zzz . . .).

Harmonizing in Thirds and Sixths

In this chapter, I talk a lot about chords, which are full-sounding and pleasant musical settings. But even two notes together can sound just as beautiful. In this section, I cover the two most common ways of playing harmonies on the violin.

Playing harmony parts on the violin most likely involves playing intervals of a third *above* or a sixth *below* a tune. These are very pleasing harmonies, easy on the ear and enjoyed by generations of Alpine folk singers!

To find the third interval above any note, count the original note as *1*, go up to the next note, *2*, and then end on the note after that, *3*. When you harmonize in thirds, you use the notes of the key you're in. So if your song is in the key of A major, you find a third above A by going through B to C♯, which is the third note above A in the key of A major.

To find the sixth below, use the same idea, but this time count through a descending scale. For a sixth below A in the key of A major, start on A as *1*, and then go down through G♯ *(2)*, F♯ *(3)*, E *(4)*, D *(5)*, and C♯ *(6)*.

You've probably noticed that the third *above* and the sixth *below* are actually the same pitch (in this case, C♯). But the third above is the C♯ *above* the note you're accompanying, and the sixth below is the C♯ *below* the note you're accompanying.

Figure 12-9 shows you a third above and a sixth below A in the key of A major, with the counting underneath.

Figure 12-9:
Counting your way to thirds above and sixths below.

TRACK 48

Count   1   2   3   1   2   3   4   5   6

Part V

Taking It Up a Notch: Techniques and Styles

The 5th Wave   By Rich Tennant

"Hey Ed, wanna hear me play 'the shower scene from Psycho,' again?"

In this part . . .

If you're comfortable with your basic violin techniques, you may be looking for more of a challenge — or looking to get fancy to impress your friends. This part helps you go beyond the fundamentals.

All three chapters in Part V introduce you to some pretty smooth moves, with more showy bowing techniques in Chapter 13 and some very nifty left hand work in Chapter 14. You even get a start on *vibrato,* which is a hallmark of violin playing. Then in Chapter 15, you meet three very different styles of playing music, because your violin is so versatile that you can take it anywhere — it's much smaller than a cello — and it fits right in.

Chapter 13

The Language of Bowing

*W*hen you go to a symphony concert, you can see the violinists moving their bows in many different ways to create a variety of *articulations* — the word string players use to describe how you begin and shape the course of each of your sounds. If you've heard the musical "effects" of the various bowings and are wondering how violinists make those sounds happen, you're in the right chapter. Of course, each bowing style has its own name so that composers, conductors, and players can let each other know what sound they want.

The names of these bowings may sound like they're delicious items on the menu at a posh French or Italian restaurant, but they're not. Each name refers to a particular way of playing your bow on the string to produce a recognizably individual sound — rather like articulating the vowels and consonants of our spoken languages. The more expert the player, the more musical "languages" that emerge from the violin.

In this chapter, I show you how the different bowings work, to add spice to your sounds and to show you what those composers are asking for when they write all those little dots and dashes over their notes. (Hint: It isn't Morse code!) This chapter is full of new bowings for you to try, so take it nice and easy, one section at a time. The information in this chapter definitely isn't fast food — it's a gourmet feast of sound for you to savor over a long time.

Two Notes (Or More) with One Stroke: Legato

The word *legato* derives from the Italian word meaning "tied together" and refers to a very smooth transition between one note and the next. For violinists, legato has a very specific meaning: Playing more than one note in the same bow direction. The English word *slur* refers to the same kind of bowing in violin playing. In fact, some string players call this kind of bowing *slurred legato,* including both terms for good measure.

Musicians who don't play the violin may use the term *legato* just to mean any notes that are played smoothly, not necessarily in the same bow. (The only "bow" they get is at the end of the piece, when the audience applauds!)

Learning to play legato allows you to fit two (or more) notes into one bow stroke without having to change bow direction for every note. Apart from the physical fun of learning to jog — and even sprint — with your fingers to play more notes during one smooth bow stroke, legato bowing can also come into play when the music is slow and singing. Changing bow direction seamlessly takes a bit of finesse, but your singer friends will be jealous when you play a long musical line on your violin — without having to take a breath in the middle!

You may notice that some of the scales you play in this chapter are also in Chapter 10. But you apply different bowing actions to play scales with slurs — and they also *sound* a lot different from the détaché style of bowing (refer to Chapter 4). Refining your control of the speeds and smoothness of the bow strokes makes the difference.

You can tell that the composer or editor is asking for two notes in the same bow direction when you see a curved line — looking just like a smile or a frown —under or over the note heads, as I show you in Figure 13-1.

Printers usually place the *slur* mark, or *legato* mark, near the note heads to make it easy for players to see the information.

Figure 13-1: Two notes legato.

Here's a "note" to any pianists who've succumbed to the urge to play an instrument that sustains and controls the whole duration of a note (violin commercial over!): A violin's slur mark may look exactly like a piano's *phrase* mark, but the mark means something quite different when it's used in violin music. A slur mark in violin indicates that you play two or more notes in the same bow direction, with a smooth sound, and with the last note receiving its full time value.

Changing bow direction smoothly

The first step toward keeping a calm right hand while having a busy left hand is to keep the *speed,* the *weight,* and the *contact point* of your bow (the trio of Old Reliables that you meet in Chapter 7) as similar as possible when you go from a down-bow to an up-bow — and, indeed, when you go from an up-bow to a down-bow. Here, I give you some more details to prepare you for the new bowings in this chapter.

Speeding ticket

Now that you're moving ahead from basic bowing, you must consider quite a few factors when choosing your bow speed. As always, the number-one consideration is the sound, which can be anything from a bold, strong sound to an ethereal whisper. Generally, using more bow speed helps make a bigger sound, because a faster stroke makes the violin's strings vibrate more energetically. Your bow speed needs to become more adjustable to accommodate the different sounds and rhythms you meet.

Weighty matters

Adjusting the depth of the bow on the string is the second factor violinists use to create exactly the sound they imagine. The more weight the hand gives to the bow stick and the deeper the horsehair presses into the string, the more the string is pulled into vibration and the richer and more powerful the sound. Just like many humans, sound digs being rich and powerful! Of course, how much pressure you can exert on the bow before it starts to choke the sound is limited. Your goal is to keep your right shoulder, elbow, wrist, and all finger joints somewhat flexible. Being flexible allows you to adjust the weight of your hand on the bow as necessary when you need to increase your leverage toward the tip.

Contact point

The bow's contact point (also known as the *sounding point*) on the string is a bit like an electrical contact point — a source of energy! But in this case, your musical power derives the benefit. Try a little scientific experiment to see what I'm talking about: Press your index or middle finger down on your A string over the very top edge of the fingerboard, just where you play your highest notes. Notice that the string is somewhat resistant but not impossible to press down so it touches the ebony of the fingerboard. But if you try the same pressure on the A string right next to the bridge (where the string is at its highest point), you can hardly press the string down at all.

By bowing where the string has less tension, you can play softer sounds, ones where you're not adding a lot of weight to the bow. However, the stronger sounds work best if you bow at various sounding points nearer the bridge, because you can bear down considerably more on those very same strings.

Starting to slur two notes

Preparing the bow and fingers for slurs means coordinating techniques that you already know but which you haven't yet put together in this particular sequence. This first exercise may remind you of a country dance, where the caller walks you through all the steps slowly and separately at first, before the band strikes up and you whirl into action.

Slurring two notes in one bow stroke is easy if you work your way through this preliminary exercise, shown in Figure 13-2, on your A string. In this exercise, the first time you put two notes into one bow stroke, briefly stop the bow on the string between notes. Try these moves:

1. **Use only half of your bow on the down-bow for the first A, and then stop your bow on the string.**

2. **Land finger 1 on the A string while the bow is stopped (and you can stop the bow for as long as you need — just move very calmly at first).**

3. **Continue your down-bow until you've bowed all the way to the tip.**

4. **Stop the bow briefly at the tip, and then begin an up-bow while finger 1 is still playing on the A string.**

5. **Stop the bow on the string when you arrive at the middle of the bow, and then lift finger 1 off the A string while the bow is stopped.**

6. **Continue the up-bow smoothly on the open A string until you reach the frog.**

7. **Use the same process, but with fingers 2, 3, and 4 in the subsequent measures.**

Moving on to smooth slurs is just a step away. When the bow distribution is even and the fingers move independently of what the bow does, you're all set for real legato. Refer to Figure 13-2, the same figure that you work on for the preliminary stopped strokes.

Play a few calm bow strokes on open A to establish the smooth sound. When the bow speed is even, try adding finger 1 during the course of the first "real" down-bow stroke of the exercise, landing finger 1 on the string as you pass the midpoint of the bow. On the following up-bow, lift finger 1 off again as you pass the midpoint of the up-bow stroke. The same steps work for all of the finger combinations shown in Figure 13-2. You can listen and play along with the smooth *legati* (how's that for being totally correct with Italian plurals!) on your CD-ROM. You can also watch me play this exercise.

Figure 13-2:
Slurring
from an
open string
to a finger
and then
back again.

TRACK 49, 0:00

Now that you have the basic idea about slurs, I give you an overview of the different slurs you meet in real music so that you can be as prepared as a Boy Scout when you encounter legato galore! Just use the preliminary stopped bows at first for each slur, until your bow distribution is even and your finger coordination is prompt. If you can play with ease and don't need to make the preliminary stops anymore, go right ahead. The technique you've practiced is available to you anytime you need it to clear up a tricky spot.

Slurring between fingers

The most usual situation in slurring involves transitioning from one finger to another. In Figure 13-3 as well as on the CD-ROM, I show you how to play a very smooth legato between any pair of fingers. Use the rest measures to get the next pair of fingers ready.

This exercise works a lot like the open-string slurs, except you prepare your starting finger on the string before you begin to bow. I walk you through the first example so that you can use the same idea for the different finger combinations. In all these exercises, the starting finger of each set can remain calmly on the string.

1. **Begin with finger 1 on the A string at the start of the first down-bow. As you begin the bow stroke near the frog, plan on using the first half of your down-bow for finger 1.**

2. **Prepare finger 2 over its spot, then land the finger decisively as you continue your down-bow into the upper half of the bow, without changing the bow speed at all as finger 2 lands. Continue bowing on finger 2 until you reach, or almost reach, the tip of the bow.**

3. **Release finger 2 from the string at the end of the stroke, just as you change bow direction, and then start the up-bow on finger 1, and so on.**

   I give you each example once, but feel free to repeat a measure a few times to pattern the moves and gain confidence.

I show you these slurs using the first finger pattern for now, with finger 2 placed very close to finger 3, which is on its fingerboard guide (refer to Chapter 5 to find out about finger patterns and how to make fingerboard guides). Later on, when you want to refine your skills or challenge yourself, try the same exercises with other finger patterns, so that you're fluent at slurring in any key.

TRACK 49, 0:22

Figure 13-3:
Slurring
between
fingers.

Adding two-note slurs to scales

After you get going with two-note slurs, apply your new bowing skills to some of the scales from Chapter 10.

Start by using music that your left-hand fingers know well: your most basic scales. Follow these steps as I show them in Figure 13-4 and on the CD-ROM, and you're slurring smoothly:

1. **Try the simple one-octave A major scale, starting on open A and using détaché bowing (refer to Chapter 4), with a separate stroke for each note.**

2. **Play the same scale a second time, but this time, use preliminary stopped bows to prepare for slurring, with two notes per bow stroke.**

3. **Play the scale a third time through, and continue your bow strokes smoothly, without stopping during finger changes on the two-note slurs.**

I put down-bow and up-bow signs in the first bar to remind you of the bowing actions, and then I leave you to continue the same bowing idea for the remainder of each example. You have one empty measure between the two scales, to set up your new finger pattern.

You can prepare slurs on any scale or song using the method outlined in these steps. Figure 13-4 gives you the scales of A major and B flat major to try out, and I also show you how on the CD-ROM.

TRACK 49, 1:00

Figure 13-4:
Two scales
with slurs (A
major and B
flat major).

Adding two-note slurs to a song

After you have your legato skills cooking in scales, try them out on Mary's lamb too — they add variety and expression to all kinds of pieces that you want to play (see the song "Mary Had a Little Lamb," later in this section).

Halving a good time

When you move on from practice exercises to playing real music with two-note slurs, you need to be prepared to play slurs and separate bows as they happen, in any sequence. In pieces with slurs, I let you know when to use only half the bow length for some of the separate bowings.

Using half a bow works really well if you remember one important fact: Your bow has two halves. Sometimes, you need to play a half bow in the *upper half* of the bow, between the middle and the tip of the bow, and other times, you need to play the half bow in the *lower half* of the bow, between the middle and the frog. If your half bow happens after a long down-bow, you play it in the upper half of the bow, and . . . well, I'm sure you get the picture. I tell you more about bow distribution in the section called "Getting Up to Speed and Figuring Out Bow Division."

TRACK 50

Mary Had a Little Lamb

After Mary had that little lamb comfortably in her arms, she calmed down and got some legato practice in! Just slur two notes in one bow where you see a legato marking. Use most of the bow for slurs and half notes, and about half the bow length for regular, separate quarter notes. Start the song with your bow near the frog and with fingers 1 and 2 ready on the A string so that when you lift finger 2, the change to finger 1 is smooth. Use finger 4 for the top E, so you practice the slurring all on one string.

Slurring across strings

Of course, you won't always play all your slurred notes on the same string. You may need to cross over to another string as the melodic line moves up and down. Slurring notes while crossing strings calls for very smooth and well-coordinated combinations of your skills.

Slurring across strings from an open string to a finger

Crossing from an open string to a finger allows you a bit of time to get the string crossing ready and the finger poised so that the bow and the finger arrive on the new string at the same time. I give you a step-by-step account of how to get this right:

1. **Begin your down-bow on the open string and relax your right elbow so that your bow hand can prepare to approach the new string as you continue your down-bow.**

   Floating your arm level slightly feels a bit like putting your car's gear in neutral on the way to a new gear.

2. **Approach the new string level as closely as possible with your bow before the actual moment when you need to sound it, to make the transition easy and smooth.**

3. **Let your finger hover over the new string, so it can be close by and ready to drop on to its spot in sync with the bow.**

4. **Drop your finger onto the new string, and adjust your arm's level slightly to switch the bow over.**

   Hey presto (or at least *allegro moderato*) — the bow and the finger meet on the new string.

Tip: Your new finger can actually land a little ahead of the bow's arrival, if it isn't in the way of the sound.

Figure 13-5 shows you some simple slurs, starting across two open strings, just to get your bow moving well, then adding fingers. You can watch how these slurs work on your CD-ROM. Later, try these same fingerings between other pairs of strings.

Figure 13-5:
Slurs across strings from an open string to a finger.

When you first practice slurring across strings, it helps to add a small stop between notes, until you get used to coordinating your fingers and bow to do the moves. But if you can slur easily and accurately without adding the "stop," by all means, go ahead — lucky you!

Slurring across strings and between fingers

The last kind of two-note slur you meet in this chapter is when the slur involves crossing the string *and* changing from one finger to another at the same time. But after playing through the previous examples and songs in this chapter, you can easily accomplish this final step. I tell you the steps even though most of them probably feel quite familiar:

1. **Prepare finger 1 on D, and then begin your down-bow, budgeting about half the length for the first note.**

2. **Drop finger 2 onto the A string soon after you begin to bow.**

3. **As you reach the middle of the down-bow, allow the bow to change to the A-string level to sound the C♯, using a gentle and smooth motion.**

4. **Begin the up-bow on the A string level and gently roll the bow over toward the D string so that you sound finger 1 at the middle of the bow.**

Each bar works in much the same way. Prepare each new finger a little ahead of time and move calmly and smoothly.

Tip: Leave finger 1 sitting quietly on the D string, because you're going right back to it on the next slur!

Figure 13-6 shows you some examples of slurring while crossing strings and changing fingers, which are also demonstrated on the CD-ROM.

After practicing the different types of slurs, you're prepared to add your new legato skills to scales and pieces. Knowing a skill in its basic form is the first step to being able to adapt it to a broad range of situations where related skills may be needed.

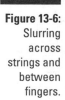

Figure 13-6: Slurring across strings and between fingers.

Moderato

TRACK 51, 0:23

Try playing your G major scale with two notes per bow (see Figure 13-7, and play along with the CD-ROM). Your fourth finger can take a brief vacation for this scale, so that you have the chance to slur from one string to the next during the same smooth bow stroke. Going upward, lift finger 3 as soon as the bow is safely playing on the next open string. In the descending scale, you need to prepare finger 3 on the next string while you're playing the open string, so that the finger is ready when the bow arrives on the new note.

Violin students traditionally use finger 4 instead of an open string when playing a descending scale, so as to keep their left hand frame well in shape over the string. But because you're learning string crossings right now, use the open strings all the way in a legato scale.

Figure 13-7:
G major
scale with
slurs.

TRACK 51, 1:01

Try out your new slurs on "Asian Mood," a song that appears with détaché bowing in Chapter 5. Now you see this song with several slurs to play, for a smooth effect.

 TRACK 52

Asian Mood

Begin with your bow set comfortably near the frog on open A, and then add finger 1 as you continue the first down-bow. Keep finger 1 on the string while you play finger 3 with the up-bow. Lift finger 3 decisively to return to the B that finger 1 is holding in place as you continue the up-bow. Measure 2 has mixed bowings: The first part of the bar involves a slur across the strings, from open A to finger 3 that's playing the note G on the D string, followed by two separate bow strokes (which each need about half as much bow as the slurs) on the note E. Each of the following pairs of measures has the same bowing pattern, except for the very last note. Use the open A string in this song so that you get lots of slurs going across from one string to another.

Playing three notes in a bow stroke

Playing three notes in a bow is just like playing two notes in a bow; you just fit in one more note. The big difference involves dividing your bow length (well, just the horsehair bit, really) into three parts when you try the preliminary stopped versions, till you feel in control. Figure 13-8 shows you what you see on the music when three-note slurs are coming up.

Figures 13-9, 13-10, and 13-11 are a few warm-ups for you to work on slurring three notes in a bow. When you do the preliminary stopped bows to sequence your coordination, make sure to divide the length of the horsehair into three equal parts.

Figure 13-8:
Three-note
slurs.

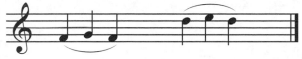

If you bought a packet of stick-on dots for marking the fingerboard to set up your left hand (refer to Chapter 5) and have been wondering what to do with the hundreds of dots you have left over, here's the perfect use for two of them: Take two dots and pop them onto the side of the bow stick that passes in front of you, one at the ⅓ place and the other at the ⅔ place. (It's just like having courtside tickets at Wimbledon!) But seriously, if you line up the dot with the string at each preliminary stop when practicing three-note slurs, you develop a sense of even bow use, which helps your legato sound excellent.

The three-note exercises shown in Figures 13-9 and 13-10, and played on the CD-ROM, use the D string, but you can try them on any string when you've mastered the original versions. The exercises use upward and downward note sequences to keep them challenging. In Figure 13-10, leave the lower finger sitting on the string while the upper finger plays.

Figure 13-9:
Three-note slurs involving open strings.

TRACK 53, 0:00

Figure 13-10:
Three-note slurs from finger to finger.

TRACK 53, 0:29

Figure 13-11 shows you three-note slurs across three strings, and you can watch them in action on the CD-ROM. You lead toward the A and E strings by letting your elbow level down slightly as you play through the down-bow. When you bow three notes in the up-bow, traveling steadily toward the D-string level, let your right hand take the lead, with your arm level following suit. Changing strings using the moves I describe helps you draw your bow parallel to the bridge, keeping the sound smooth and consistent. As for the left hand, you have plenty of time to change fingers on the E string during the time you're bowing the open Ds.

TRACK 53, 0:52

Figure 13-11:
Three-note slurs across strings.

Although I give you the musical examples in quarter notes so that you can concentrate on technical skills, legato bowings can happen with just about any note values. Later in this chapter, you get to try some different note values in slurs by playing some songs.

Adding three-note slurs to scales

Playing arpeggios with three-note slurs brings you to a new level of fluency and coordination. In Figure 13-12, I give you three examples to work on, but you can try the same idea on any arpeggio. You meet rest measures in some other exercises in this chapter, but here, notice that rest measures are worth three counts, because of the 3/4 time signature. Listen to this exercise being played on the CD-ROM.

Figure 13-12:
Three arpeggios with three-note slurs (A major, D major, and G major arpeggios).

Adding three-note slurs to a song

As for songs, you can add a bunch of three-note slurs to "Old French Folk Song." When three notes of the same pitch occur in a measure, doing a smooth legato bowing makes them sound like one long note, so keep the bow strokes separate for those bars, using the lower half of the bow, between the frog and the middle.

TRACK 54

Old French Folk Song

Begin with smooth, singing bow strokes, starting the first down-bow from near the frog and using a comfortable amount of bow (probably about half the bow) for each note. Look for the legato marks and play them as indicated, using most of the bow. You need to slow the bow stroke slightly to fit in all three notes. In the penultimate measure, slur the first two notes in one bow, and then take the B on an up-bow so that you can finish the piece with a down-bow for a naturally tapering sound.

Fitting four notes in a bow stroke

By the time you fit four notes into a bow, things are getting pretty athletic! Figure 13-13 shows you how music looks when you play four notes in the same bow direction.

Figure 13-13:
Four-note slurs.

When you see slur marks like the ones in Figure 13-14, you must fit four notes into one bow stroke. Try the same system with those office stick-on dots that I tell you about in "Playing three notes in a bow stroke" to mark the ¼, ½, and ¾ marks over the bow-hair to keep your distribution even. Keep your bow traveling smoothly and evenly on the D string while your fingers land and lift to make the pitches. The rest measure between the two parts of the exercise gives you time to get ready for the new fingering. You can watch the exercise being played on the CD-ROM.

Using a similar process to the two-note slurs, take the G major scale again, but this time, play the two-octave version for more notes, and bow four notes in each stroke (see Figure 13-15, and listen to the exercise on the CD-ROM). Use open strings (no finger 4s necessary here) to concentrate on the smooth transitions between strings. Hold the top G at the end of the ascending scale for 2 beats, and do the same thing when you finish descending and arrive back on the open G.

Figure 13-14: Four-note slur exercise.

TRACK 55, 0:00

Figure 13-15: G major two-octave scale with four-note slurs.

TRACK 55, 0:39

Getting Up to Speed and Figuring Out Bow Division

You become familiar with bow division when planning out your bow for slurs, earlier in this chapter, as well as in some other places in *Violin For Dummies*, such as the chapter about rhythm (refer to Chapter 8). Violinists always need to plan out their bow distribution so that they make the best possible use of those 24 inches or so of horsehair. In this section, I go over the most useful ways of dividing the bow so that you can get the sound you want.

Deciding how much bow to use on a note or bar

If a violinist runs out of bow, the sound simply disappears — or the bow makes a very peculiar little crunchy sound while the player tries desperately to keep bowing, using the last inch of bow. Running out of bow is a lot like running out of breath when you're singing or speaking. So violinists figure out how to divide or distribute their bows as they go along.

When you first look at a piece of music, you determine if it uses shorter or longer note values. Many of the exercises and songs in the earlier parts of this book use full bows for the purpose of beginner violin training (it's a lot like driver's ed!). But you need to become more familiar with using different amounts of bow if you want to play more intricate songs, according to the sound and character of the music. I give you some special examples here to show you how to play the bow for maximum effect.

Figure 13-16 shows a slow sustained theme, so you need to budget plenty of bow for the sound to speak out (you can see this theme being played on the CD-ROM). You're looking at using whole bows. Now observe the slurred six-teenth notes in measure 4. These notes occur on a down-bow — plus you need to use almost the whole bow on this stroke so that you have a full bow length for the next bar. In measure 6, the two notes aren't slurred, although the character of the strokes is still smooth. You know you need to be right at the frog to start the last long note, so in measure 6, be a little Scrooge-like when spending the first down-bow (add a little weight to make up for the slower speed), and make sure the up-bow before the last note moves your bow lightly to the frog.

Figure 13-16:
Deciding
how much
bow to use.

Figure 13-17 shows a cheerful little passage with eighths and sixteenths. Begin using small bows at about the lower middle of the bow for the sixteenths, playing quite lightly to sound *mezzopiano,* and use about twice as much bow for the eighths. Things change considerably for the bow at measure 3, when you slur four notes in one bow direction. For this move, plan to use more bow on each four-note slur, at least double the amount you used on the eighths, to make the bowings very smooth.

Figure 13-17:
More
bowing
decisions.

If you run into an uncomfortable spot when bowing, look at what you're doing in the *preceding* bar so that you come into the tricky section in the best possible position.

Doing the math: Dividing the bow by note values

Throughout this book, I give you several instances where you divide the bow according to the relative lengths of notes. But the greater the variety of music you play, the more bow division becomes sophisticated. In Figure 13-18 and on the CD-ROM, I show you a specific situation to prepare you for bow decisions you make to sound very fine in your repertoire.

The basic bowing pattern in Figure 13-18 is similar for several measures, so first decide how to approach the pattern. Because the music is slowish and *mf*, using a full bow for the quarter notes and half bows for the eighth notes makes sense. In measure 4, the rhythm pattern changes. Here, you need to slow the overall bow speed to allow for the whole bow lasting for 2 beats, and you need to reiterate the up-bow for the eighth note at the end of the measure. The dynamic level is constant, so add a little weight to maintain the sound. Use about ¾ of the bow on the first A and the last ¼ or so on the second A. In the second-to-last measure, use about a full bow on each quarter note, and then halve the bow speed for the final D so that it lasts 2 beats.

Figure 13-18:
Bow division by note length.

Andante   TRACK 57, 0:00

Dividing the bow strokes in anticipation of the next note

Sometimes, you play a whole bunch of short notes followed by a long note. A violinist has to be very sneaky and must creep the bow toward the place it needs to be for the next note. Deciding where you want to be for the start of the long note usually gives you a clue about where you need to do the sneaky stuff! Figure 13-19 shows you an example of needing to get to a particular place on the bow.

Play the sixteenths as much as possible in the comfort zone around the middle of the bow. Then start to push a little more toward the frog (with sneaky up-bows) as you approach the last note, so you start the whole note from the frog of the bow.

Figure 13-19:
Sneaky bows.

TRACK 57, 0:23

Adjusting the amounts of bow for dynamics

The same notes can use very different amounts of bow, according to the volume of sound you want. I show you this situation in Figure 13-20 and on the CD-ROM. Start with small bow strokes at about the middle of the bow for the *p* sixteenth notes, but increase the amounts slightly as you make the steady crescendo. A steep decline in sound occurs in the last measure of sixteenths, and you also need to sneak a little toward the frog for the last whole note, which uses a slow bow, of course.

A very general principle is that *forte* levels are best played near the frog, because the frog itself is naturally the heaviest part of the bow. The extra weight of your hand and arm on top of the frog create a powerful tone producer! So, where possible, arrange to play louder passages on the lower part of the bow, or make your way there as soon as you can.

Figure 13-20:
Adjusting the amounts of bow for dynamics.

TRACK 57, 0:37

Mais Oui, Maestro: Taking On Ze Accents

Composers let you know when they want an *accent* on a particular note for a marching effect, for a jazzy effect, for a surprise effect, or for any number of other possible reasons, by writing special signs over or under the note head. In this section, I show you the accent signs you see on printed music, and I tell you how to bow them so the sound's just right.

The musical score would get too complicated if a musical symbol existed for every possible musical effect. So performers decide how to interpret the symbols by looking at the mood and style of the music.

Kreutzer's kreations

Although Rodolphe Kreutzer (1766–1831), the famous violinist, composer, and conductor, was born at the court of Versailles, his father came from Germany to join the court orchestra, which accounts for his not very French-sounding name. Today, the name Kreutzer is familiar to classical music buffs from Beethoven's great "Kreutzer" Sonata Op. 47. Beethoven sent the sonata to Kreutzer with a personal note of admiration, but Kreutzer never even replied. He didn't like the Kreutzer Sonata, considering it to be outrageous and unintelligible, and so he never performed it.

After beginning his musical studies with his father, young Rodolphe went on to study with Anton Stamitz (one of the most famous violinists and composers of the time), and he made his solo violin debut in Paris at the age of 13. From 1785, he played in the court orchestra, which was his regular job until 1792. He composed his first opera, *Joan of Arc,* in 1790 and went on to have great success with no less than 46 works for stage. He played concert tours throughout Europe and became a professor at the Paris Conservatoire. A fractured left arm caused him to retire from his solo career in 1810, so he became a full-time conductor and assumed the position of conductor of the Grand Opera in 1816. Kreutzer was by all accounts a crusty old bird, not given to charm or popularity, but as a musician, he was highly accomplished. On his violin, he favored singing tones and sweet sounds. His legacy of violin music includes 19 concertos and the *42 Studies,* the book every violin student knows and works from.

For the fanciest bowings in this chapter, which include these accents and all the new bowings you meet from now to the end of the chapter, I've devised a short *study,* which is sometimes known by the French name *étude* (a study is a musical piece that violinists, pianists, and other instrumentalists use for concentrating on a special aspect of technique). This study is inspired by "Kreutzer 2," the most famous violin study in the world. I tell you about Kreutzer in the sidebar "Kreutzer's kreations."

Accenting the positive

When you see an *accent* on a note, you emphasize the start of the note with some extra bow weight and speed, and then you follow through the rest of its duration with a regular détaché stroke. You can control how much you accent the note according to the character of the piece you're playing and how loud the dynamic levels are around the accented note. Figure 13-21 shows you what you see on the printed page.

I add some accents to the short study "Homage to Kreutzer," shown in Figure 13-22, and I play them for you on the CD-ROM. Observe that the first bit is very comfortable to play, with accents on the first note of each group, but at the end, accents pop up on every note!

Figure 13-21:
Getting just
the right
accent.

TIP

The version of the accents that I present in this study is just one of many possibilities. Later, for a challenge, you can revisit this exercise to put accents on different notes of your own choice.

Figure 13-22:
"Homage to
Kreutzer"
with
accents.

TRACK 58

Allegro moderato

TRACK 59

Haydn: "Surprise" Symphony

Haydn was annoyed with his rich patrons for falling asleep during his concerts (which usually took place after the aristocrats had enjoyed a long gourmet dinner), so he wrote the following little "surprise" into his symphony, for a rude awakening. Beginning your first down-bow just under the middle of the bow, play little stopped bowings using about an inch of bow on each eighth note, as if you were tiptoeing around. Use a longer stroke on the quarter note, till you're just above the middle of the bow, and then bow the next phrase with the same articulation, but starting up-bow. The *pp* section starting at measure 9 can use even tinier bow strokes. Then go for it with the accent on the last note, and wake up the neighbors!

Here are a few extra ideas to perfect the surprise: In measure 7, just hop finger 2 diagonally across to F♯ on the D string. At the end of measure 8, make a circular bow retake to arrive on down-bow for the start of measure 9. (Refer to the sidebar "Getting back to your starting place" in Chapter 8 to know how to do a circular bow retake.) By the way, "*ten.*" means *tenuto*, Italian for "hold on a bit," almost as if you're looking around cautiously before you start sneaking again.

Hammering it out: Martelé

You can't beat martelé for a powerful, punchy sound (the word *martelé* is French for "hammered," after all). The stroke is very purposeful, firm, or sometimes, even angry sounding. Most martelé strokes occur during music that's military or resolute in character. Figure 13-23 shows the four symbols that composers can use to indicate martelé. The first is the most usual, but I show you the others so that you have an idea of what bowing to try if you see them on a piece you want to play.

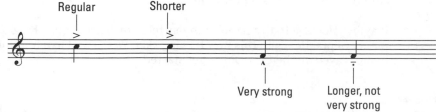

Figure 13-23:
Martelé
symbols.

Start the bow with quite a deep bite into the string, which is set up *before* you begin to draw the bow stroke. To sink the bow firmly into the string, lean mostly on the first finger of your bow hand (with a little help from finger 2 and some counter-pressure from the thumb in response) until you see the middle of the bow stick dipping slightly toward the horsehair. By preparing to play the bow with a lot of weight added to the stick before you begin to move, you ensure that the start of the martelé sound is powerful. Begin the martelé stroke with energetic speed, and then simply release most of that extra bow weight very soon after you start moving the bow so that the hammered sound is only at the very start of the sound.

Martelé is a very versatile bow stroke — you can play it with any amount of bow and in any section of the bow. This kind of stroke most usually occurs in the upper half of the bow, between the middle and the tip. When the pressure isn't released almost entirely at the end of the stroke, the tone suffers. However, you do need to control the end of the stroke so that the bow doesn't leap up off the string, so the stop has to be a little firm. If the new stroke begins before the old stroke stops, you get crunchy sounds.

Because this stroke requires a good amount of downward pressure to start the sound, your wrist level may descend slightly, perhaps up to an inch, and your base knuckles may also weigh in a little closer to the bow stick. When your fingers are prepared for the first biting action, use your arm movement to start the actual stroke.

Watch for the direction of the bow when playing martelé by aiming the frog of your bow toward a carefully chosen "target" in the room. Also, choose a fairly strong (resistant) point of contact on the string, and be ready to try a few other points of contact until you get the sound clear and strong.

If your next note is on a different string, allow the bow to come to a rest on the new string at the end of the previous stroke so that you're already there in plenty of time for the next attack.

Just to add to the complexity of bowing, some bowings are represented by more than one possible symbol — and some symbols have more than one bowing solution. The fact is, these variant symbols changed their meanings during the course of history, and some even had geographical variants. In the end, though, you make intellectual and artistic decisions based on what sounds right to you as a performer.

Playing "Homage to Kreutzer" with martelé bowing in Figure 13-24 gives you plenty of practice with this new bowing skill. Watch and listen to the song being played on the CD-ROM to get started.

Figure 13-24: "Homage to Kreutzer" in martelé.

TRACK 61

Grand Old Duke of York

The Grand Old Duke needed plenty of vigor and resolution to get up and down that hill with his 10,000 men! As you play the song, try the martelé stroke (use the upper ⅔ of the bow for a full sound) on every note, except the eighth notes, which can be bowed firmly (using smaller bows). Each dotted half note calls for a slow bow, followed by a quick up-bow on the last quarter note of the bar, so you can get back to your usual starting place for the next measure.

 Practicing "Grand Old Duke of York" with regular détaché bowing until your fingers are confident enough to try martelé is helpful for this and any other new music you're broaching (refer to Chapter 5 for more about détaché bowing). Just take it easy at first, and then add the details as you feel ready.

Meeting the Fanciest Bowings

The names of these fancy bowings may indeed sound like items on the menu at an exclusive restaurant, but you can "taste" all the sounds on your violin without paying a big bill! These bowings require a flexible bow hand and some calm, slow preparation in order to work successfully at speed. Here's my best advice: Don't skip a step when getting up to speed, just go gradually.

Slurred staccato

You already know most of what you need to play *slurred staccato*. How can that be possible? Well, in the early part of this chapter, every time you play the preparatory slur where you stop the bow between notes, that's slurred staccato! The stroke is like a slur because the bow continues in the same direction for the next note, but it's like staccato because the sound stops briefly between notes to get a little separation. Figure 13-25 shows you what signs indicate slurred staccato on the page.

Figure 13-25:
Slurred
staccato
signs.

Make the brief bite that starts each stroke by adding a little weight to the first and second fingers on the bow, just as you initiate a quick bowing movement. If your thumb bites a little underneath the stick in sympathy with your finger power, that's fine, as long as it releases right away just as the stroke begins.

Moving on to the trusty "Homage to Kreutzer," shown in Figure 13-26 and played on the CD-ROM in both video and audio, I add some instances of slurred staccato for you to get your teeth (and bow) into. Notice that I vary the number of notes within one bow direction, so get out your calculator to figure the bow speeds and divisions!

Figure 13-26:
"Homage to
Kreutzer"
with slurred
staccato.

TRACK 62

Drink to Me Only

See the slurred staccato marks on this song, "Drink to Me Only." Use the middle ⅔ of the bow, and use open strings freely while you learn the piece. You can always add a few choice finger 4s when your bowing feels familiar and comfortable. When you see a dot over the next note, you need to make a light stop of the bow on the string just before you nudge the bow for the next note. At the end of measures 4 and 12, make a circular retake of the bow during the rests, so as to land the next down-bow back at the starting place for the next down-bow. Notice that some slurs are smooth, just for an extra challenge.

Meet the off-the-string family

These bowings may be off-the-string, with the bow lifting off (or even bouncing off) the string between strokes, but they're not off-the-wall! All the bowings up to this point in *Violin For Dummies* start and finish on the string. This section introduces you to some off-the-string bowings that just drop in or make flying visits to your strings.

Brush stroke

You smile when you play the violin because playing music is fun! The brush stroke makes your bow smile too. *Brush stroke* is the name given to strokes where the bow is lifted slightly off the string at each end of the note, so your hand moves in a curved, "smile" shape for this stroke. Figure 13-27 shows you the symbols that can indicate brush strokes.

Figure 13-27:
Brushing up on brush strokes.

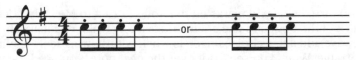

Practicing "Homage to Kreutzer" using the light brush strokes I show you in Figure 13-28 and play on the CD-ROM prepares you for meeting them in music you want to play. This stroke works best in the lower half of the bow, around the *balance point* (literally the place about ⅓ from the frog, where the bow can balance like an acrobat on the high wire, if you set the bow on its side and horizontally across your extended left index finger) of the bow. To develop a brush stroke, start with smooth bowing in the lower half of the bow, just back and forth on the string, with no stops, very fluid. Gradually start to lift off at each end of the stroke, allowing very generous movements, rather like a conductor swishing away with a baton. When these bigger strokes feel free, start to make the strokes a little smaller and faster, but always keep the smile shape happening and always let each stroke come up a little off the string. Allow your fingers to be quite flexible on the bow for this stroke, don't grip tightly, and let the tip of the bow and the point of your right elbow describe "smile" shaped movements in sync with the hand movements.

Figure 13-28:
"Homage to Kreutzer" in brush strokes.

TRACK 64

Allegro moderato

mf

Very handily, you can now try out your brush strokes on Haydn's "Surprise" Symphony that you met earlier in this chapter, playing brush strokes instead of just stopping your bow lightly on the string.

Spiccato

Spiccato bowing refers to bouncy little strokes that happen around the middle of the bow. You choose the exact spot to use depending on the speed and volume of the spiccato notes: A little higher up the bow is lighter, and the spiccatos rebound more quickly but are somewhat less powerful in tone than are spiccato strokes dropped on the string a tad below the middle of the bow.

Also called a *dropped stroke,* spiccato calls for a flexible approach from the wrist and fingers to work successfully, because they act as a spring system to cushion the landings on the strings. Pernambuco wood is used for making bows because of its special qualities of being both strong and flexible at the same time. Here's an instance where those qualities are particularly useful to you: The bow rebounds of its own accord, and you don't need to do much. In fact, the less you do, the better. Figure 13-29 shows you what to look for on the music to indicate spiccato bowing.

Knowing the difference between brush stroke and spiccato — and when to use which — can be tricky. In the brush stroke, you control every aspect of the lifting and landing of each stroke (by actually doing it yourself!), but in the spiccato stroke, the bow rebounds due to its natural elasticity, and then your hand just drops and "catches" it. Generally, the brush stroke takes place in the lower third to half of the bow in slower-moving music. Spiccato works best around the lower to upper-middle area of the bow, and you use it for faster passages.

Figure 13-29:
Spiccato
signs.

Here's how you get started with spiccato:

1. **Suspend your bow with its middle area about 3 inches above the A string, and let your hand hang ever so slightly below your wrist level.**

2. **Let the horsehair drop straight down onto the string and then rebound back up silently — just like bouncing a ball — but don't try to actually make a bow stroke.**

   The pinky finger makes this action happen by releasing its weight from the bow and then getting its power back as the bow rebounds. Letting your forearm level down a little as the bow drops, and then letting it go up again as you catch the bouncing bow, is okay.

3. **Try the same drop-and-catch idea in other parts of the bow to see where spiccato works best.**

   Observe that while the bow rebounds very briskly near the tip, the stroke is hard to control and feels a little brittle.

To make a real spiccato, add a little down-bow and up-bow action, mostly from your elbow hinge, to the preceding steps. If the stroke has more horizontal movement, the articulation is gentler and the duration of the note is slightly longer. If the horizontal movement is shorter (and this is usually needed in spiccato), the bounce element is greater. The bow doesn't need to jump too high off the string, especially when crossing to a new string. If you want the bow to rebound very actively, keep the stick directly above the ribbon of horsehair while you play. The flatter the bow hair, the greater the bounce. However, if you feel that the strokes are too bouncy, tilt the bow stick a bit away from you.

In violin playing, your playing technique is most successful when you keep your movements as simple and natural as possible.

Using dear old Kreutzer gives you a chance to try out spiccato for a few bars. Take a very easy tempo, and keep your bow grip quite flexible, no tight gripping. Figure 13-30 shows you "Homage to Kreutzer" with spiccato dots. You can watch and listen to the song on the CD-ROM too.

Figure 13-30: "Homage to Kreutzer" in spiccato.

TRACK 65

TRACK 66

Magic Flute Overture

Play Mozart's "Magic Flute Overture" to practice your spiccato bows. All the eighth notes receive light spiccato bows, but the sixteenths are slurred with four notes to a bow. Just to add to the fun, you need to play two up-bows (with a small lift between them) in a row for the first two eighth notes following the slurred sixteenths. Not to be too picky about spiccato, but I just wish to remind you to keep your bow hand flexible and light for this bowing.

Pizzicato (with all the toppings)

This chapter mainly covers fancy bowings, because bowing's mostly what the right hand does in violin playing. But because pizzicato is almost always a right-hand technique, it qualifies for a place in this section too. You can read about how to make a basic pizzicato in Chapter 5, but in this section, I show you some more nifty pizzicato techniques to complete your knowledge of this plucky little sound.

Unless a piece of music uses only pizzicato throughout, chances are that you need to play some plucked notes right in the middle of other bowed notes. Each situation calls for a different technique (I demonstrate each on the CD-ROM by playing an open A string):

✔ **When you have time to prepare:** If pizzicato notes happen at the very beginning of a piece, or after a few rests, you have time to make the following moves, which I show you on the CD-ROM:

    1. **From your regular bow hold, fold the bow into the palm of your right hand by wrapping fingers 2, 3, and 4 securely round the frog.**

    When you do this, you see the horsehair facing you directly.

    2. **Extend finger 1 and your thumb.**

    3. **Keep this same general position, and place the tip of your thumb (pointing down) against the E-string side of the fingerboard, about 1 inch from the top end of the ebony, to let it be the pivoting point you may use to adjust your hand position.**

    4. **Use the pad of finger 1 to make the pizzicatos (to pluck the strings).**

✔ **When pizzicato lasts for a few notes, with no time to change the bow hold:** This technique is used for one or a few pizzicato notes that are amidst bowed notes. Keep your bow hold regular in every respect, except extend your index finger and suspend your whole hand a little down from your wrist, so as to get a favorable angle for the pizzicato finger to do its job.

✔ **When you can put down the bow and pick it up again:** Ah! The easiest one — just put your bow across the shelf of the music stand and play regular pizzicato. You have two different choices here:

    • For slower music, or when plenty of space exists between notes, make a loose fist, extend finger 1, and then suspend your left hand a little from the wrist, just above the strings you want to reach.

    • For faster music or when lots of string crossings occur, use the same idea about making a fist as described in the previous bullet point. But in this situation, also extend your thumb and position it pointing down against the side of the fingerboard for extra support, just like when you still have your bow in hand.

You see *pizz.* written above or below the notes on the staff when the composer wants you to play pizzicato, and you see *arco* (Italian for "bow") when the composer wants you to return to regular bowing.

Your last right-hand workout, shown in Figure 13-31, is a short exercise in which you try out your new pizzicato skills. Try each technique along with the CD-ROM, so you become a plucky player.

Figure 13-31:
Pizzicato
party!

TRACK 67

Chapter 14

Putting Your Finger on It

In This Chapter

▶ Playing easy double stops

▶ Playing three- and four-note chords

▶ Shifting left hand positions

▶ Rockin' away at vibrato

▶ Tapping into trills

Doing some impressive stuff with your bow hand (refer to Chapter 13) may make your other hand feel a bit "left" out — so in this chapter, I take a look at some rather fancy new finger techniques that allow your left hand to give the right one a run for its money, and that bring your fingers into the "digital era" (ouch!). Throughout this chapter, I give you exercises and songs to build up your finger and hand flexibility and mobility a whole lot — so that you sound like a seasoned violinist.

Two Notes Are Better Than One: Easy Double Stops

Double stops may sound like some particularly amazing feat on the football field, but playing double stops is actually a special — and very beautiful — way of playing the violin. When playing double stops, you bow and finger on two strings at once. Most of the time in violin music, the violin plays a single melodic line on just one string at a time, such as in the great songs I cover in this book. But occasionally, composers ask the violinist to play two, three, or even four notes at once. In fact, when you play three or four notes at once, you're playing *chords,* rather like a pianist. At the end of this section, I show you the moves for chords, but you start by playing two notes at once.

Double stops often happen in music that's very emotional and intense, though not necessarily loud. Composers may use double stops for any number of reasons:

✔ **Emotional intensity:** The sudden change to two notes sounding out of the violin can be an unexpected and moving experience.

✔ **Fuller sound:** A composer may want music for a single violin to sound like two violins playing at once.

✔ **Shading:** If a piece of music is like a painting, then the notes are like that painting's colors. The extra tones add a new shade to the colors.

You find double stops in *cadenzas* of concertos (where the orchestra stops playing and the soloist treats the audience to a display of virtuosity based on the themes of the concerto) as well as in fiddling, where the double stops brighten the sound or, sometimes, mimic bagpipes.

Preparing your bow for double stops

The main focus in this chapter is on your new left-hand skills. But just getting your bow to balance evenly and consistently on both strings at once takes quite a bit of practice. The good news is that this kind of practice also bene-fits your tuning skills (refer to Chapter 2) — bowing smoothly on two strings helps you to hear the pitches of the open strings really clearly when tuning the violin before you play. Here's a simple, but effective, workout for you to get your bow ready for double stops:

1. **Balance the bow evenly on the A and D strings together, silently at first, so that you can really feel both strings under the horsehair of your bow.**

2. **Draw the bow gently to and fro on both strings together (or down-bow and up-bow, in violin-speak), starting with small, manageable amounts of bow at a calm speed.**

   At first, you may well hear the A string or the D string sounding alone, despite your best intentions. If so, the bow isn't yet evenly balanced on the two strings. Pressing harder may allow your bow to reach both strings, but the tone will be crunchy, so I don't recommend it. Instead, if you hear the A string alone, look over at the tip of your bow. Watch as you lower the tip's level while your bow hand's level floats up a bit, just a little, until your bow is working well on both strings. If you hear the D string alone, look over at the frog and watch as you allow gravity to lower the frog's level a tad (while the tip level of your bow rises slightly), until the bow is correctly angled to play on both strings and the A sounds along with the D.

3. **Keep expanding your bow stroke until you're using most (or all) of the bow for each stroke.**

   Using a fairly slow bow speed allows you better tone control when play-ing double stops.

4. **Keep the bow traveling smoothly, as if you're driving a very fancy limo on a newly surfaced highway.**

How double stops got started

Early composers were fascinated with the idea of a string instrument being able to produce two or more musical lines at once. In the sixteenth century, Italian composers tried writing music with double stops for the *viola da gamba,* the predecessor of our modern cello. Later, French composer and virtuoso viola da gamba player Marin Marais (1656–1728) wrote pieces that used very florid chords and double stops. The most famous examples of older music using

double stops are the *Sonatas and Partitas for Solo Violin* by J.S. Bach, dating from about 1720, and they're still very much in today's concert repertoire. Playing these double stops was certainly challenging, but because violin bridges used to have less curvature in the eighteenth century and the bows had less tension, playing on three or four strings at once was slightly less of a feat of athleticism than it is today.

Repeat the preceding steps, but play on the D and G strings together and then on the A and E strings together. Take care to adjust your right arm's level comfortably in relation to the bow stick as it balances evenly on each pair of strings.

Play the workouts, spending as much time as you need on each set of notes, and then try Figure 14-1, counting to 4 beats on each bow stroke. On the CD-ROM, you can watch me play on each pair of strings while counting steadily. If you want to play along with the video, use the 4 beats of empty (rest) measure to find your balance for the next pair of strings.

Figure 14-1:
Bowing on
two open
strings at the
same time.

After you feel fairly comfortable with bowing smoothly on pairs of open strings, you can add fingering to get a variety of double stop sounds.

In Figure 14-2, I show you double stop exercises on the same three pairs of strings, but you go on to add the first finger on the upper string, then the second, and then the third. Listen to how double stops with fingers sound on the CD-ROM. For the sake of ease and convenience, I've presented these double stops using the same finger pattern on each pair of strings: Finger 2 is close to finger 1.

Try this exercise, which starts in the same way as the previous exercise (refer to Figure 14-1) but continues with these steps:

1. **At the end of measure 2, drop your first finger onto the A string just as the bow direction is changing to down-bow again.**

2. **At the end of measure 4, drop your second finger onto the note C just as the down-bow is ready to play.**

   Because your first finger isn't in the way, you can leave it sitting lightly on the string in its spot. Use the same technique with finger 2, as well, when finger 3 plays.

3. **After the down-bows and up-bows on finger 2, drop finger 3 onto the A string just as the bow is changing direction to the last down-bow.**

Tip: Make sure your third finger is well in tune; you're playing the note D, so it needs to match the pitch of your open D string to sound just right!

Play the double stop exercises with the same fingers on the other pairs of strings — the exercises work in the same way as in the preceding steps.

Figure 14-2:
Double
stops with
fingers on
the strings.

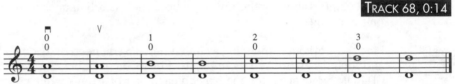

TRACK 68, 0:14

Going from one string to two and back again

Double stops don't happen that often in music, so you need to be comfortable going from playing on a single string to playing on two strings at once — and then back again. This section takes you through the stages you need to know to make a smooth transition between strings.

With separate bows

One situation you encounter often in double stops is switching from one string to two strings (and then back to one again) just as you change bow direction. This maneuver takes a little finesse with the bow levels.

Figure 14-3 shows you an exercise where you go from the D string to the D and A strings together, and then back again, using separate bows. You can also watch me play the exercise on the CD-ROM. Here are the steps:

1. **Finish an up-bow on the second D, and at the same time, allow the bow's level to start adjusting closer to the A string so that the level**

change is minimal when you begin your new down-bow on the D and A strings together.

2. **Start to float the bow's level over toward the D string when you're nearing the end of the up-bow (on the second D and A together).**

   Now you're as close as possible to the new bow level that you need to be on for the new down-bow on D alone.

3. **Play the double stops that follow in the exercise in the way as described in Steps 1 and 2, but add the new finger on the A string ahead of the bow, because adding the finger a bit sooner won't get in the way of your sound.**

On the MP3, I play on D and A, but on the video clip, you can watch me play the same exercise on each pair of strings, with a measure of rest between versions, so that it's easier to set up the bow for the next levels.

When adding a new finger and switching from one string to two strings in double stops, the "old" finger may remain lightly on the string — if it isn't in the way.

I tell you in Chapter 6 all about adjusting arm levels for string crossings, but to keep the process very simple in review, keep these points in mind:

✔ **If you're crossing to a _higher-sounding_ string (such as from D to A):** Lead the level-change with your elbow, releasing slightly downward, and then let your arm and hand follow the wave of movement.

✔ **If you're crossing to a _lower-sounding_ string (such as from E to G):** Lead the level-change with your hand floating slightly upward, and then let your arm and elbow follow the wave of movement.

The process of level adjustment may feel quite contrary at first, but I can assure you that it soon becomes second nature.

Figure 14-3:
Going from
a single
string to a
double stop
and then
back again
(separate
bows).

TRACK 68, 0:37

With slurred bows

Sometimes, the music calls for you to go from one string to two strings (and then back again) all in the same bow stroke. So as you're about to play the double stop, your bow doesn't change direction.

The trick to smooth transitions with slurred bows is to find the bow level closest to the *next* string you're going to play — very sneaky! For example, if you're bowing on your D string and the next note is on the G string, allow the bow to lean toward the level of the G string. Don't let the bow go anywhere near the A string! The distances don't look like much, but they cost you time in travel. Prepare your bow levels wisely for smooth transitions. Because violinists are a bunch of wise guys, this technique should suit you just fine.

Figure 14-4 shows you some slurred examples of getting into double stops. Playing slurred double stops calls for knowing your bow levels really well so that you don't make bumpy transitions across the strings. I tell you the steps for the first pair of strings, D and A, which I play on the MP3. You use the same process for the other two pairs (I show you the exercise for all three pairs on the CD-ROM.)

1. **Start a down-bow at the frog on the open D string, bowing steadily at a very relaxed pace.**

2. **Start lowering your right arm level slightly as you approach the midpoint of the bow, to bring the bow hair almost onto the A string.**

3. **Continue the down-bow direction, but just as you reach the middle of the bow, allow the bow to make a full transition toward the A string so that the bow is equally balanced to sound both the D and A strings together.**

4. **Begin the smooth up-bow on exactly the same level at the tip of the bow, sounding the D and A strings together and keeping the same bow speed you use for the down-bow that starts in Step 1.**

5. **Start floating up your right hand (your arm's level follows) as you approach the midpoint of the bow, to prepare for the transition to the D string.**

6. **Continue the up-bow direction and then allow the bow to make a full transition to playing the D string alone just as you reach the middle of the bow.**

7. **Land the next finger on the A string for each double stop on the A while bowing the open D string alone in the subsequent measures.**

On the video clip, I play the same exercise on each pair of strings. To play along, just follow the same sequence of steps, just adapted for the different strings. You have a measure of rest after each pair of strings, to allow you to set up your bow on the new level.

Figure 14-4:
Going from
one string to
two and
then back
again
(slurred
bows).

Ballet dancing with your fingers
on the lower string

I'll be "double crossing" you if I pretend that you've got all the moves needed
for the double stops you meet in music. Sometimes, composers write double
stops where the finger needs to play on the *lower* string, while the upper note
is an open string. These double stops may feel like taking your fingers to
ballet or tap dancing classes.

When your finger is playing on the lower string, it has to land a little more
steeply, on "tiptoe," as it were, to keep the upper string open. Try this out
with Figure 14-5. (You can watch this exercise in action on your CD-ROM.)

Figure 14-5 will go smoothly if you follow these steps:

1. **Bow evenly on the D and A strings together.**

   Playing on the open strings a few times before you start adding fingers
   makes sure your sound is clear.

2. **Drop your first fingertip onto the D string, making sure it doesn't
   touch the A string at all, after the second half note, which happens on
   an up-bow.**

   Tip: Violinists with bigger or thicker fingers may need to aim their fingertips a little toward the G string because their fingers won't be in the
   way of the sound over there.

3. **Follow the process described in Step 2, but using different fingers,
   when the time comes to add fingers 2, 3, and 4.**

   There's usually no need to lift any finger off in this exercise, because old
   fingers aren't in the way of the new notes.

Tip: Your fourth finger may not be ready to cooperate in this step, so it's also perfectly fine to play Figure 14-5 just as far as finger 3 and then back again. You can return later to add finger 4 on the D string to sound with the open A.

Figure 14-5:
At ballet class with your fingers.

You can, of course, try the "ballet dancing" shown in Figure 14-5 on any pair of strings.

Playing double stops where both notes are stopped

Another variation on the double stop (variety is the spice of life, after all) is landing two fingers at a time, one on each string involved in the double stop. When both notes of the double stop require a finger to sound the pitch, you could easily be in for double trouble — if I didn't walk you through the moves. In this section, I show you a couple of double stops where both notes require a finger, for you to get a little taste of how they work. This type of double stop makes your playing sound fancy, too.

Figure 14-6 shows you a famous piano tune, which I adapt for your violin so that you can exercise your double stop skills. You can listen to the tune on the CD-ROM before you try playing it.

1. **Set fingers 1, 2, and 3 on your D string, on "tiptoe" as in Figure 14-5, so that they don't get in the way of the open A string's vibrations.**

2. **Play the first two measures around the middle of the bow, sounding finger 3 (which is playing note G on the D string) together with your open A string.**

   Tip: As with the previous section on "ballet dancing," if you have broad fingers, or if the tiptoe thing isn't working well, try placing your fingers a tad further over toward the G string. You can also try putting finger 3 on alone for the first bar and then sneaking the next finger onto the D string just before lifting off the finger that's finishing playing.

3. **Lift finger 3 off smartly at the start of measure 3, and then play the next two measures with finger 2 on F♯ on your D string.**

4. **Hop finger 2 over to the A string, directly across from where it was playing on the D string, as if it's on a guitar fret, at the start of measure 5.**

5. **Bow out the double stop with finger 1 on the D string (playing the note E) and finger 2 on the A string (playing a C♯).**

6. **Match finger 3 well to the pitch of the open D string, because your last measure of this phrase involves an octave double stop.**

   Tip: At first, allow plenty of time to change fingers. Just stop the bow, and then make your left hand moves as needed. Bow again when you're ready. Later, you can reduce the transition time in this step.

Figure 14-6: Double stops all the way!

TRACK 68, 2:18

Playing double stops galore

After you practice the double stop techniques I talk about in this chapter, you get to play "Hunting Horn Song" to incorporate all those new sounds. I tell you the moves so you're not "hunting" for the notes! Needless to say, it's also on your CD-ROM.

1. **Prepare fingers 1 and 3 on their spots before you begin to bow, and then land your bow evenly on the A and E strings to begin the first long down-bow from the frog.**

2. **Lift off both fingers simultaneously for the next double stop, and while you're sounding the open strings with a smooth up-bow, hover fingers 3 and 2 over their next placements.**

3. **Land both fingers just as you begin the next down-bow on the D and A strings together.**

4. **Pop up finger 3 for the quarter-note double stop on the next up-bow, but keep finger 2 sitting on the D string to sound together with the open A string, and keep the same left-hand finger placement for the next down-bow.**

5. **Place finger 1 neatly on the D string for the next double stop, and slide finger 2 directly across to the A string.**

6. **Notice that the next couple of bars are played just like the beginning of the piece for the left hand, though a bit fancier for the bow.**

7. **Slur the first double stop to the single-note G on the E string in measure 7, and then switch to single-string playing for the rest of the measure, as the horn disappears into the distance.**

8. **Prepare the last octave on the two Ds by hovering finger 3 over the A string, ready to land as soon as you begin the final down-bow on the D and A strings together.**

Tip: You can play the upper line alone first, then the lower line alone, before you put them together in double stops.

 TRACK 69

Hunting Horn Song

Pulling Out All the Stops: Three- and Four-Note Chords

Often at the very end of a piece, the composer asks for an even richer sound by writing three and four notes to be played at once (or as close as possible to at once), which means you're actually playing chords on your violin. You use your bow in special ways to make these chords sound as clear as a bell.

Bowing on three or four strings requires some understanding of the curvature of the bridge and the shock-absorbing qualities of the hand and the bow. In this section, I show you the two most usual ways to play chords, so that you can deal with them in the music you play.

Chords are generally played from the bottom note to the top note. You make a richer sound, and you highlight the highest note (which is most usually the note belonging to the actual tune of the song). So always place a finger on the lowest string first, and then add the next-higher notes in sequence. The exception is if one of your fingers is already playing on the previous note, in which case, you usually add all the *remaining* fingers from the lowest string first.

Three-note chords

Getting round the curvature of the violin bridge involves some artful moves to make your three-note chords sound rich. Violinists begin three-note chords by playing the lower two strings together and then switching to the upper two strings during the same bow stroke, without batting an eyelid — or stopping the bow stroke!

I show you how to bow four different three-note chords in Figure 14-7, and you can watch me play them on the CD-ROM. Follow these moves for the first chord:

1. **Set your left hand up for the first three-note chord by simply placing finger 1 on the A string and leaving it there before you start bowing.**

   The three notes of your chord are the open G, the open D, and note B on the A string, played by finger 1.

2. **Begin your down-bow on G and D strings together.**

3. **Switch your bow over to play on the D and A strings together before you're at the halfway point of the bow, while continuing the down-bow direction, to play the top two notes together.**

After you get going, I give you an empty measure to get organized for each three-note chord. While still referring to Figure 14-7, do the following moves for the second, third, and fourth chords:

- ✔ **Second chord:** Land finger 1 on the E string, and then follow the preceding Steps 2 to 3, adjusting the steps to use the new notes and strings.

- ✔ **Third chord:** Land finger 1 on the D string, with finger 2 close by on the A string, and then follow the same bowing moves as in the preceding Steps 2 to 3.

- ✔ **Fourth chord:** Notice that the final chord is very similar to the third chord, but this time, finger 1 lands on the A string and finger 2 is close by on the E string.

TRACK 70, 0:00

Figure 14-7:
Four three-note chords.

Keep a strong bow contact as you finish a chord to make it sound rich. You may need to work a little extra weight into your bowing when you're approaching the tip of the bow, which is naturally lighter, and you want to maintain the sound.

Four-note chords

For the juiciest possible sound, four-note chords are really peachy! Bowing these takes a bit of finesse, because you can't really bow on all four strings at once without making a tremendous amount of crunchy bow noise. To get a clear sound, think of bowing four-note chords as if your bow were a seesaw (or teeter-totter), and roll across each pair of strings while you keep the bow moving steadily. In Figure 14-8, I show you two four-note chords to try, and I demonstrate them for you on the CD-ROM.

First, prepare your fingers in their correct placement. For the first four-note chord, land finger 1 on the A string and then place finger 2 close by on the E string. For the second four-note chord, land finger 1 on the G and D strings together (aim finger 1 at the black space of the fingerboard between the two strings to land on both), and then place finger 2 a whole step away on the A string and finger 3 close by on the E string.

Putting fingers on one at a time makes good sense when you first practice a chord, but later, you can shape up all your fingers together to land them in one movement.

After your fingers are in place, follow these instructions and look at Figure 14-8 to play an impressive four-note chord:

1. **Balance your bow at the frog on your G and D strings together, and then draw about ⅓ of the down-bow before stopping lightly on the strings.**

2. **Roll the bow silently over to the D and A strings together, draw the next ⅓ of the bow, and then stop lightly on the strings.**

3. **Roll the bow silently over to the A and E strings together, and then bow out the final ⅓ of your bow.**

After you're able to feel the different levels, you can reduce the amount of stopping, until the transitions are smooth. When your transitions are smooth, try the last two moves:

1. **Save some bow at the start of the chord so that you have plenty of sound for the top notes, which is usually where you need extra bow.**

2. **Try bowing "2 + 2" strings; in other words, go from the G-D string level to the A-E string level by rolling quickly across the middle of the chord.**

    This technique is useful when the chord happens quickly, and you have no time to linger on the middle strings.

Figure 14-8:
Two four-
note chords
to get ahead
with!

A grand finale with chords

Here's a fine ending that you may meet in a majestic piece of music in G major. *Maestoso*, the Italian word for "majestic," describes a grand mood. Maestoso brings to mind a king processing elegantly, or the final scene of a long and complicated opera, when everyone gathers onstage to sing a triumphant song. To play "Grand Finale," follow these moves to finish with a flourish:

1. **Begin on a firm down-bow, using a broad, accented stroke for lots of sound.**

2. **Continue in a similar character through the first phrase, just observing the two up-bows in measure 3.**

3. **Make a circular retake (refer to Chapter 8 for details on circular retakes, also known as *bow circles*) to land a *f* down-bow for the first note after the quarter note rest, and continue majestically through the second phrase.**

4. **After playing an up-bow on the open A that precedes the first chord, prepare your bow on the A and D strings together, to play the first three-note chord, which is the same one that you play in Figure 14-7.**

5. **When you finish bowing the three-note chord, begin a circular retake, bringing your bow around so that it's ready to land on the G and D strings at the same time, and while you're making the circle, switch your first finger to play B on the A string and place finger 2 close by to play G on the E string.**

6. **Bow out the final chord, which is the same chord as the first one you play in Figure 14-8.**

Getting into the First Four Positions

Playing a lot of tunes (and double stops) helps you to develop plenty of left-hand balance and agility. If you feel good about your skills, you're ready to move on to trying your left hand in different positions along the neck of the violin. *Position* is the name for the place where your hand goes on the neck of the violin in order to play the notes. In this section, I introduce you to the four main positions you need to know.

Finding first position

I bet you don't know that if you practice the exercises in this book in order, you play with your left hand in *first position* up until this point. That's because you haven't yet had a formal introduction to all the other positions. *First position* is the name for the basic left hand position violinists start with and use the most. In this position, finger 1 plays the next note up from your open string. So on the A string, finger 1 plays B (or B♭) in first position. You use first position in many other chapters in this book — without necessarily knowing its official name. The technique of moving your left hand from one position to another is called *shifting,* or *changing position,* but not, of course, because violinists are shifty characters.

Violinists *change position,* which means sliding the left hand up the neck of the violin to reach higher notes, for a variety of reasons. The most important ones are:

✔ To play high notes that can't be reached from the regular *first position*.

✔ To keep all the notes of a particular melody on the same string, maintaining the *timbre,* a term musicians use to describe the color and character of a particular sound. (That's one way you can tell whether you're hearing a flute or a violin.)

✔ Because the music is easier to play in a different position, and therefore sounds better — changing positions could facilitate string crossings or some other aspect of fingering or bowing music.

In this book, I use the actual words *first, second, third,* and *fourth* to refer to left hand position number. However, you may see Roman numerals referring to a position number in other music. So *I, II, III,* and *IV* refer to left hand positions one to four as well. Understandably, violinists stop counting in Roman numerals after about the tenth position!

Smoothing out the second position

As I mention in the preceding section, unbeknownst to you, you play in first position in all the previous chapters of *Violin For Dummies.* So in this section, you get to move up the violin's neck to . . . *second position!* Actually, the move up the neck is very small, just next door to first position, but the move opens the door to playing a new range of notes on each string.

The three moves I explain here get you to second position. Try them on the D string, silently at first, so that you can feel and see your moves before you pick up your bow to sound it out:

1. **Place your first finger on note E on the D string.**

2. **Slide finger 1 just a half step higher, up to note F (which your second finger usually plays).**

3. **Take your thumb along the same distance, so that it remains more or less opposite to finger 1.**

   Welcome to second position!

I show you how the finger placements relate to your tapes or dots on the fingerboard (refer to Chapter 5) in Figure 14-9, and I show you the notes you play in Figure 14-10. Notice that with the *natural* notes (no sharps and flats) that you play in this example, you need to place finger 1 a whole step above its usual placement in first position on the G string.

When you look at Figure 14-10 to see the notes you play in second position, notice that you have a bit of a safety net in place — you can check some of the notes (which appear as whole notes in the exercise) by matching their pitches with their corresponding open strings.

Figure 14-9:
Finger
placement
in second
position.

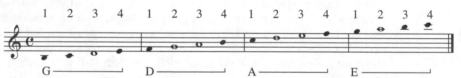

Figure 14-10:
Notes you
play in
second
position.

Putting second position to work

Finding all the second-position notes on the violin allows you a glimpse of the whole picture. But actually, playing music in second position usually involves only some of those notes, which belong to a particular musical key. (I tell you more about keys in Chapter 11.) To get started, I show you how to play the F major scale in second position, and then you play a song in second position, using those same notes.

To play the F major scale in second position, you use the same spacing as when you play the E major scale (refer to Chapter 10) — the only difference is your left hand position.

If you have tapes or dots on your fingerboard to mark the spots (refer to Chapter 5), here's a place where they can be of special value — they show your hand this new spacing. Here are the moves for the F major scale:

1. **Play a down-bow with your first finger in second position on the D string (on the note F) to sound out the tonic note.**

2. **Make a whole step to note G for finger 2, and observe that finger 2 lands exactly on your next tape (which originally marked the spot for finger 3 but has been temporarily taken over).**

3. **Make another whole step to land finger 3 on the next tape or dot.**

4. **Place finger 4 very close by to finger 3 (because it's only a half step away), probably touching the side of finger 3.**

5. **Walk finger 1 calmly across to the A string to play the note C (still in second position — don't move your left hand) while finger 4 is playing, and release the other fingers from the D string as soon as you begin the down-bow on finger 1.**

Continue up the A string in a similar manner, following through with fingers 2, 3, and 4.

Tip: The finger placements on the A string are the same as on the D string — they're just on a different string.

Figure 14-11 shows you the scale of F major in second position. (It sounds exactly the same as the F major scale in Chapter 11, but you use different fingerings to play the notes.)

You may feel more comfortable when you play the F major scale in second position, rather than in first position. So if you have a chance in a piece of music to play a musical phrase in second position, go for it!

Figure 14-11:
F major
scale in
second
position.

TRACK 72, 0:00

The new positions in this chapter have a theme song, "Joy to the World," so that you can move from one position to the next with great ease. At the end of the chapter, I show you some different songs to try with the positions.

To play "Joy to the World" (shown in Figure 14-12) in second position, first prepare your hand by climbing up (but not down) the F major scale in second position (refer to Figure 14-11). When you're ready, follow these moves to get off to a good start (you can watch the moves on your CD-ROM and play along too):

1. **Set your bow on the A string, quite near the frog, so that you get a hearty down-bow sound as you draw a vigorous stroke on the top F.**

2. **Try out a version of your slurred staccato (refer to Chapter 13) on up-bows when you play fingers 3 and 2, using plenty of bow for the dotted eighth note, and just a little bow for the sixteenth note.**

3. **Play finger 1 on the note C, using a full down-bow, then land finger 4 safely over on the D string after playing finger 1, and continue the downward scale.**

Whenever you cross from one string to the next, land your new finger on the new string and then begin sounding the new note just before you release the old finger. This technique makes for a smooth transition.

4. **Hop finger 1 lightly across to note C to return to playing notes on the A string on the last eighth note of measure 2, and then continue building back up to the top F, step-by-step, with the last notes of the song.**

Figure 14-12:
"Joy to the World" in second position.

Playing in third position

Playing in *third position* is violinists' second favorite thing to do (after first position)! I'd say it's a very "handy" position to find; your hand feels very comfortable on the neck of the violin. An added advantage to third position is that finger 1 plays exactly an octave above the next-lower string, and the outer edge of your palm (just under finger 4) is very near to, or just touching, the body of the violin.

You've probably figured out that for third position, you need to put your first finger on the spot where the third finger normally plays. If you use the same idea that you use to prepare for second position (refer to "Putting second position to work," earlier in this chapter), you start out with the following moves:

1. **Start in first position, with your first finger playing the note E on the D string.**

2. **Play F♯ with your second finger, and then G with your third finger.**

3. **Take a good look at the spot where your third finger is playing, and listen to the sound of the G so that you can match the location and sound when you shift into third position.**

4. **Release your third finger from the string, and then slide your whole hand up into third position.**

   Finger 1 plays the note G on the D string, exactly where finger 3 was playing a moment ago.

Take your thumb along with the rest of your hand when traveling to a new left hand position, to keep your hand in good playing shape.

Figure 14-13 shows you where all the fingers land on the strings in third position, and Figure 14-14 shows you the notes you can play in third position.

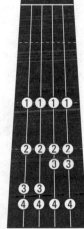

Figure 14-13: Finger placement in third position.

When preparing to play in third position, check the pitch of your first finger against the open G string of your violin, and adjust slightly, if necessary.

After finding your finger placements in third position, you're ready to set up for a scale and a song in third position. You can build a third-position G major scale by starting on finger 1 on the D string. Your fingers work in exactly the same way as they do in the F major scale you play in second position (refer to Figure 14-11), but your hand position is a step higher.

Figure 14-14: Notes you play in third position.

To find your starting note, follow the same four steps I show you at the beginning of this section about third position. When you drop finger 1 on the note G, you're all set up. Look at the G major scale in third position in Figure 14-15. You can see and hear me play on your CD-ROM (on the video, I play the scale descending, for your reference).

Figure 14-15: G major scale in third position.

I show you how to play all the scales in this chapter with separate bowings. But you can add two-note slurs (and even four-note slurs) to the scales when you're comfortable with the finger placements and ready to flow along.

After playing the notes of the G major scale in third position, you're ready to use those notes in this section's theme song, "Joy to the World." I show you how to play the song in third position in Figure 14-16, and you can hear it on the CD-ROM. Follow the same steps as you did to play second position, noting (we violinists like to take note!) that you're a whole step higher throughout.

Figure 14-16: "Joy to the World" in third position.

Venturing forth in fourth position

If your hand asks, "Are we there yet?" you can reassure it that you indeed *are* almost there. You take just one more step to arrive at the *fourth position*. Although third position gets all the attention, finding fourth position is just as easy, because as you look down the "telescope" of your strings, your first finger plays the same note as the adjacent open string to the right. For example, if you play in fourth position on the A string, your first finger matches the E of your open E string.

Figure 14-17 shows you where to place your fingers on the violin strings in fourth position.

Your thumb, which moves along more or less opposite finger 1, is now near the place where the violin's neck joins the body. The neck thickens slightly, but it has a nice curved shape underneath for your thumb to slip around. To find a comfortable (and effective) thumb placement, line up your fingers in fourth position on the D string, and then allow your thumb to slip a little lower around the neck, as if the thumb's tip is doing a demonstration of a beautiful sunset. Of course, your own hand's shape and size determine how much adjustment you need. But in mid-sized hands, the tip of the thumb arrives at (or a little below) the level where the ebony fingerboard joins the light wood of the violin's neck.

In Figure 14-18, I show you all the notes you can play when you go to fourth position on your violin.

After orientation, you're ready to set up an A major scale and prepare for your venture into songs using the fourth position. Look at the process the same way as you do for preparing the second and third positions. Start by playing fingers 1, 2, 3, and 4 on the D string in regular first position. Listen to the note A that you play with finger 4, and look at where it's playing on the D string so that you can target that spot with finger 1 when you shift up. Release your fingers, smoothly shift up to fourth position, and then place finger 1 on note A.

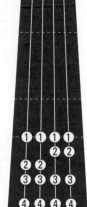

Figure 14-17: Finger placement in fourth position.

Figure 14-18: Notes you play in fourth position.

More positions to meet

In this chapter, you meet the first four positions and find out how to use them in music you actually play. Of course, you can use more positions than just the first four. By applying the same system to moving farther up the violin's neck, and even gradually elevating the palm of your hand over the body of the instrument for higher positions (just leave the very tip of your thumb contacting the right side of the violin's neck to easily descend from those very high positions), you can reach fifth position and beyond. Violinists use the first four or five positions pretty regularly, and they go up to tenth position in concertos and other virtuoso repertoire. Even higher notes exist on the violin, but most players give up counting position numbers after tenth position — so they just go into the stratosphere to target occasional notes or passages that are really high.

When preparing to play in fourth position, check your first finger's pitch, A, against the open A string to ensure accuracy, and then adjust your placement up or down a tad, if necessary.

Now you're ready to set forth on your A major scale in fourth position. When you start with your first finger on note A and follow the steps I show you for second and third positions, your resulting scale is A major. Check out the A major scale in Figure 14-19, and see me play it on the CD-ROM (I also play the scale descending on the video).

Figure 14-19:
A major
scale in
fourth
position.

And finally, the last appearance of "Joy to the World" — in fourth position, of course! After you've climbed up the A major scale in fourth position, you know what to do for this song, shown in Figure 14-20: Just follow the moves you know from second and third position, but play them all one step higher, and your world can be joyous in fourth position too. Listen to the song on the CD-ROM, and play along, if you want.

A cool thing about fourth position is that finger 4 is exactly one octave above your open A string in A major. So you have an additional tuning checkpoint between the open string and finger 4, which lets you know you've put your hand in the right place.

Figure 14-20:
"Joy to the
World" in
fourth
position.

Knowing what position you're in

Violinists usually know what position they're playing by looking at where the *first finger* is placed, and comparing it to where the fingers are usually placed in first position. Remember these quick and convenient ways to figure out which position you're playing in, or how to get to the position you need:

✔ **Second position:** Put your first finger where finger 2 usually plays in first position.

✔ **Third position:** Put your first finger where finger 3 usually plays in first position.

✔ **Fourth position:** Put your first finger where finger 4 usually plays in first position.

Changing Position

Not since the *Kama Sutra* have positions been discussed with such gusto! After you've met the positions in the preceding section, you can get some mobility happening *between* the positions as you change (or shift) positions. By practicing shifting, your left hand — and your bow — know what to do and how to get around the violin from one spot to another. Shifting positions may remind you of finding your way around a city: The first few times, you need to go slowly and carefully, checking your map, and then after a while, it becomes second nature to find the places you visit.

In this section, I ease you into shifting positions. You start without using any violin at all so that you gradually get comfortable with shifting. I also outline the different types of shifts, telling you about each kind and when you're likely to use it.

The terminology that describes position changes can be confusing. Violinists use three terms interchangeably, all of which refer to changing from one position to another:

✔ Position changes (and changing position)

✔ Shifts (and shifting)

✔ Slides (and sliding) — generally a term you might hear about in more old-fashioned books

Easing into shifting positions

Preparing your moves well before you actually have to shift ensures a successful transition. Paying close attention to three important factors makes this technique work smoothly:

✔ Know how you expect the new pitch to sound so that you can target it correctly.

✔ Make the moves fluent, and aim them well.

✔ Establish the proper spacing of your fingers for notes in the new position, after you've arrived there.

Sliding up and down the violin's neck when changing positions is easy to do with a bit of practice, but you do need to try out a couple of actions before you begin. Get out the "air violin" (refer to Chapter 3), dust it off, and then try a few breezy runs at changing position (see Figure 14-21):

1. **Get your "air violin" into playing position.**

2. **Shape up your left hand and arm for a beautiful hand frame, just as if you're a soloist standing in front of a famous orchestra.**

3. **Let your hand, forearm, and wrist move a few inches toward your nose as one unit, all at the same time, moving from your elbow hinge, and then move them back to your original position.**

   Your elbow may naturally move slightly toward the side seam of your shirt as you shift up and then away again. Congratulations, you've just completed your first shift!

Figure 14-21: Shifting with your "air violin."

a

b

Stand in front of a mirror while you play your air violin. See how the movements work before the violin gets in the way!

Nearly all your movements on the violin are arc-shaped because your joints are fixed points from which each movement swings. All your shifts have a slight but discernible circular shape to their movements.

Now try the moves with your actual violin, but don't use the bow just yet. When you're holding the violin, the trick is to find the right amount of energy for holding it securely while allowing your arm to move freely. Hold the violin in place with your right hand around the upper ribs as you try these steps. Holding the violin in this way gives you a secure feeling while you're getting used to the movements (I demonstrate this shift on the CD-ROM):

1. **In playing position, set up your left hand as usual, in a nicely rounded shape with your fingers hovering over the strings.**

2. **Keep the same general hand shape as described in Step 1, and glide your whole hand, including the thumb, all the way from the scroll end of the violin's neck to the body end of the neck (your body or the violin's body, they're both in the same general direction!).**

   Remember: While you're doing this sliding, your elbow isn't swinging to the right or left, it's moving very naturally, slightly toward your body, as your left hand shifts up.

3. **Check that your violin hold is loose enough to allow your left arm some freedom of movement, but just snug enough to keep the violin from sliding away from you when you shift down again toward the scroll.**

4. **Start to allow your hand to venture even higher up toward the bridge after the first slides are moving smoothly.**

   Oops, the side of your hand bumps into the ribs of the violin, and it won't go any farther! Well, this is where your thumb and elbow come to the rescue.

5. **Slide your thumb around under the curve of the violin's neck, just before the neck joins the body of the violin (move like one of those racing cars going round the corner in a lap on a track).**

   Imagine your left hand is being controlled by a puppeteer and the string to move your hand to a higher position is attached to the outer side of a bracelet around your left wrist. The puppeteer — who is most conveniently standing just behind your right ear — gently pulls the string toward himself, so your wrist arcs outward just enough to avoid bumping into the violin while you slide up into the higher positions.

Keeping your thumb very relaxed, so it doesn't grip the neck of the violin, is essential to moving smoothly during position changes.

Getting to know the four kinds of shifts

Now that you know some basic moves, I show you how to find the positions you need to play music of all kinds. Pick up your bow, and away you go!

Open-string shifts

An *open-string shift* is a sneaky little number where your left hand shifts (the most shifty shift!) while your bow — which you have now picked up again — is bowing an open string. No sweat! You can use an open-string shift anytime you need to shift . . . provided the shift happens right after playing an open string.

To do an open-string shift, just release all fingers from the string, keep your left hand frame in a ready-to-play shape, slide along the neck of the violin until you're at the right spot for the next note while you are bowing the open string, and then land the new finger on its note.

Now that you have the moves for open-string shifts, try them out on this D major arpeggio, which I show you in Figure 14-22 and demonstrate on the CD-ROM (refer to Chapter 10 for more about arpeggios). Playing these shifts gets you ready to play with a flourish! Pick up your violin and bow, and then follow these steps to make it all happen:

1. **Begin the arpeggio as usual, playing open D on a down-bow followed by finger 2 on an up-bow.**

2. **Begin playing the next down-bow on the open A string, then slide your hand up the neck of the violin as soon as possible during the course of that down bow, until finger 1 is over note D in third position.**

3. **Drop finger 1 onto the fingerboard at the same moment that you change to the up-bow, and then continue in third position to the top D of the arpeggio.**

4. **Use exactly the same process in reverse to come back: When you begin bowing on the open A string, slide your hand back to first position so that finger 2 can play F♮, and then finish back "home" on the open D string.**

Figure 14-22:
D major arpeggio, two octaves.

TRACK 75

0   2   0   1   3   1   4   1   3   1   0   2   0

...III pos.   ...I pos.

Same-finger shifts

Violinists use *same-finger shifts* a lot, so learning the moves sets you up to do well in your musical endeavors. You simply travel to the new position with the same finger that you're already playing (lightly) on the string, and that's it.

Shifting the same finger to a new position just requires a bit of careful sequencing, and away you go! Here's what you do:

1. **Release the fingertip weight, from fully pressing the string down to the fingerboard to just lightly touching the surface of the string before you begin to move.**

2. **Brush the fingertip lightly along the surface of the string as you slide your hand to the new position.**

3. **When you're on target, press the string down to the fingerboard to sound the new note.**

Always move your thumb with your hand when sliding between "neck" positions (first to fourth position). Moving your thumb at the same time ensures that your hand frame doesn't really change shape as you shift, which helps your fingers to go on working normally.

Figure 14-23 shows you a little meowing song to get those same-finger shifts moving (I also play this song on the CD-ROM for you to watch). Here are the moves to purr-fect your technique:

1. **Prepare finger 1 on the D string, and start with your bow on the D string too, setting it as close to the frog as possible, to allow lots of room for those meowing sounds.**

2. **Count "1, 2, 3," and then begin your down-bow on beat 4, gliding gently toward the third position in time to arrive there on the first beat of the new bar.**

3. **Shift down again during the up-bow, which is the exact reverse of the action in Step 2.**

4. **Land finger 2 on note F on the D string, glide lightly to third position during the down-bow stroke, and then go back to first position on the next up-bow.**

5. **Continue with finger 3, using the method described in Step 4 for finger 2.**

6. **Pounce on the A string with great gusto for the ending "woof."**

Intermediate-note shifts

Another type of shift involves using an *intermediate note,* which is an extra note that a player creates very discreetly to help make shifting smooth in two particular instances:

✔ When you're shifting *up* from a lower-numbered finger to a higher-numbered finger.

✔ When you're shifting *down* from a higher-numbered finger to a lower-numbered finger.

Figure 14-23:
Same-finger
shift
exercise:
The cat's
meow.

TRACK 76, 0:00

A careful sequence of actions conceals the sound of the slide very discreetly so that the actual notes of the music are clear to the listener. Shifting well is a bit like knowing that a house has all sorts of structural beams and electric wires in order to be functional, but they're concealed behind the designer wallpaper. Here's how you execute an intermediate note shift:

1. **Play the old note, the one just before the shift happens.**

2. **Begin at the end of the old bow stroke and at the end of the old beat, and use the old finger (are you starting to feel very old?) to prepare for the new note by slightly releasing the weight of the old finger from the string, sliding to the new position on your old finger, and thus creating the "intermediate note" of the name of this shift.**

3. **Land your new finger on the new note at the click of the new beat when you've concealed the shift inside the end of the old everything, and then play your new bow stroke.**

You can practice doing an intermediate-note shift in Figure 14-24. In the first measure, I show you the starting note, followed by the intermediate note in parentheses, so that you know what you're aiming for. In the second measure, I show you the new note in the new position. You actually play the measures marked *a*, *b*, and *c*, which show you how to achieve a smooth shift by concealing the intermediate note more and more, as you become familiar with the shift. You have a rest measure between each version, so you can set up the starting note again in first position. I perform the moves on the CD-ROM, too:

1. **Begin your down-bow near the frog at measure *a*.**

   This measure works like a same-finger shift on finger 1, going from first to third position.

2. **Release your finger's pressure on the surface of the string, and then slide lightly to the note G on the second half note in the down-bow.**

   The up-bow on finger 2, playing the note A in third position, is your destination note.

3. **Repeat Steps 1 and 2 for measure _b_, but hold your original note for 3 beats and shift on the fourth beat.**

4. **Treat the shift in measure _c_ like a dandelion puff, and float up to your new position at the very end of the down-bow, just touching the intermediate note for a fleeting shadow of note G.**

   This step brings you closer to the real thing.

5. **Notice that the intermediate note in measure _d_ is so light and so hidden just before the bow changes that only you know you're measuring out the distance with it!**

TRACK 76, 0:24

Figure 14-24: Intermediate-note shifts, up and down.

"My Dame Hath a Lame Tame Crane" in Figure 14-25 uses a few intermediate-note shifts in a real musical situation. On the CD-ROM, I just play this song once, so you can play it together with me. This old English song is also a _round,_ which means you can play it with one or two other friends. Each person begins to play when the person who began the song gets to the next asterisk (*), which I mark over the music.

Here are the playing instructions:

1. **Begin with the pickup on an up-bow, and then start shifting as soon as you dare, fitting the shift to third position into the up-bow and landing finger 2 on the note A right on the downbeat of the first full bar.**

2. **Stay in third position until the third beat of measure 6, when you make the downward shift to first position using finger 2, which travels to note F on the D string during that down-bow so that you can play finger 1 on the pickup E — just like in the first phrase.**

3. **Play the final shift similar to the way you played the one at the beginning of the piece, in Step 1.**

When working on intermediate-note shifts, allow plenty of extra time in practice to sound out the intermediate note clearly, just like you do in the preceding example. Taking your time has two important benefits: Your hand learns the distance accurately and calmly, and your ear learns to hear the *interval* — the musical distance between the two notes — with confidence.

Figure 14-25:
"My Dame Hath a Lame Tame Crane."

Finger-substitution shifts

Finger-substitution shifts are very subtle shifts, where you change fingers midway into the shift, a bit like runners passing the baton in a relay race. Doing the actions in the correct order helps you achieve a smooth result. When shifting up, a lower-numbered finger is passing by a higher-numbered finger, rather like passing a slower car on the highway. Follow these steps for finger-substitution shifts:

1. **Release the weight of the old finger to the surface of the string as you begin the shift on the old finger.**

2. **Touch the new finger to the string when the momentum is underway, skimming the string's surface as you move, until the new finger arrives at its new note, having "taken over" from the old finger en route.**

3. **Press the new finger down on the string to make the new note.**

In Figure 14-26, you practice a few examples of finger substitution shifts. I tell you the moves, step-by-step, and I demonstrate the ascending shift on the CD-ROM:

1. **Begin a down-bow on finger 2, which is playing note F on the D string.**

2. **Lighten finger 2, and begin to move your hand up toward third position.**

3. **Let finger 1 brush on the string close behind finger 2 as you near the halfway point in the shift.**

4. **Let finger 1 take over from finger 2, which then floats off the string.**

Figure 14-26:
Finger-
substitution
shifts in
action.

At first, when practicing finger-substitution shifts, you need to take up quite a lot of the bow and make some sliding noises just to get all the movements in order. But when you know the sequence, you can move the shifting process later and later into the bow stroke.

In Figure 14-27, you try out finger-substitution shifts in Mozart's Trio from the "Haffner" Symphony, composed in 1782. As soon as you play the first C♯ using a down-bow, shift up to note D on finger 1 just the same way that I show you in Figure 14-26 — the only difference is that you're playing on the A string now. The shift down in measure 2 is also very similar to the shift in measure 2 of the preceding exercise. You know the moves — enjoy!

Figure 14-27:
Trio from
Mozart's
"Haffner"
Symphony.

Changing position to go to a different string

Going to a new string when you shift is a lot like shifting on the same string. You follow the shifting process in every way, except at the end, you place the new finger on the new string.

Try out Figure 14-28 to get a taste of going to a new string while shifting. I show the secret shifting notes in parentheses on your music, and I demonstrate the technique on the CD-ROM.

Keep the bow moving when shifting and going to a new string, but slightly release finger pressure during the shift to avoid making extra sliding sounds that aren't part of the music.

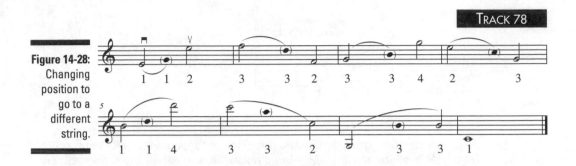

Figure 14-28:
Changing
position to
go to a
different
string.

TRACK 78

Playing a shifty song

Bonnie Prince Charlie was extremely relieved to escape to the Isle of Skye instead of being captured by his enemies, and "Speed, Bonnie Boat" celebrates that escape. The song also offers you the chance to "escape" from all kinds of positions on the violin. Here's how:

1. **Play the notes as you would normally, in first position, for measures 1 to 4.**

2. **Slide your hand up to third position during the rest at the end of measure 4 to make an open-string shift, and at the same time, make a bow circle in the air so that you can begin the next bar with a down-bow.**

3. **Remain in third position until the end of measure 8, and then shift calmly back to first position as you make the down-bow circle during the rest.**

   This is an intermediate-note shift, with finger 2 siding to a silent B in first position on the G string.

4. **Shift up to third position at the end of measure 12 using an intermediate-note shift, with finger 1 sliding to G on the D string to prepare for the new position in measure 13.**

5. **Shift one position down at the start of measure 14, and again at measure 15, using same-finger shifts.**

   Get ready for the last section, because it offers you a bunch of challenging shifts!

6. **Start by making an open-string shift to arrive and remain in third position, extending your fourth finger (just stretch the fingertip out toward the harmonic, don't move your left hand from third position at all) to just touch the harmonic at the end of measure 18, and keeping that third position placement until the middle of measure 19.**

7. **Shift back to first position mid-bar in measure 19 (an intermediate-note shift), but don't settle there, because you need to shift right back up to third position for the last note.**

8. **Make a same-finger shift up to the final note.**

When you're practicing a song, figuring out what kind of position shift you're making each time lets you perform the shifts with confidence.

TRACK 79

Speed, Bonnie Boat

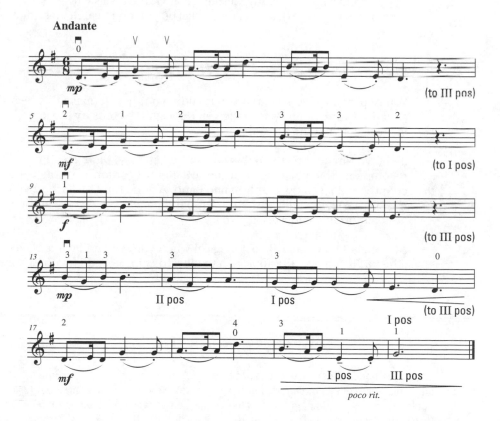

All Aquiver: Vibrato

The very word *vibrato* conjures up romantic images of a most desirable and gorgeous sound. In practical terms, violinists playing with vibrato effects are making oscillations of their fingertips on the strings to produce a slight pitch wave on any note — a sound that's very like the human singing voice. Your violin can sound like the pure choirboy trebles of the famous English cathedral choirs (who sing with almost no vibrato), or like a Wagnerian soprano (who sings *molto vibrato*) singing above a full orchestra at a chandeliered opera house — all by producing a variety of speeds and amplitudes of oscillations. Add in some slight variations in finger pressure and a generous handful of bow speeds and weights, and you can see a whole cookbook full of vibrato recipes! In this section, I show you some basic steps to get your vibrato happening.

Practicing vibrato is like trying to ride a bicycle for the first time: If you take the time to find your balance and coordination, it all begins to work together. From then on, you don't lose the skill. So try out some of these vibrato exercises, and come back to them as often as you can — don't force your hand to play the finished product until it's ready. Getting good vibrato skills can take from three to six months (or longer), so don't lose heart if you don't catch on right away.

Getting started with vibrato

You're probably very excited about finding out how to make this beautiful sound on your violin — so I take you through the steps by the shortest and most effective route possible.

If you've turned directly to this section to get some hints on vibrato, I highly recommend that you check out the "Changing Position" section, earlier in the chapter, to loosen up your arm and hand. A good time to start on vibrato is when your violin hold, bow hold, left-hand balance, and some shifting skills are comfortable and working well.

Although it may seem almost magical when you see and hear a player making a beautiful vibrato, the approach to vibrato is logical and involves some step-by-step preparation.

Vibrato through the ages

Nowadays, audiences are accustomed to hearing violins played with lots of vibrato, but this wasn't always the case. Back in Bach's time, vibrato was used very little, and it was regarded as ornamentation. There was a gradual "crescendo" in the use of vibrato as history progressed, until modern times, where it's used pretty much continually.

As far as playing decisions are concerned, you can proceed fairly confidently by using little or no vibrato in music of the Baroque era; a tasteful and discreet amount in music from the Classical era; a warmer and wider vibrato impulse in music

from the Romantic era; and mostly constant vibrato in music written after about 1910, where the composer likely specifies *senza vibrato* if no vibrato is required on a particular note or passage.

Since the arrival of the first recording techniques around 1900, modern audiences are fortunate to have some sounds captured from bygone days. For music written before that time, music buffs have to rely on "earwitness" accounts, which are notoriously idiosyncratic and contradictory, to allow them to guess how music sounded to those old guys.

Vibrato preparation

This "handy" checklist will help you develop good vibrato preparation routines. Ask yourself these questions:

1. Are my feet well balanced? And are my toes, ankles, and knees flexible? (If not, try a few sailorlike rocking motions, as if you're on deck in a swelling sea, to balance freely.)

2. Is my violin balancing lightly and comfortably on my collarbone and shoulder?

3. Are my jaw and neck locked or pulling down too much on the chinrest? (If so, lift your head off the instrument for a few seconds and then look from side to side a couple of times to loosen your neck muscles.)

4. Is my left hand well shaped and fairly loose on the neck of the violin? Can I shift with ease, with freedom of movement in my elbow and shoulder joints?

When you're well set up, you're ready for vibrato.

The amount of time it takes to develop a vibrato into working order varies from person to person, so it can be anything from a few weeks to a few months. Hurrying the process causes tension and discomfort, making the end result less satisfactory. Allow your hand the time it needs to develop each step, and keep on exercising even the simple warm-ups after your vibrato is established. Violinists who can vibrate after a short period of practice don't necessarily end up with a better-sounding vibrato than players who need months of preparation and practice.

Exercising without the violin and bow

Starting without having to deal with the violin (or bow) allows you to focus entirely on your new left hand movements. This exercise gets your wrist and arm joints moving freely while you maintain a little "holding power" in your hand — just like when you do real vibrato.

1. **Dig out an old pill box that fits comfortably in your palm, and then fill it about ⅓ full with uncooked rice.**

   One of those egg-shaped shakers from the music store also fits nicely in your palm — and produces the requisite sound when rocking back and forth.

2. **Begin by sitting in front of a table or desk and leaning your left elbow on the surface, in a close approximation of your violin position.**

3. **Hold the shaker lightly in your violin hand, loosen your wrist so that your hand flops toward your shoulder, and then send the wrist in the opposite direction so that it flops away from your shoulder.**

   In this step, your wrist and hand are moving, but everything else stays pretty much still. Keep the movements regular, so you can hear a rhythmic "swish-swish" as the rice moves around in the container.

4. **Allow the movements described in Step 3 to flow a little faster and to become somewhat bigger: Your elbow joint is opening out a bit as your hand flops outward toward the tabletop and closing inward as your hand flops toward your shoulder.**

   Tip: Go slowly at first. Using the second hand of your watch gives you some idea of a relaxed starting speed. You can feel the movements and keep them smooth and in sync with the ticking of your watch.

5. **Stand in playing position to repeat Steps 3 and 4, but this time, allow your elbow joint to open out a little more as your hand rolls outwards (and, of course, to close as your hand moves inward).**

Exercising with the violin, but still no bow

After you get familiar with the basic movements for vibrato, you're ready to put them to use on the violin. Trying vibrato moves with just the violin enables you to focus on the new movements without having to coordinate the bow.

For the following exercise, be sure to move your hand parallel to the neck of the violin when rocking:

1. **Hold the violin in guitar position, so that you can see your hand very easily, and let the scroll of your violin angle a little up toward your left ear.**

2. **Slide your whole hand (the thumb too) freely back and forth along the violin's neck, with your left elbow's hinge moving freely and your fingers lightly brushing the strings (no pressure) as you go.**

3. **Reduce the size of the brushing gradually, and let your thumb remain in one spot while your hand and fingers continue to brush the neck and strings.**

   By this point, your hand and fingers are using a scope of just an inch or two.

4. **Imagine the tip of finger 2 is glued very lightly in place, so that the fingertip stays in one spot, while the slight brushing movement continues along the neck of the violin.**

5. **Try Steps 2 through 4 again, but this time, hold your violin in playing position.**

Repeat the exercise using each finger in turn. Some fingers will find the motion easier and others will be less willing, but giving them all a workout prepares them for their job. The skills do eventually even out!

Violinists often ask one another, "Do you use *wrist* or *arm* vibrato?" But in fact, most well-functioning vibratos work when both the wrist and the arm are moving freely. So if someone asks you that question, I suppose your reply can be "Yes" or "Both"!

Exercises with the violin and bow

Playing with both hands together for vibrato may take some coordination, because of the different moves each hand makes. Try these exercises that combine the violin and bow to develop your vibrato skills.

Vibrato impulses

Alternating between playing a finger with some vibrato and then playing an open string gives your hand time to loosen again between impulses.

To play the vibrato exercise in Figure 14-29, make sure to relax your hand every time you play the open D string, and then almost throw your finger as you land it, so that you can spark a little vibrato wobble (indicated by the wobbly line next to the finger number) on each note. You can see this technique in action on your CD-ROM.

Figure 14-29:
Vibrato impulses on the D string.

TRACK 80

Rockin' wrists

Your last vibrato prep exercise involves starting vibrato in third position (refer to "Getting into the First Four Positions," earlier in this chapter) to allow your wrist a chance to rock. Try this exercise without the bow first, and then later, bow out the notes while keeping the rocking movement in your left hand. Here are the actions (no music required!):

1. **Place your left hand in about third position, so the heel of your hand is leaning against the violin.**

2. **Place a fingertip (try finger 2 first) on the D string.**

3. **Rock your hand slightly from the wrist, causing your fingertip to rock also, while maintaining the contact of the heel of your hand on the ribs of the violin.**

4. **Try Steps 2 and 3 with each finger in turn.**

The rocking motions are slow at first, but after a few days of exercising, you can gradually increase the speed of oscillation of the rocking motions. A sign of readiness to increase the tempo is that the rocking is even.

Good vibrations: Using your vibrato in a real song

Try part of the "Pachelbel Canon" using your new vibrato moves on the flowing half notes. As you play, stay as relaxed as possible, without gripping with your thumb or pressing too hard with your fingers.

Vibrato depends on the top joint of each finger and the base joint of your thumb being flexible and malleable.

You can give your vibrato an extra boost by adding it to the slower songs and pieces that you play in previous chapters.

 TRACK 81

Pachelbel Canon

Tapping into Trills

A *trill,* which involves a rapid alternation between the printed note and the next note above it, often happens near the end of a phrase or movement of music. Trills are musical ornaments, something like the glittery decorations on wedding cakes. A trill really draws the listener's attention to a particular note. You know when the composer is asking for a trill because you see the sign *tr* above the note head.

Trilling on a note can be a thrilling move — if your fingers are up to speed. This section shows you how to trill effectively and have fun with it. Trilling looks very simple, but it takes some coordination to sound really good. Taking it step-by-step sets you up to deal with trills in any situation.

Establish a firm, secure, and flowing bow action on trill notes before getting too busy with the left hand. I recommend practicing notes without the trills at first, and then adding the trills when you're in control of tone and timing.

Building speed of repetition

Your starting move is to loosen up those fingers and get them to tap with agility by working from an open string to each finger individually. When you can *spark* each finger — meaning getting it to spring quickly and lightly into action — trilling is much easier to broach.

My first piece of advice about trills is to perform them calmly: Don't make any vibrato-like hand movements on your trills. Just tap the trilling finger from a quiet hand to make it sound just right.

This little exercise, seen in Figure 14-30, involves the first-finger pattern (though you can try it with other finger patterns later to develop even more trill skills). Watch me demonstrate the moves on the CD-ROM before you try them out.

Start with finger 1 ready on the D string, and then lift each finger smartly and actively when it's time to move on to the next note. I double the finger speed every two bars, but the bow speed remains the same.

Tip: Keep your fingertips closer to the string as the speed increases, so that the fingers don't have far to travel and can get there sooner.

Figure 14-30:
Thrills with trills.

Speeding from finger to finger

In this section, I show you how to build speed and agility from one finger to the next. Trills almost always involve tapping your finger on the next note up from the main note you're playing, so that's how you practice in the prep exercise shown in Figure 14-31. Finger 1 remains *lightly* on the string, while finger 2 does the tapping action.

To help make your trills work well, avoid pressing the lower finger too heavily on the string.

Figure 14-31:
Trilling from
finger to
finger.

TRACK 82, 0:29

After you try trilling with fingers 1 and 2, try the same idea with fingers 2 and 3. If you want a challenging workout, try fingers 3 and 4 as well. Though to tell you the truth, violinists try to arrange trills to happen on other finger combos other than fingers 3 and 4 if possible, because little ol' finger 4 finds trilling pretty hard — that's where changing positions comes in very useful. I show you the difference between the two alternatives in Figure 14-32 and demonstrate them on the CD-ROM, so that you can try the two methods for yourself and have a choice if you meet a similar situation in music. The first time, you play the trill using fingers 3 and 4. Hard work, huh? During the rest measure, slide up to third position and prepare finger 1 on the note D. Then play the same trill notes as before, but using fingers 1 and 2. Just shift down to first position for the final C.

Figure 14-32:
In a good
position
to trill.

TRACK 82, 0:45

Trilling techniques

In this last section, I tell you a couple of final details on how trills work in real music to set you on your way with confidence.

A question of timing

If you're trilling on a short note, a couple of quick taps is all that's needed. If your trill happens on a longer note, stop the trilling action before the end of the note so that you can prepare the next note. Figure 14-33 shows you an example of a longer trill and indicates the spot (at the beginning of the fourth beat) where you can stop the trill (stop on the main note, B) and just play the plain eighth note. You can watch me play and stop this trill on the CD-ROM too.

Figure 14-33:
Knowing
when to
stop.

trill stops on B here

Sharps, flats, and naturals with trills

Usually, trills involve playing the notes in the key of the music. If the composer wants a trill note that isn't in the key signature, you see the extra accidental above the trill or sign (refer to Chapter 7 for more about accidentals).

Figure 14-34 has two examples to try out, and you can hear them on the CD-ROM. In the first measure, you play the trill in the regular way, tapping finger 2 on a C♯ because the key signature has a C♯. I give you a rest measure, and then you observe the natural sign (♮) above the trill indication in measure 3. This natural sign tells you that the upper note of the trill is now C♮, so finger 2 taps out a C♮ while finger 1 plays the same note, B as "B"-fore! Depending on the original key signature and on what's happening in the music, you can also find a sharp (♯) or a flat (♭) written above the trill sign that tells you what note to trill on.

Figure 14-34:
"Accidentally"
getting the
right notes
in trills.

Try out your trills on this minuet that I've composed for you in the style of Handel, with decorative trills throughout. I've written it so that you play trills on different fingers, for a thorough workout.

The notes are fairly simple, but I do have a bit of bowing advice: Use plenty of bow throughout, and slow the stroke a little to last for the 3 beats of each trill. The trills don't need to be very fast at first, just a few taps set you on the right path, and you can return to the song later to add more zip to the trills when you're ready.

TRACK 83

A Trill a Minuet

Chapter 15

Styles of Music

· ·

In This Chapter

▶ Fiddling around with country music

▶ Grooving to jazz

▶ Enchanting with the gypsy violin

· ·

*W*hen you know the basics of violin playing, you can mix your techniques into various combinations to play different styles of music. From traditional playing styles to modern, highly experimental styles (where you knock on the violin's back like a percussion instrument and then bow just behind the bridge to create a shrill and disturbing shriek), your violin is a versatile instrument.

Today, increasing numbers of classically trained violinists are learning other musical styles — because they're fun to play *and* they aren't usually performed in a tux! Three popular styles are fiddling, with its dancing, lively rhythms; jazz, with its laid-back moods, sophisticated syncopations, and complex harmonies; and gypsy violin, the most romantic and exuberant of all styles. In this chapter, you taste the main features of each of these three styles and sample some sounds and techniques you can try yourself.

Fiddling Around with Country Music

When your mother told you to stop fiddling around, she wasn't pleased. But that's because you weren't doing that fiddling around on your violin! People often wonder about the difference between a violin and a fiddle. Actually, very little difference exists between a "classical" violin and a fiddle used for folk and other styles, except that fiddlers often use all-metal strings to produce the more folksy sound. In fact, the violin started out as a simple folk instrument. Even when courts and churches hired orchestras to play at aristocratic events and religious ceremonies, those same musicians supplemented their incomes by playing popular music at local weddings, funerals, and festivals — just like today. But anyone who has seen great fiddlers play realizes that the distinct musical style — and all that agile bowing — lead violinists to try fiddling.

Familiarizing yourself with fiddle music

When you hear fiddle music, you notice right away that many pieces are short and lively, with a few more mournful numbers interspersed. Because much fiddle music is based on reels, jigs, and waltzes, you want to tap your toes to the music as you catch the beat — you and generations of Celts have experienced the same invitation to the dance. This is music of the working people, not of the aristocrats. You hear it at barn dances, weddings, and such occasions when whooping it up is the order of the day.

Fiddling includes a whole bunch of exciting styles under the large umbrella of its title. For now, you meet four of the most popular genres in fiddling: Celtic, bluegrass, country and western, and Cajun. In case you're not familiar with fiddling, I suggest a few recordings — and even a video or two — just to give you a taste of the variety of sounds and styles that are popular with fiddling buffs.

If you want to know more about fiddle music than what I tell you in this book, a whole world of information is waiting for you. Get an issue of *The Old Time Herald,* or browse through a copy of the book *Appalachian Fiddle* by Miles Krassen (Oak Publications) to start on more tunes.

Celtic

These titles introduce you to the sights and sounds of Celtic fiddling:

- ✓ *Traditional Music from Cape Breton Island* (Nimbus), by Buddy MacMaster, one of the greatest . . . well . . . masters of Celtic fiddling. He's from Cape Breton Island, off the coast of Nova Scotia on Canada's east coast, a place that received thousands of Scottish immigrants in the seventeenth and eighteenth centuries. His recordings give you a taste of the characteristic sounds, and you can also watch him live on video in *Master of the Cape Breton Fiddle* (SeaBright Productions).

- ✓ *Leahy Family: Live* (Koch Entertainment). On CD and DVD and bursting with energy and drive, the Leahys show you the sounds (and the step-dancing) of the Irish traditional fiddling style.

Bluegrass

I recommend these albums to give you a good feel for the bluegrass style:

- ✓ *Heroes* (Warner Brothers), by Mark O'Connor. This groundbreaking album exemplifies bluegrass (and gives a delicious taste of most other fiddle genres), with appearances on its tracks of other great violinists such as Jean-Luc Ponty and Stéphane Grappelli.

- ✓ *Bill Monroe: The Essential Collection* (Spectrum). Monroe is the daddy of Bluegrass, but he's mainly a mandolin player. (Many musicians can play violin and mandolin because they're essentially the same instrument, although one has frets and is played with a pick, and the other doesn't have frets and is played with a bow — no prizes for guessing which is which!) Listen especially for Tracks 11, 15, and 16 for a pair of agile fiddlers in Monroe's group.

Country and western

In country and western music, the fiddle is important, but it's essentially a backup instrument along with the pedal steel guitar. The fiddle is front and center in the western swing style and in the hurtin' songs that characterize much of country music.

For fine playing in this genre, listen to *The King of Western Swing: 25 Hits (1935-1945)* (ASV), by Bob Wills and His Texas Playboys. Hear Bob Wills's violin sounding out at the start of the "Osage Stomp," Track 2, and weaving around the vocalist in "Right or Wrong," Track 7.

Cajun and zydeco

For a great sampling of the Cajun and zydeco genres, check out *The Rough Guide to Cajun and Zydeco* (World Music Network). Listen especially to Michael Doucet's fiddling on Track 8, "Bayou Pon Pon," and Wallace "Cheese" Read's playing in "Fiddle Stomp" on Track 14. (Readers may be inspired to know that Michael Doucet first began his fiddling when he was already in his 20s.) The first master of this genre was Doug Kershaw, featured on the Mark O'Connor album *Heroes*, which I mention at the very start of this section.

The origins of fiddling

Celtic fiddling as we know it today originated in the seventeenth century in Scotland and Ireland. In those days, when traveling was much less usual, roads were virtually non-existent (and recording hadn't even become a twinkle in anyone's eye), so each region evolved its own distinct style. In Scotland, for example, you can hear Scandinavian sounds in the fiddle music of the remote Shetland Isles, whereas the fiddle music of the Highlands frequently evokes the flavor of bagpipes.

In Ireland, too, many regional influences fuse into the style known as Irish fiddling. Dancing and playing at the same time is one of its trademark features. As early as the mid-eighteenth century, dance masters would go to houses to teach steps for the reels and jigs, probably carrying tiny fiddles called *kits* in their pockets. The pocket-sized violin was popular with dance masters and street musicians alike, giving easy and immediate access to all kinds of fiddle music. Nowadays, people throughout the world have heard of the Irish style (with a modern touch) through blockbuster shows such as *Riverdance* (1995), which showcases the lively step dancing associated with Irish fiddling music, and the traditional Irish band The Chieftains.

Fiddling made its way to America with a wave of immigrants who brought their own music along with them from Scotland and Ireland starting way back in the seventeenth century. Because many of these people settled in rural areas, over a period of time, their music became known as "country music."

Fiddling in different styles

If you listen to any of the recordings I suggest earlier in this chapter, you know that fiddlers, traditionally, have different playing styles. This section explains some of the styles and how they sound:

- **Celtic:** Within the broad heading of fiddle music, Celtic fiddling is a particularly popular style stemming from Scottish and Irish origins. Celtic fiddlers play reels (energetic dances, mainly in 4/4 time), jigs (tunes mostly in 6/8 for lively dancing), hornpipes (usually in 4/4 time and ranging from moderate to fast tempos), and strathspeys (characterized by snappy short-long rhythms, in 4/4 meter, but with more unusual rhythms and a more deliberate speed than in reels and jigs).

  Most of this music is still passed on by _rote_ learning (or learning by imitation, not to be confused with _note_ learning). Keen fiddlers travel across America to jam with other fiddling fans and learn new songs. Many countries have their own versions of fiddling; for example, Cape Breton fiddling is a Canadian regional variation of Scottish fiddling.

- **Bluegrass:** _Bluegrass_ refers to the fact that the nickname for Kentucky since the 1800s has been "The Bluegrass State." Bluegrass, which emerged on the scene around 1945, has an energetic feel that people love, with high, screaming violins and really fast tempos. Bluegrass bands use banjos and slides (see later in this chapter) to give this music its characteristic sound.

  Most bluegrass fiddling requires some improvisation, while Celtic fiddling doesn't. One element that they do share, though, is that neither style uses vibrato. People consider Bill Monroe (see the list of suggested recordings at the beginning of this chapter) to be the originator of the style.

- **Country and western:** A little simpler than bluegrass, this style uses catchy melodies and mostly single notes with no slides. But you often hear a second violin playing a harmony line. The tempo changes are much less drastic than in bluegrass.

- **Cajun and zydeco:** Cajun music has its roots in the music of French-speaking settlers in Louisiana. Many of the songs feature sad ballads, reflecting the sense of loss of the exiled population. Two fiddles usually play these songs, one playing the tune and the other the accompaniment. Over time, the style became fused with local Louisiana music. The style uses a lot of double stops (for volume) and strongly accented bowing.

  Zydeco is closely associated with Cajun music. The Creole people of Louisiana play this style, which has French, African, Spanish, and blues influences. The fiddle often features prominently in zydeco, but the accordion is the main instrument.

Sounding like a fiddler

Fiddle music might sound simple, but playing like an authentic fiddler sure isn't. It takes years of practice to get those fiddly techniques just right. But with a few nifty moves that I show you in this section, you can soon be on your way to a hoedown.

Shuffles

The *shuffle* (the fiddler's name for the separate "long short-short" bowings that I show you in pieces and rhythms in Chapter 13) is used to imitate train sounds. Country-style fiddlers can play or accompany just about any tune with a bow shuffle. The bow shuffle adds rhythmic drive and energy to simple tunes. Shuffling is one of the signatures of fiddle music, and because it's a fairly basic skill in this particular form, you can use it to add the flavor of fiddling to any folk tune. More complicated and intricate shuffles exist too, but begin shuffling with this kind, which is the most playable one.

Fiddlers generally don't use a whole lot of bow, and some fiddlers even hold the bow with the thumb on the outside of the ferrule (see Chapter 4 for more about that fascinating ferrule!), to allow them to play short strokes with lots of power and agility. Figure 15-1 shows you what this bow hold looks like.

Try holding your bow with your thumb on the outside of the ferrule for other bowing practice too. This bow hold helps promote a comfortable, rounded hand shape, good for improving flexibility — and tone production.

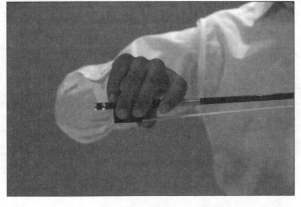

Figure 15-1:
Holding your
bow like a
fiddler.

The best example of the shuffle is in the traditional showpiece "Orange Blossom Special," named after a train and composed by two young fiddlers, Ervin Rouse and Chubby Wise, in 1939. Even if I don't show you how to shuffle off to Buffalo, I show you how to shuffle up and down the D major scale in Figure 15-2. First, listen to it on the CD-ROM. Then try playing this pattern around the middle of the bow, using about ⅓ of the bow for the quarter notes, and half of that span for the eighth notes— or less if the music is moving fast. When you have the shuffle happening, you can apply it to songs.

Figure 15-2: Shuffling up the D major scale.

TRACK 84, 0:00

Double stops

Double stops, where you bow (and often also finger) on two strings at once, provide a bit of harmony when added to the basic melody of any song. (You meet double stops in detail in Chapter 14.) Double stops can also evoke the drone of bagpipes for extra Celtic flavor. In Figure 15-3, I show you a simple example of double stops to get you going for the real stuff in your songs at the end of this section.

In double stops, make sure that any note matching an open string is really in tune with that string — you can adjust a finger to match the pitch of an open string while you're playing, but you can't stop and crank the pegs to adjust the open string. Open strings are very powerful bosses! In this example, take a moment or two to match finger 3 to its corresponding open string (D) before you start, and remember to bow smoothly and evenly without undue pressure. You can also listen to how it works on the CD-ROM.

Slides

A *slide* creates a vocal effect. A finger slides along the string, moving from one pitch to the next either slowly or quickly to scoop the pitch up (or occasionally down) to a note. A slide is fairly easy to add in to a song, and it gives a song some instant authentic flavor — a sort of soup cube for your music. Quick slides usually begin about a half step lower than the note you slide into. If slides are notated on your music, you see a diagonal line leading toward the note head.

TRACK 84, 0:14

Figure 15-3: Double stops in action.

Figure 15-4 shows a couple of typical slides. In the first example, immediately after you begin the down-bow, slide finger 1 into its spot from about a B♭. After the rest measure, play both the open E string and finger 4 on the A string at the same time on a down-bow, but place finger 4 deliberately a little low and then slide it until it matches the pitch of the open E. You can watch and listen to how slides work on the CD-ROM.

Figure 15-4:
Slides.

TRACK 84, 0:27

Tags

Tags — short and rhythmically catchy final phrases *tagged* on to the end of a melody — are used by musicians to let their group know that a piece or section of music is ending.

The tag "shave and a haircut, two bits" is a well-known example. You can give this tag a listen on the CD-ROM and try it out in Figure 15-5. Make sure you observe the quarter rest at the start of the second measure, to add the tension of the unexpected silence.

Figure 15-5:
Tag —
you're it!

TRACK 84, 0:45

Fiddling your way to songs

To finish up this section with a bit of fun, I show you two fiddle tunes to try your new moves on.

TRACK 85

Cripple Creek

A classic Bluegrass tune, named after a town in Colorado that experienced an evocative history: a gold rush, abandoned mines, hauntings, and gambling. And here's a perfect opportunity to try out your shuffles. First you play the tune in its plain form, and then you fancy it up with the shuffle bows. This tune is in A major and uses quarter notes and half notes. Play mostly around the middle of the bow, and use about twice the amount of bow for the half notes to sing them out. When you begin the shuffle, use the middle part of the bow for agility. Your left hand plays exactly the same fingerings for both the tune and the shuffle. Using open strings wherever possible gives you the right sound.

TRACK 86

Chicken Reel

You get to play with slides in "Chicken Reel," a tune in the style of western swing. It's "reely" fun to give your first finger a squishy slide from F♮ to F♯ each time. Start your first down-bow near the frog so that you arrive at the middle section of the bow to play the eighth notes. Notice that the slur occurs on a down-bow on measures 1 to 2, and then it's an up-bow on measures 3 to 4. The up-bow into measure 4 allows your bow to travel back toward the middle portion of the bow.

Grooving to Jazz

The style known as *jazz* developed mostly around New Orleans at the beginning of the twentieth century. Jazz is actually a fusion of several kinds of music played in America at the end of the nineteenth century. Although the origins of jazz are in West African music sung and played by slaves, the genre branched off into many individual styles — such as sacred music (spirituals) or blues — influenced by the social and geographical conditions that the slaves and their descendants encountered in America.

Listening to some jazz violin

To really get your head (and ears) around jazz music, I recommend a few interesting recordings — all of which feature orchestral or solo violin — that you can find at local stores or online:

✔ *Satin Doll* (Vanguard), by Stéphane Grappelli. I talk much more about Grappelli in Chapter 18's discussion of great performers, but he has to head any listening list, because he's still top of his class. This album features Grappelli's violin artistry in such favorites as "Ain't Misbehaving," "On the Sunny Side of the Street," and "Pennies from Heaven."

✔ *Stuff Smith: Masters of Jazz Vol. 6* (Storyville). Listen to Track 11, "Swingin' Bach," for a jazz version of the famous Bach "Double" Violin Concerto, and hear Smith's incredible violin technique and artistry throughout this eclectic collection.

✔ *Wild Cats* (ASV), by Joe Venuti and Eddie Lang. Venuti's tremendous facility, creativity, and humor shine through in this compilation of his recordings with brilliant guitarist Eddie Lang. Listen for the casual way he segues into double stops in just about every number. A hilarious duet with a solo bassoon in Track 13 showcases Venuti's speedy fingering and bowing — he could outrun just about any violinist — and further evidence of his facility sounds out clearly in Track 12, "Wild Cat." For a unique and incredible sound, listen to Track 8, "Four String Joe," where Venuti may have been using his bow in his trademark way — loosening the hair so much that it could wrap round all four strings at once, and play all four notes, while the bow stick ran under the body of the violin!

✔ *Livin' with the Blues* (Acoustic Disc), by Vassar Clements. Steeped in the sadness and nostalgia of the blues, Vassar Clements worked in both blues and bluegrass styles. Track 1, "Cypress Grove," features a haunting violin solo by Clements that incorporates slides and bending the pitches to give a vocal quality to the music. Track 6, "Green Onions," features a more up-tempo and light-hearted mood, with colorful interactions between the violin and Charlie Musselwhite on harmonica. Listen to Track 13, "Fiddlin' and Faddlin'," for a jazzy take on fiddle music.

✔ *The Inner Mounting Flame* (Legacy), by the Mahavishnu Orchestra. This is a powerful album, with every track a testament to the unique sound of this orchestra. Track 2, "Dawn," features a cool violin and guitar opening unison theme with violinist Jerry Goodman adding some amazing riffs throughout, and Track 4, "A Lotus on Irish Streams," showcases Goodman's artistry with a folk-inspired theme.

Getting the jazz sound

As with fiddling, when you get deeply involved with the style, you find many subtleties to master and make into a fluent musical language. In this section, I show you some of the characteristic sounds so that you can get a taste of this highly energized style. One thing: Jazz violinists use very little vibrato — they try to sound like horns! (Refer to Chapter 14 to understand vibrato.)

Syncopated rhythms

Jazz rhythms are much more complex — and fancy — than rhythms in just about any other style of music. Their main characteristic is *syncopation,* where notes often occur before or after the main beats, which can disturb the listener's feeling of security, or even sound a little shocking. Although syncopation happens sometimes in classical music, it's fundamental to jazz styles, happening in just about every song.

Coping with syncopation takes a little persistence, but is worth the effort. To try out some syncopation for yourself, I show you a G major scale with a syncopated rhythm in Figure 15-6. Clap and count the rhythm before you play it on your violin. I include the counting words on the figure.

All that jazz

Music dictionaries divide jazz into numerous branches, including *ragtime, blues, big band, improvisation, music to dance to, music to listen to, bop,* and *progressive jazz.* A brief glance at history shows how these different strands developed. Before 1900, early string bands playing jazz usually featured the fiddle (showing the excellent taste of the early jazz musicians!), guitar, banjo or mandolin, and double bass. Early jazz was seldom written down, and it relied on the players doing some improvising as they went along. In the beginning of the era, one of the most popular kinds of jazz was *ragtime.* Ragtime music started out as music to listen to, and its original tempo wasn't fast, but later on, it sped up to become dance music. The genre's elements of *syncopation* — rhythmic effects where the music often avoids the main beats, creating many surprises — are fundamental to the jazz style. (I explain more about syncopation in the section, "Getting the jazz sound.")

Around 1920, Louis Armstrong — the most important figure in American jazz — emerged on the scene. He introduced solo improvisation into jazz pieces. Also in the '20s, the Original Dixieland Jazz Band immediately captivated listeners with its bright sound and energetic rhythms. Gershwin's "Rhapsody in Blue," originally scored for piano and jazz band, appeared around the same time and was an immediate hit. The scene was well and truly set for jazz styles that still sound fresh and exciting almost 100 years later. And with the advent of commercial radio broadcasts in the '20s, jazz reached a much broader audience then ever.

The 1930s saw more interesting events in jazz history. Such icons as Duke Ellington, Count Basie, and Cab Calloway formed jazz orchestras. Many orchestras included string sections from time to time, and Duke Ellington's trumpet player, Ray Nance, doubled on violin, improvising solos with the band. A number of all-women jazz ensembles flourished in the '30s and '40s, including Lil Armstrong's (Louis Armstrong's first wife) All-Girl Band, and the Harlem Playgirls. Some white band leaders worked in jazz, notably Benny Goodman and Glenn Miller, playing in a style known as swing. Jazz became somewhat more integrated in the 1930s, with black and white musicians having the opportunity to work together after years of segregation.

The '40s and '50s brought jazz to a wider and more diverse audience through Duke Ellington's Carnegie Hall concert, a milestone event, and the founding of the Newport Jazz Festival.

Miles Davis introduced a cooler sound of jazz in contrast to all the hot, fast jazz that had been popular in the '30s, '40s, and '50s. His lyrical tunes and relaxed sounds influenced many players, including Chet Baker, and set the stage for a whole new generation to enjoy a variety of great jazz music.

As far as violin is concerned, one of the most famous jazz violinists of all time was the French violinist Stéphane Grappelli (see Chapter 18 for more about him), who led the Quintet of the Hot Club of France in the 1930s. He reached the pinnacle of success together with Django Reinhardt, his amazing guitarist, who himself was Roma and a product of Roma culture.

If your interest is piqued by all this history, you may want to read a couple of famous books about the era: Albert Murray's *Stomping the Blues* (Da Capo Press) and Eileen Southern's *The Music of Black Americans* (W.W. Norton & Company).

Sul ponticello

To express intense, raw emotions, jazz uses an array of unconventional sounds. In this section, I show you how to produce a string sound, *sul ponticello,* that's used quite a bit in jazz but is very different from the singing tones you expect to hear from a violin. *Sul ponticello* is an Italian term for bowing (almost) on the bridge. You don't actually bow right on the bridge, but the closer you dare to go, the more metallic and raunchy the sound! You know to use this technique when you see the term *sul pont.,* or *s.p.,* on the page of music. *Posizione normale* (meaning normal position of the bow), or *p.n.,* on the page tells you to get back to your regular sound.

Try Figure 15-7 beginning by bowing very close to the bridge to hear the possibilities of *sul ponticello,* then steer your bow closer to its normal path as you progress. You can watch the technique in action on the CD-ROM. Notice that here you play your first note on an up-bow.

Swing rhythms

If it ain't got that swing . . . it ain't going to sound very authentic. When jazz musicians see a pair of eighth notes, they sometimes *swing* the rhythm, playing the first one longer than the second, giving a dancing, triplet-like effect for an easy-going, relaxed sound.

You can try this technique in Figure 15-8. The first part of the figure shows you what jazz musicians see on the page (known as *straight,* when the eighths are played evenly), and the second part shows you what you actually play when you swing the eighths. I demonstrate the "swing" version on the CD-ROM.

Blues scales

Blues, originating from African work songs that the slaves brought with them to America, reflect great sadness and a sense of loss. Scales known as *blues scales* include three of their notes, typically the third (III), fifth (V), and seventh (VII) degrees of the scale, affected by "blueness," a lowering of the pitch by about a half step, to evoke an oppressed and hopeless mood. (Refer to Chapter 10 for a list of the degrees of a scale.)

TRACK 87, 0:00

Figure 15-6:
G major scale with syncopation.

Figure 15-7:
Sul ponticello.

Figure 15-8:
Swinging along.

In written music, blues notes appear as a half step lower than usual, because the five-line system doesn't really accommodate intervals of less than a semitone between two notes, but blues artists usually bend the pitch down a little less than the full extent when they perform the songs. Jazz violinists use the notes of blues scales a lot, particularly in sad songs.

Rockin' with violin

You don't expect to find the delicate violin among all those amplified guitars and drum sets of rock music. But in fact, versatile violins feature in some very famous numbers of rock music, adding rich lyrical qualities to the rhythmic drive of the songs. There's even a fiddle wailing away on the second version of The Rolling Stones' "Honky-Tonk Woman" (1969), called "Country Honk." An early appearance of electric violins in rock took place in the '70s in Curved Air's numbers, and another great British band, Jethro Tull, featured the violin playing of Eddie Jobson (formerly with Frank Zappa) on their album *A* in the early '80s. Perhaps the most influential and active rock violinist of all is Jean-Luc Ponty, who is also a very accomplished classically trained artist. Ponty played with Frank Zappa on *Hot Rats* (1969), and Elton John asked Ponty to play on his *Honky Château* album (1972). A current band notable for use of the violin is Final Fantasy, an internationally known Toronto project whose violinist, Owen Pallett, makes heavy use of the electronic looping of violin parts.

Accolades to Joe Venuti

One of the first jazz violinists was Joe Venuti (1903–1978), an offbeat (must have been all those sycopations!), iconoclastic, brilliant jazz player who included many double stops in his stylings. He loosened the bow hair and then put his bow stick under his violin to be able to bow on all four strings together. Born to Italian parents who immigrated to the United States, Venuti learned classical violin as a child and possessed a well-developed technique before he began to apply his considerable talents to jazz music.

A blues scale can begin on just about any note, and can have different patterns. Figure 15-9 shows you a typical six-note blues scale starting on D, so you can try it out for yourself. You can also listen to the scale on the CD-ROM.

Using flowing bow strokes, begin quite near the frog on the open D string, and then land finger 2 "low" on F♯. Finger 3 plays on G in its usual place, and then finger 4 plays A♭ very close to finger 3. Use open A for the A♮, and then follow the same finger pattern as before for fingers 2 and 3, but this time, play on the A string.

TRACK 87, 0:46

Figure 15-9: Blues scale.

Jazzing up your violin

If you've ever wanted to sound like a jazz musician, playing these songs gives you a chance to put your new sounds and rhythms into some real tunes.

 TRACK 88

Country Club

One of Scott Joplin's memorable ragtime numbers for you to try your syncopation on, this song moves at a steady and relaxed pace. Bow with a quite strong pulse on the first quarters, using most of the bow. In measure 3, you play the first sixteenth note with a quick up-bow, which brings you back toward the middle of the bow for the rest of the bar. Then in measure 4, observe the two little up-bows in a row, which take you back to the lower part of the bow so that you can syncopate the held-over Es on an accented down-bow. Allow the three slurred notes to bring you back to near the frog to start the next bit of the tune. At the end of measure 6, play E♯ with a "low" finger 1, and then slide finger 1 up a half step for the F♯ (which is only a semi-tone higher) at the start of measure 7. Making a crescendo into the last bar gives a strong effect to your ending.

TRACK 89

Sweet Georgia Brown

This favorite standard was composed in 1925, and it's also well known today as the theme song for the Harlem Globetrotters. Take the song at a steady pace. Look out for the slight change when the theme comes back in measure 5, and play F♮ instead of F♯. Make a circular retake at the end of measure 12 so that you can start measure 13 with a quick and firm down-bow. When you first learn to play this song, use plenty of open strings and keep the fingerings simple while you learn the catchy rhythms. You can always come back later to try finger 4 (or even a little shift to *third position* here and there — refer to Chapter 14).

Enchanting with Gypsy Violin

The very words *gypsy music* conjure up thrilling images of people in gorgeous, colorful costumes dancing around a campfire, or of a wonderful solo violinist serenading a couple who are enjoying a romantic dinner at a restaurant. The rich musical tradition of the Roma and the presence of Roma communities throughout Europe, many of them traveling communities, have long inspired writers and composers all over the world.

Listening to some great gypsy violin

If you've never heard gypsy violin in action, prepare to get swept away with these recordings I recommend every violinist hear:

- ✔ *The Gypsy Violin* (Alula), by Laszlo Berki Gypsy Ensemble. This album has lots of Hungarian flavor in these foot-tapping czardas and polkas, and a luscious, full sound.

- ✔ *Master of the Russian Gypsy Violin* (Arc Music), by Oleg Ponomarev. Descended from famous gypsy musicians, Ponomarev carries on the tradition handed down through generations of virtuoso violinists in this exciting compilation.

- ✔ *Gypsy* (Well-Tempered Productions), by Lara St. John. The dramatic and brilliant Canadian violinist Lara St. John performs gypsy-inspired works from the mainstream repertoire with fire and passion.

Rooting around for origins

The Roma people (who were once referred to as *Gypsies* because people believed they came from Egypt) actually originated in India. Gradually, over several centuries, they traveled through Turkey to Europe, bringing their music with them. Mainstream classical music's admiration for gypsy technique and musical ability existed even when Roma people were excluded from mainstream society. In fact, Tolstoy's Roma friend Michael Erdenko became a violin professor at Moscow Conservatory in the nineteenth century.

What we know nowadays as *gypsy violin* music comes largely from Hungary, where the Roma had a profound influence on popular culture.

The Roma also traveled through Spain, where they left a similar imprint and inspiration. Today, gypsy elements are most apparent in Flamenco music, a Spanish folk music, which is a fusion of many different styles — also influenced by Moorish culture.

Throughout Europe, famous composers such as Sarasate, Ravel (listen to his *Tzigane*), and Kreisler wrote works for violin while inspired by Roma music, often using an exotic scale they heard in gypsy folk groups. This same scale appears throughout Eastern Europe and the Middle East. You can find out how to play the scale in the section "Romancing the violin."

Romancing the violin

Gypsy violinists love a violin with a rich and dark sound, in order to tug at listeners' heartstrings. Players of this style often sand down the bridge to reduce the curvature and height a little, making fast fingerings and double stops easier. Signature elements of the gypsy style bring color and drama to your playing. As with fiddling and jazz, it takes a long time to become authentically steeped in the gypsy tradition, but you get a taste of the techniques — and benefit your own playing — by trying out some of the characteristic sounds.

The gypsy scale

When you hear gypsy music, you may realize that the scale patterns have a very different feel to them. Perhaps the music reminds you of the soundtrack of a movie set in the Middle East, but you may not know why. Well, you're actually hearing a special scale known as the gypsy scale. I tell you how to play this scale so that you can find your way through the special spacing of the notes.

Heard in music throughout Eastern Europe, the gypsy scale is a lot like the harmonic minor scale in Chapter 10, but with the fourth note raised a half step. Figure 15-10 shows you an A harmonic minor scale changed into the gypsy scale, and you can listen to it on the CD-ROM. As you go from measure 1 to measure 2, just observe the busy first finger, which slides from "low" placement for D♯ to regular placement for E on the D string. To help you see all the *augmented seconds* (which you meet Chapter 10), I have marked them with an asterisk (*).

Figure 15-10:
The gypsy
scale.

Glissando

You meet short slides in "Fiddling Around with Country Music," earlier in this chapter. *Glissando* — meaning "sliding" in Italian — is a left-hand fingering technique where the violinist literally slides the fingertip along the string toward the next note, and it can be far away! Think of ice-skating with your fingertip. Composers tell players they want a glissando effect by writing a line from one note head to the next, as you see in Figure 15-11.

Try this E♭ major scale and arpeggio on the D string, using the sliding fingers as printed. Shift your whole hand up the neck of your violin (with your thumb sliding along in sync, opposite finger 1) for each glissando finger. Release about half of the pressure of the fingertip on the string as you begin your slide. Check out how this technique looks and sounds on the CD-ROM.

All on D string

TRACK 90, 0:18

Figure 15-11:
Glissando
effects on
E♭ major
scale and
arpeggio.

Tremolo

Tremolo, meaning "trembling" in Italian, is a technique where you play near the tip of the bow and produce a shaking sound by playing rapid, tiny up- and down-bows in quick succession — producing an intense (or even downright scary) effect. Allowing the bow to sit calmly on the string before beginning the motion ensures you begin from a solid starting point. Most players use a combination of wrist and finger motions to make tremolo happen. Watch the tremolo and listen to how it sounds on the CD-ROM.

Figure 15-12 shows you what you see on the page when a tremolo effect comes along. Usually, three lines through the stem of the note indicate tremolo. If the tremolo is on a whole note, the lines that mark it sit under or over the note head.

Figure 15-12:
Shaking
things up
with tremolo.

Harmonics

A *harmonic* is a high-pitched flute-like sound that makes your violin seem almost magical. You can make a harmonic by just touching your fingertip — no pressing down at all — on the surface of the string at specific places while you draw a quite firm bow stroke. These special spots, called *nodes,* occur at various fractional points along the strings. Two nodes of note are at the quarter-way mark and at the halfway mark. (Figure 15-13 shows where those two nodes are located.)

In this section, I cover two ways to play harmonics: *octave harmonics* and *third-finger harmonics.*

Octave harmonics

An *octave harmonic* is, as its name suggests, the note sounding one octave above any open string. If you shift to *fourth position* (refer to Chapter 14) and press finger 4 down in the usual way, so that the string touches the finger-board, you get a regular, stopped note one octave above the open string. But if you just touch the surface of the string with finger 4 at that same location, you get the harmonic, which has a very different tone quality.

You can play a harmonic exactly one octave above any open string by touching any finger (though 4 usually gets the honor) on the string at the halfway point.

If you find it helpful, you can measure up your string length to locate the halfway point between the bridge and the nut at the end of the fingerboard and then mark the spot with a tape or dot until your hand knows its way (refer to Chapter 5 for more on fingerboard tapes).

You know the composer is asking you to play the special sound of an octave harmonic when you see that the note is written one octave above the open string but still has "0" indicated as the fingering, as if it were the actual open string. I show you these four notes, one for each string of your violin, in Figure 15-14.

Sometimes you see "4" written over the "0," which simply means you touch the harmonic spot with finger 4.

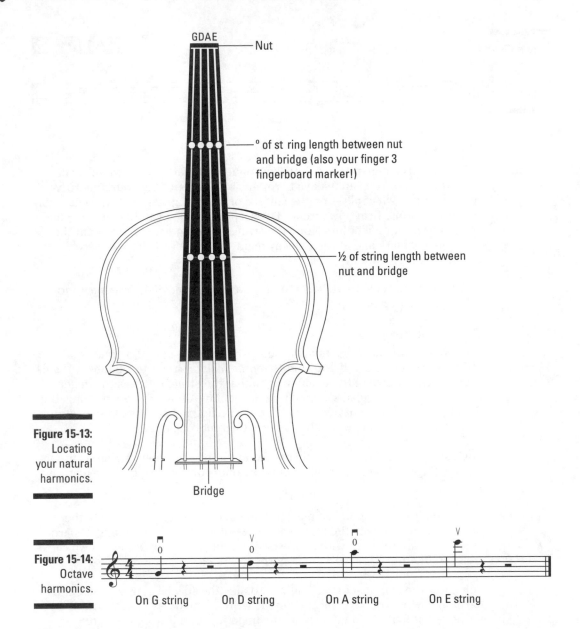

GDAE

Nut

° of st ring length between nut
and bridge (also your finger 3
fingerboard marker!)

½ of string length between
nut and bridge

Bridge

Figure 15-13:
Locating
your natural
harmonics.

Figure 15-14:
Octave
harmonics.

On G string   On D string   On A string   On E string

To sound out octave harmonics, just shift up your left hand to around *third*
or *fourth* position (refer to Chapter 14 for details on left hand positions), and
then extend finger 4 slightly to just touch the surface of the string at the
exact halfway point of the string's length. Draw a firm bow stroke with a fair
amount of speed, using the full length of the bow. (Take a look at the video
clip on your CD-ROM to see octave harmonics in action.)

If a harmonic doesn't sound clear right away, keep bowing calmly and adjust your fingertip location very slightly higher or lower, without pressing down at all, till you center on the node.

Third-finger harmonics

If you thought it was cool to get that harmonic sound one octave above an open string, you now meet the higher-ups. You can play harmonics sounding *two* octaves above each open string by touching finger 3 in its regular spot (which is one-quarter of the way up the string), but floating like a feather on the surface of the string.

You know that the composer is asking for this kind of harmonic when you see a note head with a diamond-shaped outline in place of the usual oval note head. Many possible harmonics exist on your strings, but for now, all you need are the ones you play with finger 3 in its regular spot. Figure 15-15 shows you the four possible harmonics you can play with finger 3.

Figure 15-15:
Your first diamonds!

To sound out the first harmonic, place finger 3 in its usual spot on the G string. Bow the note the normal way. You hear the note C, as you expect. Now "unpress" finger 3, taking care to keep the fingertip on exactly the same spot on the string as before, but now on its surface. Bow this harmonic with a long, fairly fast and firm bow stroke. The note you're now playing sounds much higher, two octaves above the open string note. I show you the sounding note in parentheses after each harmonic so that you know what's going on. (I demonstrate how to play third-finger harmonics on the CD-ROM.)

Both octave and third-finger harmonics are *natural* harmonics, which means you can play them by touching an open string at the right spot. If you continue with the violin, you may encounter *fingered* harmonics, where you create harmonics on any note by just touching finger 4 lightly on the string while finger 1 is pressing the string fully down.

Trills

Trills are musical decorations, something like the icing on a cake, which can ornament any special note. (I talk about trills in detail in Chapter 14.) This effect is a favorite feature of gypsy music, which is often quite flashy.

Trilling is just a finger action. Be sure to keep your wrist and palm calm, and use the finger tapping itself as the trill action. If you're trilling so fast that you feel other muscles and joints starting to tighten, reduce the speed of the tapping action. Trills don't have to be extremely fast. Also, don't press the lower finger very hard on the string — the trill will still sound fine, and the hand will be more flexible.

Playing in the gypsy style

I finish up this chapter by showing you two songs with strong gypsy influences for you to try and play —with style!

TRACK 91

Kalinka

A favorite gypsy tune, "Kalinka" tells about a small tree that blooms in winter, producing bright orange berries. This version opens with a long tremolo note on E, which you play with finger 2 in third position on the A string, to whet the audience's appetite before you launch into the song. You shift right down again to first position in measure 1. Listen carefully for the key of A minor, and place finger 2 close to finger 1. At first, you play quite steadily and deliberately, not very loudly, but you step up the tempo and the volume of sound on the repeat so that by the end, you're whirling along at a *forte* level. Gypsy music loves the excitement of sudden tempo changes, *accelerandos* and *ritardandos* (refer to Chapter 9 to know the names for different tempos).

poco a poco accelerando e crescendo*

*getting gradually faster and louder

TRACK 92

Hungarian Dance No. 1

Brahms borrowed this theme for the first song in his popular collection of Hungarian dances. It is a Csárdás, a Hungarian dance of the early nineteenth century. You can play this tune all in first position, too, just to hear how it goes and to enjoy the music. But for an authentic gypsy sound, also try the fingerings I suggest on the printed music, starting in fourth position on the G string. (Check finger 1 against open D to match the pitch before you place finger 2 a whole step above 1, on the note E.) Use full bows with a rich, singing sound. I give you several shifts, which may be played with a slightly "slidey" sound. At the very end, float your left hand up so that finger 4 can touch the octave harmonic on the A string, and then try harmonic and tremolo together for a grand finale of your new techniques.

If playing the shifts feels like overload when you're getting to know any new piece with quite a few shifts, just play in first position till you feel confident with the notes and bowings. You can filter in the fancier left-hand stuff later.

Part VI
Getting into Gear, Staying in Gear

The 5th Wave   By Rich Tennant

EDWARD PLAYED A MEAN VIOLIN

Your nose is too big, and your ears are grotesque.

In this part . . .

With so many possibilities out there, finding your own violin and bow may seem overwhelming at first, but I can help you with that. Chapter 16 gives you tips on how to succeed in choosing the perfect violin and bow to suit your needs. That chapter also helps you decide whether you should buy or rent an instrument. Then, after you've found your musical match, Chapter 17 tells you how to take good care of your violin and bow, so you can make beautiful music together for a long, long time.

Chapter 16

Finding the Right Violin and Bow for You

. . . .

In This Chapter

▶ Choosing the violin that's right for you

▶ Sizing up your violin options

▶ Buying the best bow

▶ Deciding whether to buy or rent your violin

▶ Searching for your perfect match

▶ Getting plugged into electric and electronic violins

. . . .

*E*merging from a store with your very own violin and bow, in your very own case, makes you feel as if you're walking on air — but getting to that point involves some pretty down-to-earth decisions.

Buying a violin is a big commitment — both financially and emotionally — so you need to ask yourself whether you're ready. If you're just starting out, you might not yet have enough of a feel for the instrument to determine just what's right for you.

If you've decided to buy a violin, look around to find a store that suits you, and try out several instruments and bows until you choose "The Ones."

My advice is to enjoy the process. Have a really good look around at what's available, and have some fun trying out violins to figure out what you like. In this chapter, you find out what to look for when you're buying a violin and bow, what kinds of stores to look in, and what decisions may work the best for you when you make your choice.

Picking a Violin That's Right for You

Finding the right violin isn't like buying groceries, or clothes, or even a car, where the label, make, and model number ensure uniformity. Each violin is unique, even if it's largely machine made, because the qualities of each individual piece of wood can vary. You may be keen to get your own violin, but spend time looking around at what's available before you commit to one specific instrument.

Your violin may look nice tucked away safely in its case, but what about when it comes out to play? You can spend a lot of money on a violin, only to discover that it has a crack that's hard to fix, or that the measurements are problematic, or that it simply doesn't make a sound that you like. In very general terms, you get a better violin when you pay more money, but you also need to know the main points to watch out for as you shop. Reading the following sections about what to look for and how to find it get you off to a good start.

The definition of a "good" violin is both objective and subjective: A "good" violin is in excellent playing condition (no open cracks, peeling varnish, or obvious faults in construction), has a clear sound that you like, and its price bracket is right for you.

The price is right

Before you establish any specific preferences in sound or appearance, or venture further into the actual buying process, decide on a price bracket that works for you. Establishing your price range right away keeps you from wasting your time looking at instruments you can't afford and helps you keep your expectations for your first violin realistic. So start by knowing what you can afford (about US$500 for a basic outfit, US$1,000 for a superior outfit, US$2,500 for a workshop violin with a suitable bow, and so on). Establish a likely price range — US$400 to US$600, for example — before actually trying some violins.

The number-one step in finding the right instrument for you is deciding on a price bracket and then being firm about it when you visit stores and dealers.

When figuring out what you can afford, factor in the instrument plus basic accessories to your equation, plus any applicable taxes, for the full estimate. You aren't just buying a violin, but a whole set of items:

- ✔ Violin
- ✔ Bow
- ✔ Case
- ✔ Rosin
- ✔ Set of spare strings
- ✔ Shoulder rest (if you, like most players, use one)

Buying a handmade violin

As you find out in Chapter 2, violins made by a *luthier,* a professional violin maker, can be any age, from newly minted off the workshop bench to more than 300 years old. Not all old violins are the handiwork of luthiers, however. Some older violins come from woodworkers who made all kinds of wooden artifacts, or from farmers who whittled away the winter months by making fiddles.

When you buy a handmade violin, you own a unique instrument that took months, or even years, to build. But as with all other crafts, some makers are superior to others, so the mere fact that a violin is handmade isn't in itself a guarantee of quality.

If you really love the idea of having your own unique instrument, consider buying a new violin made by a reputable maker in your area. You may even get to see your violin during the making process, and if it needs adjustments from time to time, the right person is close by. The violin may also be more stable (less susceptible to weather-related changes) because it was made in your home climate.

Find a maker in your area by checking out the *Yellow Pages* under "Violin Makers," asking local musicians, or checking the Web site of the Violin Society of America (www.vsa.to) or the sites of other professional bodies, such as the American Federation of Violin and Bow Makers (www.afvbm.com). These sites provide information about makers, valuable links to other sites, and a treasury of information.

When buying a violin, remember to budget for sales taxes if you're shopping in an area where these are tacked on to the retail price.

Most beginner and student violins come in *outfits* (the violin, bow, case, and all accessories come as a package deal). You buy workshop violins and handmade violins individually, and then you buy the bow and case separately. A violin shop has everything you need. If you want to do it all at once, you may be lucky enough to find a bow and case that you like at the same store where you buy your violin.

Here's a ballpark price guideline for what you can expect to pay for your instrument and accessories:

- ✔ **Factory outfits:** About US$300 to US$1,500, depending on the quality of the materials and the amount of hand-finishing (these violins come as an all-in-one deal with the bow and case).

- ✔ **Workshop violins:** Starting from about US$1,000 for the violin only. At the top end of the range, an excellent older violin from the Collin-Mézin workshop can cost you US$10,000 or more. You can find workshop violins at every price in between those "bookend" levels, with the majority retailing around US$2,000 to US$3,000. And then factor in at least US$300 for the bow for a basic workshop violin and US$200 or more for the case. Save up about US$50 to US$100 for your rosin and an extra set of strings.

✔ **Handmade violins:** These start at about US$3,000 and go up, up, up from there! A modern violin made in the United States by an established professional maker comes in at around US$10,000 to US$15,000, and an older, good-quality handmade violin costs about US$8,000. A good bow to match a moderately priced handmade violin can be about US$800, and for a fine violin, you're looking at bows priced around US$2,000 and up. A strong and well-furnished case may cost US$250 or more. The cost for rosin and extra strings is the same as with workshop violins.

Know that lots of factory and workshop violins have "Stradivarius" or "Guarnerius" labels inside. These labels aren't intended to defraud you — they're an open indication that the models of these violins are based on the shapes of the great instruments, something like marketing a Joe DiMaggio baseball glove.

Tip-top condition

Assessing every aspect of a violin takes a great deal of professional expertise. But the regular buyer can spend a few minutes checking out a violin's various parts to be sure they're in good condition. Check these features especially:

✔ **Bridge:** Look to see that the bridge sits between the notches of the f-holes. When you bow on the strings, a properly shaped bridge allows you to play on each string without touching the next string with your bow — but it also allows you to change from one string to the next without a bump! The bridge should be high enough so that you can land each finger on the strings and press down without great effort. But if the strings are too close to the fingerboard, you hear all kinds of extra buzzes from vibrating strings touching the fingerboard.

✔ **Cracks:** If it's an older instrument, check to see that any cracks that have happened over the years have been repaired with care, not left with gaps, or misaligned when glued together.

✔ **Neck and fingerboard:** Check that they're at a straight 90-degree angle to the body of the instrument. If the strings run closer to one side of the fingerboard than the other, or if the bridge is a bit off-center, the neck and fingerboard are crooked. The curvature of the fingerboard should match the shape of the bridge, though the bridge should be a bit lower on the E-string side. At the nut end of the fingerboard, just before the strings disappear into the pegbox, make sure that the four grooves for the strings are set equidistant from one another, and that the spacing between the grooves is comfortable for your fingers.

✔ **Wood and joints:** A good violin is in healthy condition in the wood and joints — no obvious warping, no wormholes or buckles in the body of the violin, and no cracks in the scroll. Check both the top and bottom plates of the violin where they join with the ribs — you shouldn't see any openings at all in any seams.

Ask the dealer whether the store's workshop has adjusted the violin's bridge, pegs, fingerboard, and sound post for a proper fit; otherwise, the bridge may buzz, the pegs may be hard to turn, playing in tune may be difficult, and the instrument won't project clearly.

Old news

Older violins can be charming and often have a mysterious history. The term "older" usually refers to violins about 50 to 100 years old, "old" means about 100 to 200 years old, and "very old" means over 200 years old. The oldest violins regularly in use today date from the last half of the 1600s, and the earliest surviving violin dates from 1560. You may not see the maker's name, even in some very fine instruments, because the label fell out long ago and the maker didn't leave any sign or mark inside the violin.

Old instruments can have the visual attraction of fine antique furniture (aged wood with that hard-to-describe but distinctive patina) and the deeper, richer sound that seems to evolve as instruments age. Generally, the more-expensive price tag reflects the antique value of the instrument because, obviously, the maker will not be producing any more like that.

Musicians have always been drawn to old violins, and this attraction doesn't seem to be changing, despite the recent renaissance in violin making. If you plan to go the antique route, watch carefully for all the pointers I give you in the "Tip-top condition" section, and buy from a trusted violin dealer or shop. Don't buy a "Stradivarius" on the street corner or in any other circumstances other than from an expert and reputable dealer. Fine instruments come with papers from an established dealer certifying their authenticity.

Sound advice

A good violin should have a clear and carrying sound, but your own sound preferences also guide you toward the violin that's best for you. Perhaps you like one with a more soprano timbre? Or a more alto timbre?

Trying out the violin yourself is important when deciding whether you like the sound. Make sure to play every regular note from open G to quite high up on the E string. Listen to each note carefully to hear if it sounds clear. Also climb up to high notes on each string. Although each string is distinct, the strength and quality of the sound should be similar as you play from one string to another. You shouldn't notice a drastic contrast between strings.

Fine workshops

France and Germany developed a significant business exporting workshop violins to Britain and North America between 1870 and 1950. These instruments are attractive today because they have a more mature sound and an antique look. Some top violin workshops include Roth, Heberlein, Neuner, and Hornsteiner in Germany and Laberte, Mougenot, and Collin-Mezin in France. Some successful new Chinese workshops include Eastman Strings in Beijing and the Jay Haide and Scott Cao workshops in Guangzhou. These companies are enjoying a business advantage due to the low cost of Chinese labor, and they're using the opportunity to make well-designed violins made almost entirely by hand.

Most violins have a *wolf note,* a note that may sound wobbly when you play it. You typically find this note high on the G string. If you find a wolf note on your violin, check all other notes of the same name to be sure the wolf doesn't affect the whole violin. One wolf note, if not very big and bad, is nothing to be afraid of. But look at other violins if you find more than one, or ask the shop to check the adjustment of the violin you're trying.

If, after playing, you decide that you like a particular violin, ask someone else to play it for you too. Most specialist violin shops hire music students or young graduates to assist you, or you can bring a violinist friend or your teacher along with you. When someone else plays the violin, you can really focus on the sound, without distractions. Occasionally, a violin sounds strong and bold under your ear, but strident or tinny when you listen from across a room. Have the person play the violin in a good-sized room, to make sure that the sound travels well and continues to retain the qualities that pleased you when the violin was snuggled under your ear.

"Will I be happy every time I open the case?" is a good diagnostic question to ask yourself if you're unsure about buying a particular violin.

All about appearance

Traditionally, violin makers stain and varnish the wood when the violin is near completion. Violin colors range from a blonde champagne to almost black, with most instruments in the mid-range of slightly golden brown to chestnut-colored. Nowadays, some student violins are available in funky finishes, such as bright blue.

Carbon fiber violins

To keep right up to date, you need to know about violins made of carbon fiber, which have arrived on the market in recent years. Luis Leguia, a cellist in the Boston Symphony Orchestra who's also a sailing enthusiast, took his inspiration for the idea of building a carbon fiber cello from the lightness and durability of sailing boats. A few trial models later, he arrived at a fine-sounding solution, and from there, his company, Luis and Clark, went on to build violas and violins using the same principles. These instruments sound excellent and are very stable in different temperatures and climates. Having no seams to open, no varnish to ruin, and a very cool look are also big advantages. The shape is a little more like a guitar, with rounded corners, but the playing experience is physically similar to playing any other violin, in terms of overall dimensions, string length, neck shape, and response. Retailing around US$5,000, a carbon fiber instrument can sound quite a lot better than many wooden ones in the same price range.

Appearance doesn't directly affect how good your violin sounds. But if you like modern, new, perfect-looking violins, you may not be happy with one that is older and a bit beaten up. Similarly, if you love the look of dark, old wood, think carefully before you buy a violin with a bright, shiny varnish. Often, however, appearance becomes a less important consideration when you really like the sound of an instrument.

Sizing Up the Violin

Unlike the piano, which comes only in full size, violins can be scaled down to suit smaller players. A 3-year-old beginning the violin can use a tiny violin and feel very comfortable. These smaller violins are called *fractional size* violins, and they have nothing to do with your grade-school math class. The fraction is rumored to refer to the volume of air inside the body of the violin — but I haven't poured water inside each size of violin to substantiate this claim!

The smallest child-size violin is $\frac{1}{32}$ size, which would usually be suitable for a 2- or 3-year-old, and then young students can grow through seven other sizes: $\frac{1}{16}$, $\frac{1}{10}$, $\frac{1}{8}$, $\frac{1}{4}$, $\frac{1}{2}$, $\frac{3}{4}$, $\frac{7}{8}$ . . . till they finally reach full size, also referred to as $\frac{4}{4}$ size. Most students skip over $\frac{7}{8}$ size because, by then, they're growing pretty fast and reach full size directly from the $\frac{3}{4}$ size. By the way, the fractional-sized violins don't look quite as tiny as their names suggest, although a $\frac{1}{32}$ violin is pretty tiny by any standards.

On the other side of the equation (because we're discussing mathematics!), no special, big, full-sized violin exists for football players. A $\frac{4}{4}$ violin has to work for everyone, because making the violin's body any bigger would affect the sound and make it too deep. Deeper sounds belong to the violin's cousin, the viola.

Generally, ¼ violins have a back length of approximately 14 inches and are all made from the same basic pattern. But some variations do exist that may affect the fit of a violin to a particular player. For example, a person with small hands may prefer more gently sloping shoulders on a violin because they're easier to get around for shifting. (I explain about shifting in Chapter 14.)

Here are a few considerations about physical proportions for adults trying out violins:

- ✔ **Small in stature (about 5 foot to 5 foot 4 inches tall):** You may need a "ladies"-sized violin, which has a back length of 13¾ to 13⅞ inches.

- ✔ **Tall in stature (more than 6 foot tall):** Try out a 14⅛- to 14¼-inch model of violin, usually French.

- ✔ **Smaller hand span:** You may play better with a string length that's slightly shorter than the normal length of 327 millimeters.

Never buy a child a violin that's too big, thinking he or she will "grow into" it — the physical stress causes playing discomfort and, possibly, injury.

Violins come in all sizes

If you're looking for a violin to suit a child (or someone who is quite small) and you can get to a specialist violin shop that deals in fractional-sized instruments, an expert salesperson can help you choose the right size of violin. Also, music teachers can help with the choice. If you don't have access to live advice, here are a few pointers for finding the right size:

- ✔ Have the child hold the violin in playing position (refer to Chapter 3), and reach his left hand out, palm up, to grasp around the scroll from underneath (see Chapter 2). If he can curve his fingers easily around most of the scroll and his left elbow is very slightly bent, the violin is the right size.

- ✔ If the child is lightly built, you should test the overall weight of the violin, as well as the balance, to make sure it won't be too heavy for the child to hold up and play.

- ✔ Sometimes, a child has hands that are larger or smaller than average for her body size, so it's worth considering the next size up or down. Also, because the fractional sizes aren't standardized, two ¼-sized violins can vary in size and width. Try a few different makes before choosing.

In case you're wondering, the world's smallest violin was made by Eric Meissner of Queen Anne, Seattle, in about 1977. It measures 1⅝ inches and emits a tiny but clear sound when bowed. The minuscule violin would probably be the right size for Tinkerbell!

Buying the Best Bow

When I say "best bow," I really mean "best bow for you." Those two extra words are important because not every bow is a good match for you or your violin. The choices of available bows are pretty stunning. If you don't stick to a predetermined price category and description, you risk getting overwhelmed and missing out on the right bow.

Believe me, buy the bow *after* you buy your violin. The violin is the bigger investment, and a perfectly good bow can sound much better on one instrument than on another — for mysterious acoustical and physical reasons that would take a whole other book to explain!

Your bow should cost about a quarter of the price you pay for your violin, as a general guideline. So if you paid US$1,000 for your violin, try a bow in the US$200 to US$300 price range. (I just put that in to show off my great math skills.)

What bows are made of

Not all bows are made of the same material. They vary in balance, strength, flexibility, and above all, price. This list helps you to consider the pros and cons of each bow material:

- **Pernambuco:** Bows made of this traditional material are resilient, flexible, and strong (refer to Chapter 4). But a pernambuco bow can set you back a fair bit of cash, anywhere from about US$400 and up.

- **Brazilwood:** Bows made of brazilwood have almost as much resilience and strength as do pernambuco bows, but they're more affordable. There's a price difference because the wood is very similar to, but not quite as fine as, pernambuco.

- **Composite bows:** In the last 20 years or so, composite bows have gone from being rigid bits of plastic, useful for walloping your high school stand partner on the head, to being a viable alternative to wooden bows. Composite bows of good quality don't come cheap, but they're worth considering if you live in an extreme climate where wood bows may be too unpredictable or if you like innovative products. Most composite bows are made of carbon fiber, a polymer with special bonding qualities that make it strong and flexible — perfect attributes for a violin bow (and, incidentally, for mountain and road bikes, canoes, high-end basketball shoes, and violins too!).

The best reason of all for choosing a bow is that you've found one that sounds good on your violin.

Dr. Bow's checklist for good bow health

Just as your family doctor has a specific checklist when you go for your annual physical, so do violinists when it's time to give their bows a careful once-over. Here are your bow health indicators:

✔ **Look down the stick from the screw end towards the tip.** Close one eye and treat the bow like a telescope to check that it's straight. If a bow bends sideways when you're playing, you lose tonal power and fine control.

✔ **Compare the plane of the frog and the tip to check for twisting.** Close one eye and hold the bow pointing straight out in front of you at about waist level, centering the stick above the frog, to see if the two ends are upright. A twist in the stick causes several playing difficulties.

✔ **Look carefully at the frog, stick, and white bow tip for cracks.** Cracks weaken the bow, and may even cause it to break completely at inconvenient moments (not that *any* moment seems convenient for a bow to break!).

✔ **Look for a straight grain in the bow stick, ideally without knots, which may affect the smoothness or tonal qualities of the bow.** Some knots do "knot" affect the playing characteristics, though.

✔ **Check the screw for smooth functioning.** The threads in the eyelet inside the frog may be about to fail, which is a mechanical problem that requires a new bit, or the screw may simply need a spot of oil to restore its functions.

✔ **Flex the bow gently to verify the reasonable strength of the stick.** But don't twist the head when you flex the bow.

In addition to this list, you can give a bow a look-over to check its general condition, especially to see that the frog fits well on the stick, with no wobbles, and the eyes on the frog are present and correct.

How the bow feels

Quite simply, the right bow feels comfortable in your hand, which depends mainly on two factors: weight and shape. Two bows may weigh the same amount, but their weight can be distributed more toward the frog end or the tip end of the bow. If the tip is a little heavy, you may feel the bow is stable when landing on the strings. However, if the tip is too heavy for your hand, your pinky finger may become sore from overwork. Choosing a bow is a delicate balance.

The shape of the frog can vary too; one frog can suit your hand better than another. Bow sticks are available in round or octagonal shapes, but all sticks are octagonal at the frog end.

A matter of ethics

Your teacher may advise you when you're buying a violin and bow, but it's not a great idea for a teacher to actually sell an instrument to a student, because of the conflict of interest.

Suppose you're looking at two instruments, one from your teacher and the other from a shop. If your teacher doesn't like the one from the shop, your teacher may well be right, but how can you feel certain that your teacher's opinions are objective? On the other hand, your teacher may actually recommend the one from the shop, even if it isn't quite as good, in a concerted effort to be impartial. So even with a well-intentioned teacher — the great majority, I add — your relationship can suffer.

It may make sense to do the deal through your teacher when another student from the same studio is selling an instrument and your teacher gets you in touch with that student, because the violin could be just right for you. In that case, the financial details can be settled directly with the other student, leaving your teacher free from conflicts of interest.

A teacher can spend a lot of time looking at instruments with you, often with no compensation other than knowing that you've found the right instrument. You may decide to compensate your teacher by offering to pay them an agreed fee for looking for a violin with you, or by using some prepaid lesson time to look at instruments.

Deciding Whether to Rent or Buy Your Violin

Another big decision that goes along with finding your perfect instrument is whether you want to rent a violin or buy one. Both options have their ups and downs, so consider them carefully to know what's right for you.

If buying a violin is beyond your budget — or if it seems like too much of a commitment before you're sure you want to keep playing — starting off with a rented violin may be just right for you. In this section, I go over the reasons why you may want to buy a violin and why you may want to rent a violin. I also discuss that wonderful hybrid, the rent-to-buy program.

Buying

Buying your first violin is an exciting moment if you know that you get enough joy out of music to want to continue playing for a long time. I list a few indicators for you to consider when deciding if the time is right for you to buy your own instrument, such as, if you

✔ Are in it for the long haul.

✔ Enjoy the idea of playing (and caring for) your very own violin.

✔ Have enough money to pay for the violin, the bow, and a case. (I give you some ballpark prices for violins and accessories earlier in this chapter.)

✔ Have an established and trustworthy dealer in your area, or have a friend who's really knowledgeable about instruments to advise you.

Some large and established violin stores have online buying options, and they're happy to send you an instrument on approval.

Negotiating for a discount can possibly be an option, especially if you're buying the bow and case at the same store. However, the business side must happen fairly discreetly because violin stores aren't geared to overt bargaining! One way of finding out about discounts is to ask if the store gives a discount when you buy the bow and case there too. A good moment to ask is when you've decided on a violin and are about to look at bows.

Usually, you can't get a discount on an outfit, because selling outfits is very competitive between stores. The package deal is already set at the lowest price a store can offer without losing money.

Also, you can ask if the price is negotiable. If a store is selling a violin for a private seller, you may have some leeway — the seller may be keen to sell sooner rather than later, and the store receives a percentage of the sale price. If a violin was purchased by a store and then put through their workshop, the price probably isn't flexible, because the store has their investment and overhead to consider.

If your child is starting on the violin and you can afford to buy him his own instrument, I believe that's a good idea. Pride of ownership and having one's very own violin are important feelings for children to have. Although each violin size typically lasts a student for a couple of years, most shops are geared to giving back a certain credit when you return to buy the next size up from them. This is a long-term investment for the shop, but it's a good one — if your child is fairly serious and makes good headway, each violin he goes through is a bit of an upgrade in quality, and buying the full-sized one can be a substantial investment.

Renting

When you're just starting out, renting a violin from a reputable store for a few months can be just the ticket. You don't have to make a significant financial investment right away, but you do have the chance to get comfortable with a starter violin and gain some playing skills before you choose your own instrument.

Some music schools offer rental instruments, but you need to be sure that the instruments are of good quality in craftsmanship. Find out if the violins go through a workshop each time they change hands, to ensure the best playing condition.

With a good-quality rental, you can explore the instrument and enjoy learning. You won't feel stressed about paying off a chunk of money for a violin you've only just begun playing.

When renting a violin, people typically sign on for a six-month or one-year contract, paying a monthly rental fee. Renting for longer than a year starts to add up to more than the cost of a student outfit, so by that point, buying makes a lot of sense.

Some stores apply the first three months' rental fees directly to a purchase, and if at that point you decide to buy the violin you've been renting, you end up with the rental costs deducted from the price of the outfit. If you continue renting for longer than three months, you may be able to apply a percentage (typically up to 50 percent) of the rental fees toward a purchase. Check your contract, and ask about this arrangement at the store.

Most stores offer the option of drawing up an insurance contract for your rental, if you aren't able to cover the violin under your household insurance policy. A quick call to your insurance company tells you whether you need the store's insurance connection. If you insure through a store policy, check what's covered. You may be insured against accidents and theft but not careless events, such as forgetting your violin on a bus. Factor in the deductible, too, when making a final decision.

Renting to buy

And finally, some stores offer rent-to-buy programs, where part of the rental fees you have accumulated are discounted from the purchase price of a violin. The closest comparison in regular daily life is leasing a car. You have some security because you can return the "goods" if you aren't satisfied or if you choose to discontinue, but you pay for these options, and the total cost is greater. Opting for a rent-to-buy program works if money is tight, because you don't have to put out a large sum all at once. You gradually "save" a considerable sum toward purchasing your own violin, and the credit that you accumulate may be used toward buying an upgrade violin, too, not just the one you have been renting.

Some music stores have a connection with a financing company that can arrange a loan toward buying instruments from that store. Compare the interest rates involved in such a loan (or a loan from your bank) with the total cost of a rent-to-buy option. Doing so clarifies which choice is best for you.

Say hello to Stradivarius

Antonio Stradivarius is the only violin maker's name that is well known to the general public. One of a family of instrument builders, Antonio had the most successful and famous violin-making business of all time, based in the Italian city of Cremona, which is still a violin-making center today. His career arrived on the crest of the wave of violin making that swept through Italy as violins evolved into their modern form and became such desirable instruments.

The combination of beautiful craftsmanship and a flawlessly golden sound makes these instruments the most sought-after of all — even after 300 years. A Stradivarius violin sold for more than US$3.5 million at an auction in 2006, the record price to date.

With both rental and rent-to-buy programs, conditions and details vary quite a bit between stores. So make sure that the quality of the violin (refer to "Picking a Violin That's Right for You," earlier in this chapter) and the details of the contract are to your liking before you sign on the dotted line. Take a magnifying glass, read the small print, and ask any questions you need to have answered before you sign. You can even take the contract home to read it.

Finding Your Violin

Having a plan of action before you set out to find yourself a violin can involve making a couple of calls. If you know a violinist or a music teacher at a local high school, ask that person about leads on good violins. Your expert may be able to connect you with a good store, a maker in the area, a former student who's selling an instrument . . . there are all kinds of possible connections. You can also search via several other options, which I tell you about in this section.

- **Music stores:** Looking at general music stores may be a fine option, and they're certainly a good source of rental instruments (refer to "Deciding Whether to Rent or Buy Your Violin"). But depending on the store owner's interests and the demand for violins, the violins can be excellent, or they can be a mere afterthought in the business. Ask a few questions before you commit to buying a violin from a general music store:

  - Do you have a professional violin maker setting up and repairing your instruments?

  - Do you have a trade-in policy if I want to move to another instrument?

- May I take this instrument on a week's approval to try it out and to show it to my teacher?

  If you take an instrument to try it out for a week, you're required to sign a form to take liability for the safety and condition of the instrument.

✔ **Specialist violin stores:** Shops that deal exclusively in violins (and other string instruments) offer more choice than stores that sell only a few violins. Because a specialist store's livelihood depends on selling violins and having local string players recommend their store to colleagues, friends, and students, it has to do things right. The violins probably have been through the workshop for adjustments and fixings before they arrive on display.

Prices are sometimes a little higher at specialist violin stores, so if you're looking at a basic violin outfit, compare among a few stores before you buy.

You may not have a specialist violin store in your area. But if you know of one that's within a few hours' drive, taking the trip is definitely worth it. You can speak to the expert staff, check the wide selection, or just gawk at the gorgeous violins.

✔ **Private dealers:** Private dealers usually stock a combination of a few student outfits, instruments that they're selling on commission, and, perhaps, some instruments they've invested in at auctions or estate sales. If the dealer is a knowledgeable and fair person, you can do well. But as with other situations where you need an expert opinion, such as finding a good dentist or plumber, get a recommendation. Dealers aren't obliged to be part of a professional body that guarantees competencies and ethical standards. However, because of the lower overheads from not operating out of a store, you may do well with a private dealer, so long as you have some good guarantees in place.

Most stores give you credit for the instrument you buy there, if you go back a few years later to upgrade. When you buy from a private dealer, an individual, or an auction, you probably won't have a safety net for reselling the instrument at a later date.

✔ **Individual private sellers:** Looking at the classified ads in newspapers sometimes yields a lucky find. You may find an instrument in good order, like the sound, and then buy it for less than its retail price. However, you need to show the instrument to an expert before you buy, just to be sure that you aren't investing in some extra woodworms along with the violin, or that you aren't chancing any other disappointment.

✔ **Auctions:** Big auction houses in major cities hold musical instrument sales two or three times a year. Dealers come from all over the world to try to spot the right violin for a potential customer, or to stock up with a few instruments to sell at their stores. Viewing the violins is interesting, but the choice is overwhelming. Smaller auction houses sometimes sell musical instruments as part of an estate sale or general art sale. You can keep your eyes open for such sales, but again, you need an expert to come along with you to make sure you're buying a healthy instrument at a fair price. Violins sold at auction are often in disrepair, or they're unplayable, so assessing the sound is difficult.

Auction prices for instruments are generally more reasonable than store prices. But that difference is mostly because the store spends money on repair and setup before displaying the instrument.

Although online auction sites are popular, I don't recommend them as good places to buy your violin. You can't try out the instrument or view it before buying, so you can't be sure of what you're getting.

Getting Plugged into Electric Violins

If you're a rocker at heart, or you dig other nonclassical styles, you may find the sound you're looking for in *electric,* or *electronic,* violins. Folk, fiddle, country, and rock players use these violins to get power and projection, along with a more strident tone that can hold its own against the guitars and percussion. Blues violinist Stuff Smith (find out more about him in Chapter 15) was one of the first performers to try using an amplified violin sound. Although electric violins were available in the 1930s and '40s, they weren't universally popular until the end of the century.

I know that electric violins are cool, but if you're a beginner, I recommend you start off with a traditional acoustic violin. Then, when you're a more experienced musician with solid playing techniques (like the ones in this book), you can add a pickup, which I talk about in the next section.

Acoustic pickups

Adding a *pickup* (also known as a *transducer*) for your regular acoustic violin gives your violin that rocking sound. The pickup is a small, metallic gizmo, about the size of a fingernail, that's usually wedged on the side of the bridge. The pickup takes your sound vibrations and converts them into electric signals that are augmented through an amplifier. The input jack (better pickups have a ¼-inch jack) attaches to the side of your violin, just to the left of the chinrest, and even uses a similar kind of bracket to attach to your violin. You can buy a very inexpensive pickup for as little as US$10, or a quality pickup for US$200 or more.

Some pickups (called active pickups) are battery-powered and feature electronic components inside. These components turn your sounds into signals for the amplifiers, although active pickups are usually reserved for electric violins. You don't have to use an amplifier that's specifically made for the acoustic violin, although it gives you the best sound. A keyboard amp is fairly well adapted to violin sounds, and a guitar amp may work as well.

Classical players tend to prefer microphone pickups, such as the Shure, which is truer to natural sounds. Jazz and bluegrass players prefer *piezo* pickups for more stable output. (See "Electric violins" for more about piezo pickups.) Any musical instrument with an acoustic chamber, such as your violin's bodacious body, may encounter *feedback* problems (high-pitched shrieks or crackly noises) from all the reverberations. So if you don't have a really good amplifier to use, you need to use a pre-amp too, such as a Fishman Pro EQ-2, after which the violin sounds fine with an average-quality amplifier. The *transducer,* a neat little device, filters out extra tones, keeping the sound clear and distinct.

Check out the Web sites of these fine companies for more information about available products:

- **AMT:** www.appliedmicrophone.com
- **Fishman:** www.fishman.com
- **Headway:** www.headwayelectronics.com
- **Schatten:** www.schattendesign.com

Electric violins

In the previous section, I talk about adding a pickup to a regular, acoustic violin, making it acoustic-electric. If you want to have a fully electric instrument, violin models are available without hollow acoustic chambers.

These electric models, which usually look a bit like the outline of a traditional violin, have virtually no sound when played unamplified. In these violins, the piezo transducer typically does its work from under the feet of the bridge, to pick up the reverberations of the violin sounds. *Piezo* is a crystal composite, sensitive to mechanical pressure, that can "translate" the sounds into various electric impulses. Electric violins are available from many major manufacturers, including Yamaha, Fender, and Zeta, and they retail from about US$300 for a basic model to over US$2,000 for a very fancy violin.

You can use your regular violin bow and strings on electric violins.

Taking a bow to Tourte

Although his father and brother were bow makers, François Tourte originally began his professional career as a clockmaker. Tourte's knowledge of metals, physics, and mathematics helped him in his second career, too, and after he moved over to bow making, his innovations in bow structure led to the kind of bow we still use today.

Tourte's achievements include establishing the standard length of the bow and making the tip and the frog both a little heavier and denser for more versatility of sound. Also, he most likely designed the silver ferrule to keep the bow hair flat and even. Earlier bows used snakewood, chinawood, and ironwood, but Tourte established that pernambuco wood offers the best combination of lightness, strength, and flexibility for string players.

Interestingly, he may have had access to pernambuco wood from casks containing sugar imported from Brazil. He was closely associated with the violinist Viotti, whose style promoted a full singing tone, and great clarity of articulations — perfect attributes of the Tourte bows!

Chapter 17

Polishing Your Assets:
Violin Care and Maintenance

Taking good care of your violin isn't rocket science, but it does take some specialized knowledge. With a good mix of time-honored methods combined with new-fangled technologies, you can easily take great care of your violin. In this chapter, you find out about caring for your instrument and bow — from cleaning and polishing the violin to changing the strings and putting on a new chinrest. I also alert you to some useful accessories that violinists use to make life easier — and more fun.

Cleaning Up

This bit may remind you of when guests come to visit, and you have to clean up your place so you appear to live in a state of perfect suspended animation. The one time all violinists always remember to dust off their instruments is before concerts, when they want to look (and sound) their best. But also, on a regular basis, violins and strings need general dusting and cleaning to stay in tip-top condition.

Violins actually sound better when their vibrations aren't impeded by dust and their strings are clear of ingrained rosin.

Daily dusting

The most frequent cleanup you do is dusting off your violin after playing. Little rosin flakes and dust build up on the top of the violin, just under the strings. Rosin debris may start out like dust, but with warmth and time, it melts and adheres very strongly to your violin's varnish — that's why cleaning it off right away is so important. So keep your violin happy by giving its table a quick and light wipe every time you put it away, while the rosin dust is fresh, easy to see, and easy to wipe off.

Figure 17-1 shows you where to dust: First, give a general swish over the body of the violin, and then wipe specifically under the main bowing area. Use a soft cloth, such as a traditional yellow dusting cloth or one of the new microfiber cleaning cloths, which are very effective. Dust off the table of your violin with a few light strokes, as if you were dusting a dining table before visitors arrive. Then make sure you dust the wood directly under the strings between the bridge and the fingerboard, where most of the rosin dust accumulates as you bow.

Figure 17-1:
Dusting off
the top of
your violin.

Cleaning the strings

The body of the violin doesn't get all the special treatment — your strings need attention too. Most violinists cut up an old T-shirt to use for cleaning the strings, because this job involves some surprisingly mucky results! Pay particular attention to two different areas of the strings when you clean them off: Rosin builds up on the strings where you play the bow, and grease, dirt, and sweat from your left-hand fingers build up on the strings and fingerboard. Now isn't that a romantic thought? Washing your hands before you play helps keep the strings and fingerboard clean.

Using the same soft cloth to wipe the two areas simply won't do; you spread finger grease on the bowing areas and sticky rosin on the fingering areas.

As suggested, if you're using old T-shirts to clean your strings, cut up two different T-shirts into cleaning cloths, each about 6 to 8 inches square. That way, you keep the two areas separate: For example, a white T-shirt can serve the fingerboard, and a pale blue T-shirt can clean the bow area of the strings.

To clean the strings, gather the cloth in the palm of your hand, and then wipe lightly along the length of the strings as they pass over the fingerboard. I show you how to do this in Figure 17-2.

About once a month, give your strings and fingerboard an even more thorough cleaning using a little rubbing alcohol to keep them in tip-top condition. (Get in the habit of doing so at the beginning or end of each month.) Simply follow these steps, which I demonstrate in Figure 17-3 and show you on the CD-ROM:

1. **Put a small spot of alcohol on a cloth, making it damp but not dripping.**

2. **Wipe the strings and fingerboard using a smooth and firm up-and-down motion along the length of the strings, so that you clean the surface of the fingerboard as well as the strings themselves.**

Some student violins have fingerboards made of cheaper wood than ebony. The fingerboard is then painted or stained black to look like real ebony. If you notice black stain on the damp cloth, don't continue with alcohol, just wipe the fingerboard with a dry duster.

3. **Clean off the strings between the bridge and the top of the fingerboard, where the bow plays, with a different piece of the damp cloth.**

    You can rub quite firmly on each string until the rosin deposit is cleared off.

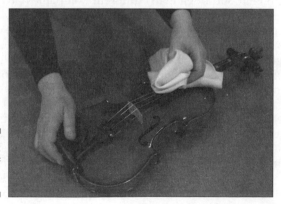

Figure 17-2:
Dusting off
the strings.

Figure 17-3:
Cleaning the
strings and
fingerboard
with rubbing
alcohol.

Getting rubbing alcohol on the varnish of your violin seriously damages it.
Slipping a soft plastic bag or an absorbent cloth between the fingerboard and
the top of the violin while you clean the strings and fingerboard prevents
mishaps.

Polishing the wood

In addition to daily dustings and monthly string cleanings, you can give your
violin another special beauty treatment: About once a year, take a soft cloth
and treat the wood to a shine-up.

Don't use any old garden-variety furniture polish for cleaning violins. Violins
need a special compound. Although many different companies produce violin
polish, most of them contain similar ingredients, such as linseed oil, wax, and
turpentine. Polish comes in attractive little bottles (about the size of those
shampoo bottles in hotel bathrooms) and costs a bit more than rosin, but
one investment lasts you for several applications. You can buy polish from a
violin store or from some general music stores that also deal in violins. One
drop of polish is enough for the whole violin body.

Use a soft cotton cloth to apply the polish in small circular motions, rub it till
it's dry, and then use a clean rag to wipe off any residue. Small polishing
motions work best, rather like when you polish your glasses, and elbow
grease is not required.

You hear a little rubbing sound when you are polishing your violin thoroughly.

Polish must go on only the varnished parts of the violin's main body — not on the strings, neck, chinrest, or anywhere else — because its oil ingredients would make nonvarnished areas too slippery to play. Test the polish on a small area of the violin before you use the polish on the whole body of your instrument.

You may be tempted to use a lot of polish, but using a lot only causes sticky gunk to build up on the surface of the instrument. The main point of polishing your violin is to clean any dust off the wood and to remove any little drops of sweat or spit that may have found their way onto your precious instrument. When you're done polishing the violin, it should look lovely and clean, just as when you bought it.

Some violin makers and repairers believe that polish can eventually damage the varnish of a violin, through buildup and through attracting more dust if it isn't properly wiped off. Also, manufacturers aren't obliged to list the ingredients of their polish compounds, so you don't really know what's in the bottle. If you're not sure about using polish, don't bother with it. By good daily dusting habits, you keep your violin pretty clean anyway.

Changing Strings

Your relationship with the violin isn't one of those "no strings attached" kinds of things! Beyond cleaning the strings regularly (as I describe in the section "Cleaning Up"), you have to change the strings every once in a while too. An experienced violinist makes changing the strings look simple: She just pops off the old string and winds on the new one in the space of about one minute. So how come when you first try to change a string, you get into a complete tangle and can't get the peg to stay in place? Actually, you need to know quite a few steps, and I take you through the moves so that you can do this for yourself. I also demonstrate them on your CD-ROM.

Set the violin down safely on a secure horizontal surface (a sofa, a bed, a table with a towel spread on it) for changing strings. Then if you sneeze, or the cat pounces on you, nothing can happen to the fiddle.

Taking off the old strings

You may need to remove the old strings in a few different situations, each of which requires its own special treatment. In this section, I tell you about the most frequent situations you encounter, and I take you through the steps to deal with them.

I must stress the importance of removing and replacing the strings *one at a time.* This process ensures that the bridge stays safely in place and the sound post inside the violin remains vertical.

Undoing a string when it's time for a change

Your string has done noble service, but you may notice that it just isn't doing its job like it used to. Here are three telltale signs that let you know your string needs replacing:

- ✔ The string is becoming frayed and rough for your fingers to play on.

- ✔ Part of the string (usually at the high-tension places, like where the string runs over the bridge or at the nut) is beginning to break, and it looks as if it may pop at any moment.

- ✔ The string has been on for a long time (maybe over a year), and its sound is less clear and consistent than it used to be.

In any of these cases, watch my demonstration on the CD-ROM and then follow these steps (and see Figure 17-4) to remove that old string:

1. **Turn the peg to loosen the string, slowly at first, until the string's tension is reduced.**

2. **Unwind the string completely from around the peg.**

3. **Pull out the very end of the string from where it's threaded through the little hole in the peg.**

   Hold on to the end of the string as you pull it out from the peg so that it doesn't escape you or scratch your face.

4. **Pull the top end of the string out of the slot in the tailpiece.**

   Just pull the end of the string toward the round part of the slot. The metal ball or the knotted end of the string comes out of the tailpiece easily, and then the whole string is free!

After you remove the old string, make sure you keep track of the peg. Pegs can easily fall on the floor and roll away, or get eaten by the family dog, when they aren't kept attached to a string.

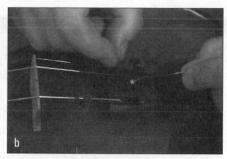

Figure 17-4: Unwinding the peg and removing the string from peg and tailpiece.

Taking off a broken string

Sometimes a string just breaks suddenly, and you have two ends to deal with separately. Here's how to deal with this tricky situation (check it out in Figure 17-5):

1. **Take hold of the string near the tailpiece and then pull the knot or metal ball end through the top of the slot in the tailpiece, and the string will come out easily.**

   You take off the part that's attached to the tailpiece first, because that's the end of the string that's usually pretty straightforward to deal with.

   If your string is fitted into a fine tuner, you just need to pull it in an upward motion out of the slot.

2. **Remove the part of the string that's wound round the peg by gently pulling on the broken end and unraveling the rest from the peg.**

If the peg is sticky, you need to turn the peg to loosen it first. Go slowly, because the end of the string can flick into your face if you pull it too enthusiastically, and the peg can become dislodged from the peg hole, drop on the floor, and then roll to some obscure place that's hard to find.

Occasionally, the string pops with such force that the end gets tangled around the peg. In this case, loosen the string gently and then use tweezers to pry the string loose from around the peg. If your tweezers are AWOL, unfurl a paperclip slightly and then sneak it around or under the recalcitrant string, just like undoing a wrong stitch in knitting.

Keeping a pair of tweezers in your case compartment, for grabbing tangled strings, is certainly a very well-organized move! And while you're being perfect, add a tiny pair of scissors for snipping off bow hairs that snap occasionally.

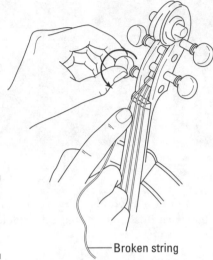

Figure 17-5:
Removing a
broken
string.

—— Broken string

Prepping the pegs and string

After you have taken off the old string, you need to get the pegs and new
string all ready before you can replace the old string. If you find that the peg
isn't turning smoothly, this is a good chance to apply peg dope or graphite to
the peg. I talk more about applying peg dope in Chapter 2. If you're happy
with the peg, no need to apply any compound.

You can buy strings in sets or individually. If you're a beginner violinist, buy
a full set of strings, because any major maker will have a set that suits your
violin, and you get a better price by buying all four strings together. When
you've been playing for a while and have greater skill (and a fancier instrument), you may want to buy individual strings so that you can mix and match
for your ideal sound and response.

Strings usually come in envelopes with labels that identify what string is
inside. Strings that don't come in envelopes (gut strings need to be stored in
tubes because bending them causes damage) have small labels (like little
baggage tags) tied on to them to identify the strings (I=E, II=A, III=D, IV=G).
Checking the gauge or thickness of strings is not a good way to identify a
string. The differences are subtle, and string thickness varies between makes
and materials.

When you take the string out of its envelope, notice that manufacturers wrap
silk thread around the string at each end to protect it from wear and tear,

using different colors of thread to identify each string. One end of the string has the colors that signify the make of the string, and the colors are the same for all strings of that set. The other end shows the color code for the string's pitch (G, D, A, E). Sometimes, the pitch colors are at the tailpiece end of the string, and other times, they're at the peg end. Just to make things more fun (ahem), each company uses its own system, so a Dominant-made A string may have a different colored thread than one made by Pirastro, for example. But the color-coding is clear after you get to know the system and are familiar with the colors for the set and manufacturer you use.

Prepping the string is pretty straightforward: Just remove it from its envelope (strings usually come in envelopes these days), and then unfurl the string to its full length. The end with the knot (or small metal ball) slots into the tailpiece or fine tuner, and the other end goes into the peg.

Putting on strings attached at the tailpiece

If your string attaches to the violin directly at the tailpiece, follow these steps to attach the new string (I illustrate the move in Figure 17-6.):

1. **Hold the top end of the string, which has a knot or a small metal ball in it, between your thumb and index finger.**

2. **Insert the ball or knot downward into the little hole at the top end of the slot in the tailpiece.**

   Make sure the knot or metal ball at the end of the string has gone through to the underside of the tailpiece.

3. **Give a little tug in the direction of the violin's scroll, so that the end of the string slips snugly right into the bottom end of the slot.**

Usually, it works to "post" the string in from on top of the tailpiece, but occasionally, the ball end of a string is too big to fit through from on top. In this case, thread the string through from underneath the tailpiece, between the tailpiece and the violin. Start with the far end of the string, the one that's going to wrap around the peg, and then thread the whole string through the tailpiece until the ball end is lodged safely in its slot.

Occasionally, the winding at the tailpiece end of a string is just too wide to fit in the slot of the tailpiece. You may have to ask your friendly neighborhood luthier to widen the slot slightly — not a big deal.

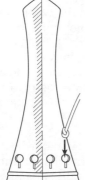

Figure 17-6:
Attaching a
string at the
tailpiece.

Putting on strings attached to fine tuners

If your string goes into a fine tuner attached to the tailpiece, you need to determine what kind of attachment you have in your violin. Typically, A, D, and G strings have a ball-end attachment, so I describe that first.

Ball-end strings

Your fine tuner may be a metal gizmo that's attached to the tailpiece, or it may be built in to the tailpiece itself. Either way, the method for attaching the string is very similar.

Take the top bit of string near the ball end between your finger and thumb, and then slot the ball into the little groove in the fine tuner so that the ball end is snugly in place. I show you the moves in Figure 17-7.

If your string is too thick to fit in the fork of the fine tuner gizmo, just take a pair of nail clippers, open out the nail file bit, slot it into the fork, and then gently widen the space very slightly.

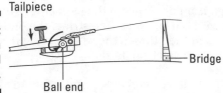

Figure 17-7:
Attaching a
ball-end
string.

Tailpiece

Bridge

Ball end

Loop-end strings

Some E-string fine tuners have a hook for attaching the top of the string. In this case, you buy a string with a loop end. E string packets always tell you whether the string has a loop end or a ball end, so that you know which one you're buying.

Attaching the loop may remind you of your grandmother's crochet hooks. Start by making sure your loop can fit on to the little hook on the fine tuner. Thread the peg end of the string through the E peg, and then tighten the peg gradually. Pause now and then to make sure the loop is still attached before you tighten the string fully. (See Figure 17-8.)

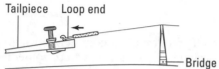

Figure 17-8: Attaching a loop-end E string.

If you're not sure what you need, take your violin with you to the store, and the assistant will, well, *assist* you to buy the right E string.

Tightening the strings

After you manage to thread the ball or loop end through the tailpiece, attend to the other end of the string, the one that goes around the peg, so you can prepare to tighten it. Look at Figure 17-9 and follow these steps to wind the string correctly:

1. **With your finger and thumb, skim along the string from the tailpiece end to the peg end, making sure the string doesn't have any weird twists (it isn't like the plot of a thriller).**

2. **Insert the very end of the string into the little hole that's drilled through the peg, making sure that about a half-inch or more of string has emerged through the other side of the peg.**

3. **Begin to turn the peg in a motion that goes toward the scroll end of the violin, so that the string runs over the top of the peg first.**

   If possible, as you turn, make the string wind over the little end bit of string that you stuck through the peg hole, to hold it firmly in place, something like securing the end of a thread when you're sewing.

The string should be set up on the peg so that it winds outward toward the pegbox wall. The winding action works rather like the thread of a screw, so winding the string outwards toward the edge of the pegbox keeps the peg snugly in place as you turn.

Scout types among you may be tempted to put a knot in the end of the strings after you've threaded them through the little hole in the peg, to stop your string from slipping out again (in case it has a mind to do something so unsuitable). But scout types must always be prepared — to resist such temptations!

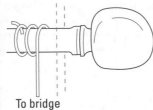

Figure 17-9:
Winding
the string
around
the peg
correctly.

To bridge

Strings are tricky to put on, and if you don't feel confident, or if you're getting in a stew about it, just take your violin to the store, where someone will be pleased to help you. And even better news is that I have never heard of a store charging money for this service.

Protecting Your Violin

The violin is a surprisingly sturdy instrument, considering how delicate it looks. Its sturdiness explains why we still have violins that date back to 1700, and even earlier. You can make sure that your violin remains in top condition by treating it just right. (I tell you about basic ways to keep your violin safe in Chapter 2.) In addition to the basics, always put your violin away in its case after each practice session, and close and latch the lid.

I know of two surprisingly frequent causes of damage to precious violins, so be aware of them! One is when coffee gets spilled on a violin that's left lying around, and the other is when a violin falls out of its case because the case lid is closed but not latched.

When you join an orchestra, the same ideas for preventing accidents apply just as they do in your living room, only more so. No matter how many violinists you see leaving their violins on their chairs at break time, it's still a very dangerous thing to do. These careless musicians may get more of a "break" than they bargained for. Take a moment to put your violin and bow away safely in your case and latch it closed. Keeping your case alongside your chair or close by makes this an easy habit to get into.

During the times when you're playing in an orchestra or group, make sure you have enough room around you to avoid bumping into the next person. Play a few full bows to check to see if you have bow space.

Chances are you take your violin to all kinds of places: to lessons, to rehearsals, to jam sessions — it really gets around! So here are some thoughts for keeping your precious instrument safe while it's in transit:

✔ **Car:** This warning's very weird, but a frequent cause of broken violins is getting distracted when you're getting into the car. Perhaps the phone rings, your kids start talking to you, or some other distraction occurs. Well, the next thing you know, you're driving off with the violin sitting on the roof of the car, or you've reversed over the violin. So always finish putting the violin safely in the car before you do anything else. Keeping your violin lodged snugly between the front and back seats of the car is probably the safest place. And I advise taking it with you when you leave the car.

Above all, if you've backed over your violin with the car, do *not* (as my wonderful violin maker friend Quentin Playfair has witnessed) put the car into forward gear and then drive over it a second time, but in the opposite direction. Doing so does not reverse the damage.

✔ **Train or bus:** If you're traveling on public transit, keep the violin case upright between your knees, or right next to you, when you sit down. Don't leave it in the aisle. Fellow travelers can trip over it; someone may easily make off with your violin; or you may be engrossed in *War and Peace,* suddenly realize your stop has come, and rush off, leaving your violin behind.

✔ **Plane:** Most airlines allow you to bring your violin on as carry-on luggage, because violins fit easily in the overhead compartments. If you're uncertain, call the airline to find out how things work.

The people who say yes at the airline office are different from those who say no at the terminal. Each airline has regulations, and those regulations are on the computers at the terminal. So if you can say something such as "I'm referring to paragraph 74, section c," you can get your way without having a stand-up argument. To be doubly secure, make a note of the name of the agent you spoke to at the airline office.

In all events, do not allow airlines to put your violin in the luggage hold unless it's specially packed, because the hold is far too cold for a violin. Plus, the way that freight is handled is often way too rough for your precious instrument. Speak to someone at the store where you bought your violin about having it packed securely.

With the post-9/11 conditions surrounding flying, regulations change as often as rock stars dump their current squeezes. So be prepared for plan B if you are flying with your instrument. Consider leaving your violin at home unless you absolutely have to bring it. You may be able to borrow one when you arrive at your destination, and thus avoid a whole lot of worry.

Wherever and however you're traveling, make sure your violin is not sitting by a heating or air conditioning duct.

Professional players have special insurance policies for their instruments because they travel with them a lot. But for most players, outings are the exception, and violins can go on the general household insurance under an extra clause. Check with your insurance company to find out the conditions. For a few dollars a year, you can be covered if your violin is broken, lost, or stolen.

Coping with an accident

If you have an accident with your violin, how the situation resolves itself — and how much that resolution costs — depends very much on what you do after the accident.

First, since a crack in the wood can significantly weaken the instrument, reducing the considerable tension on the strings is important. Don't unstring the violin; just slacken the strings a bit. But loosening the strings creates a second problem: The tailpiece is loose, and because the bridge may well be on the other side of the room, the tailpiece, or the string ends in it, can scratch the top of the violin. Crumple up a tissue and then slide it between the table of the violin and the tailpiece. The violin is now stable, so place it somewhere safe.

Next, start thinking about the repair. Look at the violin. Are any parts missing? Is a white gash where the corner used to be? Has the scroll disappeared? Find each and every fragment, no matter how small, and save them carefully. Reassembling existing parts can be time consuming, but rebuilding areas of a violin in a copy of its original style is more expensive still. Besides, it offends the basic mandate of the repairer, which is to preserve as much of the violin as possible, and you don't want to offend the repairer.

Finally, avoid absolutely the temptation to gently stroke the damaged area. This technique should be reserved for children and baby seals. On a violin, it does two things: It rounds off the tiny rough edges of the broken surface, which, if left untouched, fit perfectly together. Having ruined the chances of a fit, you have also left an invisible film of sweat or oil, which makes a good glue joint harder to carry out.

Don't be surprised if the repair quote you get seems to bear little proportion to the extent of the damage. If a fingerboard breaks off, for example, the result looks horrific, but the work involved is quite straightforward. But if a small crack has appeared around the bridge foot on the E side of the table, you probably need a sound post crack repair, which could be a major undertaking.

If you're insured, take notes as to when, where, and how the accident occurred, and notify your insurance company as soon as possible. Say clearly and simply what happened, and the insurance company will lead you through the claim.

Upgrading Your Case

When you start playing, you're probably not that conscious of your preferences in cases. And most likely, your violin, bow, and case come as an outfit, all together (refer to Chapter 16 for more about the kinds of violins you can buy). Later, the case may get worn, or you may become aware that another case may suit your needs more conveniently. In this section, I talk about the properties of some different cases, just "in case" you want to upgrade!

Whatever the shape and layout of a particular case, look at the qualities of its interior and hardware when you want to upgrade. Some flashy and gorgeous-looking cases turn out to have intrinsic problems, just to prove once and for all that looks aren't everything! I tell you about some best "case" scenarios.

The interior lining is usually velvet or a similar soft material, to cushion the precious cargo. The part under the violin should be padded a little. Press on it to feel the quality of the padding. Whether you choose velvet, plush, or corduroy for the interior is largely a matter of personal taste and what you like to see when you open the case.

On the outside of the case, you use the handle, latches, and hinges a lot, so they need to be sturdy. The hinges are most likely to bend if they aren't good quality, so look at a few different cases, just to compare these features.

As for the shape of the case, you have two main types: violin-shaped and rectangular-shaped cases. You can also find dart-shaped cases and crescent-shaped cases, both of which are somewhat lighter than a fully rectangular case. Figure 17-10 shows you all four styles, for comparison.

I like oblong, rectangular-shaped cases. They're convenient because you can store music in the outside zip pocket, and your case is easy to balance when you rest it down somewhere. The inside compartments provide plenty of room for storing your rosin and strings. The shoulder rest fits easily inside too, which is often not the case with violin-shaped cases. Oblong cases usually have room for four bows, which may seem a little excessive right now, but you don't have to buy four bows to fill the case! Violin-shaped cases are usually very light, and because you can't really store music in these cases, they stay light.

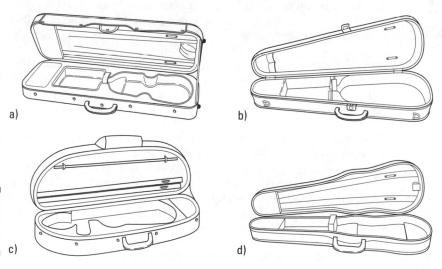

a)

b)

Figure 17-10: Shaping up with cases.

c)

d)

Testing circumstances

Just to give you some idea of the efforts some case companies make to keep your precious cargo safe, let me tell you about two wacky and very effective tests that cases have been made to undergo. Bobelock Case Company tested the strength of certain models by backing a Chevy truck over the cases. And Musafia tested some waterproof fabric for a case cover by tying a case to the roof of a house for a year (and the fabric was, indeed, waterproof)!

Having a lightweight case is a real boon if you aren't very strong, or if you're small in stature. Nowadays, lightweight cases are available in various formats, including Styrofoam, molded polyurethane, plywood-based materials, and carbon fiber. The advantages are obvious: comfort and portability. If you're using the violin at home or taking it somewhere in your car, one of the lightweight cases should be fine. However, most of these cases don't offer the same accident protection as heavier, wood-shell cases. If you slip on the ice and fall on top of your violin, or onto your back like a turtle (if you're carrying it backpack-style), you could squash your violin. Generally, though, lightweight cases are excellent and well worth considering. The interior is similar to other cases and offers your violin the same cushioning.

By the way, considering the weight of your violin case is a good idea. A lightweight case can weigh as little as 2 pounds, whereas a very solid case may weigh in at 7, or even 8, pounds. When you add a couple of pounds for the violin, bow, and accessories, it all adds up.

Most cases have a cover over the hard shell. The cover is usually made of canvas or nylon, and it needs to be waterproof, or at least water-resistant. A helpful feature is an extra flap that covers the opening of the case along the handle side, to protect the violin while you walk along in the rain.

Sales blurbs for violin cases chat merrily about suspension systems, and everyone oohs and ahs — but what is a suspension system? In a violin case, *suspension* refers to the fact that the violin is supported on two points: the top block, near the tailpiece button, and the bottom block, where the neck joins the main body of the violin. A good case does this, but a less effective case rests the violin on the middle of its back and on the back of the scroll, which can be a recipe for disaster.

Just like the human head, the best model for a violin case has a hard outer shell with a soft lining beneath. These features combine to ensure that the important stuff inside is safe. Unfortunately, a surprisingly small number of cases combine these features. They're either very tough on the outside *and* inside or the exact reverse!

Watch out for the following problems that occur with cases, and make sure that your case doesn't have them:

- The case falls over backward when you open the lid or take out the violin: a big no-no.

- The lid doesn't open far enough to stay open while you're unpacking the violin.

- The lid isn't properly aligned with the main body of the case.

- The bow toggles or clips are sharp, and they scratch your bow when you take it out or put it away.

Put your violin and bow in the case to try it out *before* you commit to buying it, to make sure the case works for your needs. If you have a high-arched violin, it may not fit some cases. Put a chalk mark on the top of the bridge, place the violin in the case, close the lid, and then see if the chalk mark has transferred onto the fabric above. If so, don't buy that particular model of case.

A violin case may also have a lot of additional fixtures and fittings, some of which are quite nifty. Look for some of these features when upgrading your case:

- **Carrying strap:** A strap allows you to sling the violin over your shoulder while you unlock the car, or just walk along. Almost all cases feature metal rings at either end of the case for attaching the carrying straps. Some cases even have backpack-style straps, which are more comfortable for many violinists.

- **Compartments for accessories:** You may find compartments inside the case, usually at the scroll end and sometimes alongside the neck of the violin. These compartments have lids, and the lids have little handles. Be sure that the lids open and close well and that you can get a grip on the handle.

- **Humidifier:** A humidifier can adjust the dryness inside the case, which is especially useful in countries where the central heating is switched on for several months in the winter. Some cases have a small bottle-like system installed, usually in the section of the case where the violin neck goes. You can also easily buy a humidifier as a separate accessory.

- **Hygrometer:** The case might have this kind of humidity indicator inside to show you the current humidity level. If a hygrometer isn't included with the case, you can buy one separately.

- **Instrument blanket:** Included with just about all better-quality cases, a matching blanket, perhaps with a little extra padding, keeps your violin insulated against temperature changes and any sudden bumps.

- **String tube:** Some cases have a string tube clipped inside across the bottom of the lid. This tube is useful if you use gut strings or other strings that don't come in convenient little envelopes.

✔ **"Subway" grip handle:** A useful addition for urban violinists is an extra carrying handle on the outside of the case, at the scroll end, for holding on to when you're standing up in the transit system.

✔ **Tie or Velcro fastener:** These important fittings secure the neck of the violin after you've put the instrument away. If something happens to the case — if it falls or receives a hard knock — your violin remains snugly in place.

Try carrying the case by the handle and then with the shoulder strap to make sure you feel comfortable. After all, you're the one carrying this along — no caddies are available to violinists!

Changing Chinrests

After playing your violin for a few months, you may want to look at chinrests again to find one that fits your evolving violin hold. Violin stores often have large selections of chinrests for you to try. (Refer to Chapter 3 for more about the types of chinrests.)

Don't listen to violinists who tell you that you have to have the same chinrest or shoulder rest that they have because it's the "best" one. Chinrests need to fit your personal chin, jaw, and neck — they're very individual.

You need to remove the old chinrest before putting on a new one (okay, I guess that's obvious). Chinrests come with a special key that you use to remove the old one, to fasten the new one, or just to give your chinrest a little tightening if it gets loose. Also, a few chinrests have custom mechanisms that come with their own little screwdrivers or keys (just like IKEA furniture), but generally, they all work in similar ways. These steps, which are illustrated in Figure 17-11, show you how to remove your old chinrest:

1. **Place the violin on a safe, horizontal surface.**

2. **Insert the special key that comes with the chinrest into the little hole on the shank of the metal clamp.**

   Most shanks have two or three holes arranged around their circumference so that you can insert the key easily and then transfer it into another hole as you keep turning the shank.

3. **Turn the key a few times to the left.**

4. **Turn the key a few times in each shank to loosen the chinrest enough to remove it from the violin.**

If turning the chinrest key becomes difficult, loosen the other shank an equal amount so that their levels match closely.

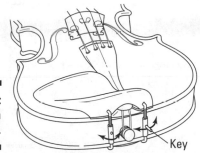

Figure 17-11:
Taking off a
chinrest.

Key

If you push the shank key in too far when removing a chinrest, you can
scratch the varnish of your violin.

Your poor violin probably looks a bit strange without its chinrest. Here's how
to attach the new one:

1. **Make sure your violin is on a safe, horizontal surface.**

2. **Put the new chinrest in its approximate place,** very close to the saddle.

3. **Tighten each shank using the special key so that the chinrest fits
   snugly to the violin.**

   The shanks need to be tightened symmetrically, in turn (if you tighten
   one of them too much before you go on to another, the threads can
   become cross-grained or resistant). The chinrest is securely on when it
   doesn't slip around. Beware of tightening it too much, because you can
   damage the violin.

Keep the key for your chinrest safely in the compartment of your violin case.
Sometimes chinrests come a bit loose and need tightening. The little pieces
of cork on the feet of the chinrest should touch only the very edge of the
violin, near the purfling — *there,* I managed to say "purfling" more than once
in this book!

Rehairing the Bow

Eventually, the horsehair on your bow becomes too smooth to catch the
string enough, or it becomes a bit greasy at the frog end, just from contact
with your thumb. Then it's time for a rehair. Now I don't recommend that you
head down to the stables with a large pair of scissors when it's time for a
rehair, but rather that you find a reliable violin store or bow specialist to do
the job for you. Professional players typically rehair their bows twice a year:
just before the colder season begins and at the beginning of spring. Bows
need longer hair in the winter when the insides of houses and halls are dried
out by heating.

The rehairing process (no Rogaine!)

Rehairing your bow is easy for you. Just drop it off looking all ratty at the violin shop, and then pick it up a few days later, looking shiny and perfect. But what actually goes on in the rehairing process? Here are the steps that a bow maker follows to rehair a bow, according to Jaak Liivoja-Lorius of Ottawa, Canada, a violin and bow expert and the former editor of *The Strad* magazine (one doesn't get more expert than Jaak!):

1. The bow specialist removes the old hair by snipping it off just near the ferrule.

2. He pulls the hair forward and takes out the head plug, which holds the hair in at the tip of the bow — and he hopes it's not glued in!

3. He throws away the old hair; it's biodegradable. (Occasionally, teachers ask to keep the old hair to show their students that it really is from a horse's tail.)

4. He takes the frog off of the bow stick and then takes off the ferrule.

5. He slides the mother-of-pearl slide forward to reveal the interior of the frog (and he usually keeps the ferrule, slide, and frog in a little box on the bench).

6. He pushes the horsehair up and then takes the block out of the frog.

7. He gives the stick and silver bits a good cleaning and polishing.

8. He selects a bundle of hair for each bow (100 to 150 strands fit the bill) and discards any hairs that aren't perfect, which is often up to a third of what he buys.

9. He ties a knot to fit into the head of the bow, using nylon or cotton thread.

10. He puts a block in the head of the bow to hold the horsehair firmly in place.

11. Next, the bow head fits into a little V-shaped receptacle on the work bench, to stay secure, and the bow maker pulls the hair toward the back of the stick and combs the hair out.

12. He puts the frog back on the bow and then pushes it fully forward in its slot on the stick.

13. With the hair sitting on top of the frog, the bow maker marks the hair with a pen, about a ¼ inch behind the head of the *mortice* (the rectangular slot cut into the underside of the bow stick, where the frog fits into), all the way across, judging the length of the hair according to the climate.

14. He makes another mark at almost the full length of the mortice, inside the frog.

15. He ties a knot that covers the space between the two marks.

16. He puts the ferrule back onto the hair — in the right direction — and puts the frog back onto the stick and the slide back onto the frog. He puts the screw in.

17. He tightens the bow a bit to keep the hair even, and he checks it every hour, loosening it slightly as the hair dries.

18. He puts the wedge back into the frog, making sure the hairs are straight by combing from head to frog so that no crossed hairs affect the bow's playing.

19. He finishes by putting rosin on the bow.

If you're a handy type, you may be tempted to try rehairing a bow yourself. But it's a very tricky job, so it needs to be left in the hands of a qualified expert.

For players who don't play so many hours a day, rehairing the bow about once a year is fine, or even every couple of years. You can check with your bow maker if you aren't sure whether your bow needs a rehair.

All specialist string stores and many bigger general music stores offer bow rehairing services. Take your bow to the store where you bought your violin, if you like the store. You drop off the bow, take your receipt, and then set a date to pick up the bow again, usually a week later (kind of like getting your clothes dry cleaned). If you go to the store where you bought your violin, they may provide a "loaner" bow for you to use in the interim.

Some stores offer same-day rehairing services, usually for a slightly higher fee — you just call to set up a time. A same-day service involves dropping off your bow in the morning and picking it up again several hours later, because proper rehairing requires a few hours.

You may save a few dollars by taking your bow directly to the bow repairer. The bow specialist probably operates out of a home workshop and doesn't have to pay the rent. Also, this option gives you more control over who works on your bow. But you may not be able to borrow a substitute bow while your bow's in the workshop.

You may think that an actual bow maker may be the ideal person to rehair your bow, but not all bow makers are keen to take on rehairing jobs. And in fact, bow makers may not do the job as well as someone who does rehairing for a living. The biggest part of a rehairer's skill comes from repetition (assuming a good system and reliable hand-eye coordination, of course), and a bow maker is more involved with the woodworking aspect of bows.

From time to time, give your bow's health a checkup, and include several observations. Check these areas of your bow:

- ✔ **Bow stick:** Check that the stick is straight. Close one eye and then look along the bow, like you're using a telescope, from frog to tip, to see if the stick has developed any sideways twists.

- ✔ **Rosin buildup on the stick:** Check whether the bow stick feels sticky, or doesn't look clean. The repair person can clean excess rosin off your stick and then return the bow in a clean and healthy condition.

- ✔ **Tip ivory and the frog:** Check whether they've developed any small cracks, and whether the lapping is starting to unwind.

- ✔ **Thumb leather:** Usually the thumb leather needs replacing because your thumb wears away at it when you play, perhaps every two or three years.

Finding Useful Accessories

When it comes to the violin, you need to have certain accessories, while other accoutrements aren't necessary but may be really cool to own. How do you separate what you need from what you want?

You can do fine with a few basic accessories, or you can go to town and equip yourself to the max. In this section, I divide violin accessories into lists of those you probably need and those you may want to get.

Necessities

A whole lot of accessories are available on the market to keep your violin healthy and to make your practice time easier and more fun. Here, I list the must-haves for your playing enjoyment:

- ✔ **Music stand:** A collapsible stand is useful for taking to rehearsals; a sturdier, adjustable stand such as a Manhasset is useful at home (refer to Chapter 3).

- ✔ **Rosin:** It's that sticky cake that you don't eat — essential for keeping the horsehair in close contact with the string (refer to Chapter 4).

  Hypoallergenic rosin is available for violinists who are sensitive to traditional rosin. Check at your local violin shop, or find it via the Web site of a bigger retailer.

- ✔ **Shoulder rest (if, like about 90 percent of violinists, you use one):** Shoulder rests help hold the violin comfortably between your jaw and your collarbone and shoulder area (refer to Chapter 3).

- ✔ **Silk covering cloth or bag for your violin (it can also be homemade):** A cover protects your violin from changes in temperature and humidity.

Extras

After you establish which accessories you need, you can look into some of these neat little gadgets. Just to guide you through this dizzying array of stuff, I tell you about each item, and I arrange them in the approximate order that you're likely to need them:

- ✔ **Mute:** A mute reduces the bridge's vibrations, resulting in a less brilliant and projecting tone. If a composer asks for this special tonal effect, you see the words *con sordino* on the score. Mutes exist in two basic varieties: detachable mutes and mutes that slide onto the bridge from the tailpiece end of the string.

Usually, the detachable mutes look like little combs with three prongs, and they're made of wood. You attach a detachable mute when you need it, and you put it in your case when you've finished. Although the tonal quality of these wooden mutes can be very pleasing, they're easy to lose, and they can be awkward to put on and take off when the music calls for frequent changes.

Mutes that remain on the strings and slide on when required are very convenient for orchestral situations, when the music may allow little time to get the mute in place. Most of these mutes are rubber, or they're made of a combination of rubber and wire.

✔ **Practice mute:** A practice mute follows the same principles as does a detachable mute, but it muffles as much sound as possible so that you can practice at 3 a.m. in a hotel room, for example. Practice mutes are considerably chunkier than regular mutes so that their mass can inhibit more vibrations from the bridge. To my mind, the rubber practice mute is preferable to the metal kind because if it happens to drop onto the table of your violin as you attach it, it won't harm your instrument. Figure 17-12 shows you the rubber practice mute.

✔ **Case strap:** As I mention in "Upgrading Your Case," most cases have metal loops for straps to clip on so that you can sling the strap over your shoulder and keep your hands free.

✔ **Spare bow:** Keeping a second bow is not a necessity, but if you upgrade your bow, consider keeping your original basic bow as a spare. Occasionally, the eyelet becomes worn on a bow, and if the hair won't tighten (inevitably, just as you're about to perform at Great-Aunt Dorothy's birthday party), a spare bow saves the day.

Figure 17-12: Strange mutations.

✔ **Case bags:** If you live in a country where winters are cold and you're frequently going outside with your violin, consider getting a case bag for extra insulation against cold, snow, or rain. Cushioned, waterproof case bags often feature backpack-type straps and a convenient external document pocket for keeping important papers at hand.

✔ **Humidifier:** Not all violin aficionados believe that a humidifier is necessary. But most violinists do like to protect their instruments the best they can, and so they opt to have a humidifier available in their violin cases — just "in case." Most important, you need to protect your violin from sudden changes in humidity, such as when the central heating goes on in the fall, when the summer is very dry, or when traveling to a different climate.

Humidifiers are available in two basic styles: snakelike tubes to put inside the violin via the f-holes, and small cylinders that live inside the case to humidify the violin's environment. Most players use the tube kind because they're easy and convenient. You just put the tube in water and then allow the spongelike materials inside the tube to soak up the moisture. You dry the outside of the tube thoroughly with a towel and then slip the tube through the f-hole of your violin until it is fully inserted, with the end "stopper" keeping it from slipping completely inside your precious instrument. Check it regularly for humidity, and re-soak when needed.

✔ **Cleaner, polish, and cloth:** Keep these cleaning supplies at home, on a shelf with your music and other violin-related gear. I discuss these items in "Cleaning Up," earlier in this chapter.

✔ **Pencil shelf:** This device slips over a music stand's shelf and provides a place to put pencils, erasers, mutes, or other small items.

✔ **Stand light:** A sturdy stand (not the light, wire, foldable kind) can support a stand light, which casts light directly onto your sheet music. Lights are useful for older eyes, for not-so-good eyes, and for playing in dark rooms and in the orchestra pit.

✔ **Music stand extenders:** Extenders are useful when playing longer musical pieces, when you may want to see three or four pages of music side by side.

✔ **Bow case:** You can buy a special case just for carrying your bow. This isn't an essential piece of equipment unless you're going to be carrying bows around a whole lot, or if you want the convenience of being able to carry your bows to be rehaired without schlepping the whole violin case along too.

You can carry your bow safely in an excellent homemade case made of black plastic plumbing tubing: Just wrap foam around the bow itself, slide it into the tubing, and then put a cap (or good ol' duct tape) on each end of the tube.

✔ **Electronic humidity and temperature sensor:** Violins don't thrive in dry air, especially in winter when the heating is on, so you need to keep an eye on the humidity in your violin case. The ideal temperature and humidity for violins is about 65 degrees Fahrenheit and about 50 percent, respectively. If the sensor registers outside the safe range (40–60 percent is considered safe) for your violin, you need to set up a humidifier in your music room, or the room where you're storing your violin. (However, a violin that has become used to lower humidity can be fine — the sudden changes from one degree of humidity to another cause the problems.)

✔ **Violin/viola amplifier:** Amps give your violin a great big sound. (Refer to Chapter 16.)

✔ **Plastic rib protector:** (For the violin, that is, not you!) Over time, the varnish and ribs of your violin can become eroded if you don't protect them. If your hands sweat a fair bit, and if the sweat is acidic, you can ask a violin shop to install a plastic film that protects the ribs of your violin. The plastic film won't damage your violin at all — though if you want it to come off, have it removed by a professional.

Part VII
The Part of Tens

"Apparently, Amadeus Mozart had a younger brother named Dizzy Mozart who was also a composer. Here's a symphony he wrote called, 'It Don't Mean a Thing, If It Ain't Got That Vienna Symphony Orchestra.'"

In this part . . .

Three cool tens await you in this part, all of which help you to become a better violinist. To truly appreciate the violin, you need to know about more than just the nuts and bolts (not that your violin actually has any!) of the instrument and playing techniques. Finding out about some of the greatest violinists gives you a sense of the instrument's incredible scope — and gives you fascinating cocktail party conversation. Chapter 18 tells you about ten violinists who have made huge individual contributions to the art of playing and lists some recordings you may want to check out. If you're really getting into playing (and I hope you are!), Chapter 19 suggests ten ways to go beyond this book to broaden your violin knowledge. Finally, Chapter 20 gives you ten tips for finding the best violin teacher possible, to help you along and keep you motivated after you're done reading these pages.

Chapter 18

Ten Performers — and Their Recordings

● ●

In This Chapter

▶ Getting to know late, great violinists

▶ Catching up with contemporary masters

● ●

*V*iolinists who have changed the face of musical history arrive on this planet only every now and then. In this chapter, I tell you about ten outstanding violinists who have made, or who continue to make, special and unique contributions to music. The performers are arranged in chronological order, and many have connections with one another, even if they're separated in time and place — the violin is universal and crosses all boundaries!

Niccolò Paganini (1782–1840)

Paganini almost single-handedly invented the cult of the performer (although luckily, he performed on his violin using both hands — and how!). Even though we can only access eyewitness accounts of his performances and get hold of copies of his compositions, Paganini is still universally recognized as the most remarkable solo violinist of all time. The effect of his performances on the public would be the envy of today's top rock stars!

Famous for spectacular feats of all kinds on the violin — including supposedly sawing through two or three of his four strings so that he'd be left playing on only one or two strings — Paganini's "24 Caprices" for solo violin still represent the pinnacle of violin virtuosity. Indeed, the *caprices* (improvisatory-sounding showy solo pieces) he wrote were so admired that pianist-composers such as Rachmaninoff "borrowed" his themes and wrote their own virtuosic variations for piano.

Unfortunately, Paganini lived before recording was possible, but his thrilling violin works are available on CD today, interpreted by the some of the finest artists:

- *Paganini: 24 Caprices* (EMI), by Itzhak Perlman

- *Michael Rabin: The Early Years* (Sony), by Michael Rabin. This CD contains 11 of Paganini's Caprices, which Rabin recorded in 1950, just after his 14th birthday. Rabin was a remarkable violinist, but his life was tragically cut short.

- *Paganini: 24 Caprices* (Sony), by Midori (at age 17!)

- *Accardo Plays Paganini: Complete Recordings* (Deutsche Grammophon), by Salvatore Accardo (with the London Philharmonic Orchestra)

Fritz Kreisler (1875–1962)

Kreisler was a son of Vienna who never lost the charm and elegance associated with his city of birth. Added to his birthright, the fact that he studied in Paris for two years means he had the most polished of musical influences developed into his personal style.

A child prodigy, Kreisler graduated from the Vienna Conservatory at the age of 10 and from the Paris Conservatoire at age 12 — with the *Premier Prix* (a special prize for being the top graduating violinist of his year, of course, way ahead of much older students)! Apparently, he didn't have to practice a whole lot to sound great, and his use of a very warm and vocal vibrato changed the concept of violin tone forever. He loved playing chamber music as much as he loved playing solo in performances with orchestra and in solo recitals.

Kreisler was the first violinist to make a substantial number of recordings, which contributed greatly to his renown and popularity. He was also a brilliant and prolific composer and arranger, activities that led to a remarkable page in music history: Many of Kreisler's "arrangements" of violin works by "old masters" were eventually revealed to be his own original compositions. His works are still featured regularly on programs at concerts today, so universal is the charm and appeal of his music.

- *Fritz Kreisler Plays Kreisler* (RCA)

- *Beethoven/Mendelssohn: Violin Concertos* (Naxos Historical)

- *Bruch/Brahms: Violin Concertos* (Naxos Historical)

Jascha Heifetz (1899–1987)

Jascha Heifetz is known for his phenomenal perfection as a violinist. In tone, intonation, and in every detail of performance, he achieved astounding accuracy and polish. Heifetz studied in St. Petersburg with Leopold Auer, the greatest teacher of his time. Young Jascha was a remarkable child prodigy, performing works such as the Ernst and Tchaikovsky Concertos when he was 11 or 12 years old.

His onstage deportment was serious, almost like a classical statue, but the emotion and fire came through in his interpretations. Apart from his solo playing, he also formed chamber groups with Arthur Rubinstein, Emanuel Feuermann, and William Primrose — all outstanding artists in their own right. The perfection and beauty of his playing make him the greatest violinist in recording history.

✔ *Heifetz Rediscovered* (BMG Classics)

✔ *Tchaikovsky, Wieniawski, Sibelius: Violin Concertos* (Naxos Historical)

✔ *Vieuxtemps: Violin Concertos Nos. 4 and 5* (Naxos Historical)

Stéphane Grappelli (1908–1997)

Born in Paris to Italian parents, pioneer jazz violinist Stéphane Grappelli founded the famous Quintet of the Hot Club of France with Django Reinhardt — it was the first jazz group to consist of string instruments exclusively.

Grappelli began playing the violin at age 13, and he picked it up with little formal instruction. Such formal instruction as he did have was on the piano at the Paris Conservatoire for four years (1924–1928), and he played the piano for silent movies to earn some much-needed money for his family. Grappelli and Yehudi Menuhin (see the next section) combined their prodigious talents to produce famous and successful records together.

✔ *Nuages* (ASV), with Django Reinhardt

✔ *Menuhin & Grappelli Play . . .* (EMI Classics), with Yehudi Menuhin

Yehudi Menuhin (1916–1999)

Yehudi Menuhin was a child prodigy with an old and beautiful soul, who was born in New York City to recently landed Russian immigrants. Through the growing availability of recordings and through the constant efforts of impresarios, the public had heard plenty of remarkable young players by the time Menuhin came on the scene — but his natural and direct expression of the music won hearts wherever he played. He studied with Louis Persinger in New York, and later, with Georges Enesco in Paris. His 1932 recording, as a 16-year-old, of the Elgar Concerto (with Elgar himself conducting the orchestra) still counts as the absolute pinnacle of performance art.

In good company: Famous people who played the violin

Apart from famous violinists who dazzle us with their virtuosity, several famous historical figures were also keen violinists. Here are a few for you to read about:

✔ Although the violin hadn't yet evolved, Nero supposedly enjoyed playing the violin so much that he's gone down in history as fiddling while Rome burned. (Not the most shining example!)

✔ Einstein was an avid violinist, and who knows, he may have been tuning his E string when he suddenly realized that "E"=mc^2.

✔ U.S. presidents Thomas Jefferson and Woodrow Wilson played the violin, as did Benjamin Franklin.

✔ In fiction, the detective Sherlock Holmes retreats to his den to stroke out mysterious melodies on his Stradivarius (which he bought for some 55 shillings in a junk shop on the Tottenham Court Road!) while solving complex whodunits.

✔ The painter Marc Chagall came from a musical family. He played the violin himself, and he often painted violinists in his magical style.

✔ Meryl Streep played her own music on the violin in *Music of the Heart*.

✔ Charlie Chaplin played on a left-handed violin — all the other way around.

✔ Jack Benny, the comedian, was an accomplished violinist, although he purposely played badly on his TV show for comedic effect.

He founded the Yehudi Menuhin School for gifted young musicians and became involved worldwide as a humanitarian and musical ambassador. He was also among the first famous performers to endorse health for musicians by promoting yoga. The Queen of England honored him with a knighthood in 1985, and he became a baron, Lord Menuhin, in 1995.

Menuhin loved collaborating with all kinds of musicians to explore all kinds of music. Apart from his recordings with jazz great Stéphane Grappelli, he also made recordings with the famous sitar player Ravi Shankar.

✔ *Bach: Sonatas & Partitas for Solo Violin* (EMI)

✔ *Yehudi Menuhin: The Violinist* (EMI Classics)

✔ *Paganini Concerto No.1, etc.* (EMI) — recorded in one take!

✔ *The Young Yehudi Menuhin* (Biddulph Records)

Itzhak Perlman (1945)

Known as much to concertgoers worldwide as to the preschool crowd who watch PBS's *Sesame Street,* Perlman has perhaps the most universal appeal of any classical violinist in history. He began his studies in Tel Aviv after hearing the violin on the radio and asking for lessons. Apart from his total facility and ease with the violin (and the admiration and delight his performances bring), he is also an ambassador for music who has made historic visits to all parts of the world.

Perlman is an icon of encouragement for people who are living with physical disabilities — because his legs were affected by a bout of childhood polio, he sits to perform onstage.

Apart from his beautiful, warm, and rich tone and his attractive, welcoming personality as a performer, Perlman has brought classical violin to huge audiences (some of whom may not have the opportunity to attend classical concerts) by appearing on *The Tonight Show.* He's very eclectic in his musical tastes; he recorded a jazz album with Oscar Peterson and also plays *klezmer* music (secular Jewish music mostly including happy dancing pieces).

- *The Perlman Edition* (EMI Classics)
- *The Art of Itzhak Perlman* (EMI Classics)

Nigel Kennedy (1956)

As a small child, Nigel Kennedy used to sit under the piano listening to his mother teaching piano lessons, but soon, he wanted to play too. Now the most famous alumnus of the Yehudi Menuhin School, Kennedy has popularized classical music while crossing over to different styles such as rock and jazz. Onstage, he's more like a rock star than a classical wonk, eschewing tailcoats for stylish outfits. His landmark recording of Vivaldi's *Four Seasons* has sold more than 2 million copies, reputedly the best-selling classical record of all time. When he's not on tour or in the recording studio, Kennedy is an avid soccer fan — his favorite team is Aston Villa.

- *Nigel Kennedy's Greatest Hits* (EMI Classics)
- *Vivaldi: The Four Seasons* (EMI Classics)

Mark O'Connor (1961)

Mark O'Connor was born in Seattle, Washington. Both in his compositions and in his live performances, he offers audiences a spectacular expression of the richness of American music today. His eclectic style combines traditional fiddling with other musical influences, including jazz, to bring a new sound to American music. Like Paganini, he's also skilled at the guitar and mandolin. O'Connor hosts an annual fiddle camp in San Diego.

- *Heroes* (Warner Brothers)
- *Liberty!* (Sony), with YoYo Ma, Wynton Marsalis, and James Taylor

Natalie MacMaster (1973)

Natalie MacMaster is a fiddler from Cape Breton, Nova Scotia, who can step dance while she fiddles. Born into a musical family, she's a worldwide ambassador for traditional East Coast music. She picked up her first fiddle at the age of 9, and she's been putting her amazing energy into her playing ever since. MacMaster has performed with a huge variety of other artists, from Pavarotti to Santana.

- *Blueprint* (Rounder/UMGD)
- *Natalie MacMaster Live* (Rounder/UMGD)

Vanessa-Mae (1978)

Vanessa-Mae is a violin superstar who's famous throughout the world. In April 2006, *The Sunday Times* of London ranked her as the richest young entertainer in the United Kingdom, with an estimated wealth of £32 million, which currently translates into over US$60 million.

Since her teens, she's been at the forefront of the fusion between classical and pop music. It certainly helps that she's also very beautiful and glamorous, but if people didn't find her music exciting, her appearance alone wouldn't sell the CDs!

- *The Best of Vanessa-Mae* (EMI)
- *Ultimate Collection* (EMI)

Chapter 19

Ten Ways to Go beyond This Book

*N*ow that you're up and running with your violin (just don't sprint too fast — you might drop it!), you can look beyond this book and out into the big, wide world. This chapter provides a few suggestions for broadening your musical horizons en route to becoming a bowmeister.

Of course, a book can offer all kinds of advice and neat information to set you on the right path, but it can't quite substitute for a live teacher. (I devote all of Chapter 20 to essential info on finding a teacher.)

Subscribing to a Magazine

Because you're consulting *Violin For Dummies* to get all kinds of information about playing your violin, I know you enjoy reading. A fun and easy way to keep up-to-date on musical topics is by subscribing to a magazine, where there's certainly plenty of info to interest you. Here are some music magazines that I recommend:

> ✔ **The Strad:** The revered grandfather of magazines for string enthusiasts, *The Strad* has appeared faithfully since 1889. The magazine is aimed at all string players, including those "other" guys — the violists and cellists and bassists — and it covers everything from detailed descriptions, replete with fabulous photos of famous instruments, to reviews of recent concerts at major venues. *The Strad* is a very good read.

- ✔ **Strings:** An excellent and more recent addition to the world of violins, *Strings* magazine began publication in 1986. Besides reviews and listings of concerts and news, *Strings* provides very practical and up-to-date articles on teaching and studying, making, and buying string instruments.

- ✔ **The Gramophone:** This magazine is a venerable institution and was founded by the famous author Compton Mackenzie in 1923. *The Gramophone* contains general-interest articles about composers and performers.

- ✔ **BBC Music Magazine:** This magazine appears every month, offering a CD with each issue. *BBC Music Magazine* covers new recordings and publishes articles of general interest, such as new research on the lives of composers and news about performers.

- ✔ **Maestronet:** An online magazine about violins and string instruments that hosts discussion forums. *Maestronet* also provides a database of instruments for sale and all kinds of string instrument–related information. Even if you're not a Californian teenager, you can have fun with this kind of surfing, and you can find out all kinds of neat info.

Attending Concerts

Sometimes, classical music concerts have a very stuffy image — snooty audiences dressed in evening clothes and long, boring pieces on the programs — but nowadays, most concerts aren't like that at all. Sure, many big-city symphonies still put on formal concerts with rich, well-dressed patrons in the audience. And why not? Affluent patrons are the main source of funding, donations, and bequests — a significant part of an orchestra's operating budget, which allows it to continue playing for everyone.

But for the most part, today's concerts are geared more toward a variety of audiences. In one season, orchestras usually schedule several different series to suit all kinds of tastes. If you're a fan of Bach and Vivaldi, sign on for a "Baroque Series." If your tastes run to cutting-edge music, sign on for a "New Music Series" to surprise your ears. If you have eclectic tastes, you can always buy tickets for individual concerts — there's no need to commit to a whole series. And most orchestras also schedule Sunday afternoon concerts, which are great if you have a long way to drive to get home, or if you can't come out in the evenings.

Why spend time and money going to a live concert, when you can sit in the comfort of your den and listen to a great performance on CD via your state-of-the-art sound system? Well, as a violinist, you gain a sense of how players move and express the music by watching them in action. And you feel the audience's excitement and intensity around you, even if people don't scream like kids did in the '60s at a Beatles concert.

You see and hear a whole bunch of violinists anytime you go to a symphony concert: The whole *Violin I* and *Violin II* sections — which are the top two voices of the strings — play in just about every piece written for orchestra. (You can tell just how important those violins are, because all the other strings get only one section per instrument!) And then, if you look out for concerts featuring a violin soloist performing a concerto, you benefit twice over from attending the concert: In addition to the two violin sections, you also see and hear a *virtuoso* player (a brilliant technician and exciting solo performer) jumping through some musical hoops to play a great piece written specially to showcase the violin.

If you're not such a classical buff, look for jazz, bluegrass, and even rock groups featuring strings performing in your area — at halls, clubs, and even shopping malls. Look for concert information in your local paper, on orchestra Web sites, and on billboards. When you start looking, you'll find a huge variety of opportunities to attend live music events. And going with a friend or two is fun. You can enjoy the music together and talk about it after the concert.

Joining a Community Orchestra

Even if you haven't been playing long, you may be able to join an orchestra in your area. Some community orchestras are at a semiprofessional level and expect players to have several years' experience. But many local orchestras welcome string players of all levels and can fit you in at the back of the section while you become more familiar with the violin. Ask about opportunities at your music school, community college, or university.

Playing with an orchestra is worthwhile on so many levels: You get to rehearse and perform some great repertoire; you improve your reading, listening, and counting skills; and you get to socialize with a bunch of music friends — a whole different circle than home and work! And when you play a concert, your family and friends can come along to see and hear what you've been up to on your violin.

Going to Summer Camps

Nowadays, summer camps aren't just for children. Many camps are geared to young professionals and advanced students, but you can find a good selection of summer programs for all ages and stages. The fiddle camps and the country music gatherings do take the biscuit on this one, but a few playing opportunities are available in the classical area too. Most summer programs offer daily classes, with faculty concerts in the evenings and some social activities.

The Suzuki Revolution

Shinichi Suzuki (1898-1998) led in a new era in violin playing and teaching when he devised the Suzuki method, which he evolved in Japan through the 1940s and '50s, and which he introduced to the United States and the rest of the world in 1964. His idea — that violin students could learn music in the same way that they first learn to speak, also known as the "mother tongue" method — allowed students to learn with greater ease, and to begin their violin studies earlier than in previous generations. In Suzuki education, the weekly private violin lesson is supported by the parent (who attends each lesson along with their child) working daily with the student at home to practice the assignments and by having regular (weekly or fortnightly) group lessons together with other students at the same stage of learning.

At first, many traditionally trained violinists and teachers were openly skeptical about the value of this method, but the results have been excellent. The main advantages of Suzuki's method are that students usually begin study between 3 and 5 years of age, before they can read, and they learn by ear and by observation (watching and listening). The method promotes the idea that every child can learn, and is insistent on respectful treatment of students. The group lessons promote skills already in development and they allow students to perform with groups and in front of groups — good for socialization and for performance confidence. The books include pieces that appeal to children, and they introduce the skills in a well-structured order.

Suzuki students only move on to the next step when they have mastered the previous one. They review their old pieces and exercises regularly so that they don't lose old skills as they advance. Suzuki was a pedagogue of inspiration and vision, and also a practical genius.

Camps vary widely in programming and accommodations. Many use university or college accommodations, while others are very rustic, with participants staying in cabins or tents. Look at brochures and Web sites for details before you apply. For programs geared to adults who play music for pleasure, check out Blue Lake Fine Arts Camp in Michigan. Or head to camp in Canada for beautiful surroundings and some fine playing at all levels with the CAMMAC (Canadian Amateur Musicians/Musiciens amateurs du Canada) organization, which runs camps in Ontario and Quebec. *The Strad* magazine lists summer programs every year, and the Internet provides more information. Naturally, you need to plan ahead of time and make sure you register for the right program.

Costs vary quite a lot between different camps, depending on the amount of individual instruction and the accommodations, but these recent ranges give you some idea:

- **Blue Lake:** About US$250 (including the registration fee) for a specialty four-day adult string orchestra session. Players find their own accommodations in nearby hotels or motels.

- **CAMMAC:** About US$850 for a week (instruction, activities, concerts, and meals are included), plus about US$200 for a shared room.

- **Mark O'Connor Fiddle Camp:** About US$750 for a week's instruction. Participants can camp for free at the site, or they can book into nearby hotels or motels.

Playing in Small Groups

From very early on in your study of the violin, you can begin to play in small groups. Your first ensemble experience may involve just playing a duet with your teacher, but soon, you can find people to play with in groups of two or three, and you can play music suited to your purposes.

Most usually, you find another violinist to play with at first, or you get together with a pianist. Later, you can find more music for string quartets (two violins, viola, and cello), or even groups of mixed instruments, such as flute quartets (flute, violin, viola, and cello), and so on. Good avenues for finding a group could be via your teacher, by chatting to people at a local music store, or through contacts at your church, community center, or workplace.

Check out the following publications for information about organizing small ensembles or for playing with a pianist friend:

- *Folk Strings, More Folk Strings, Festive Strings,* and *More Festive Strings* **(Alfred Publishing), all by Joanne Martin:** Martin created these books especially for her Suzuki students (see "The Suzuki Revolution" sidebar for more information) to enjoy with their families. The books have been so successful that she's publishing more, by popular demand! Particularly useful is the idea of having players at various levels participating successfully in the same group. The flexible scoring is available in a number of different instrumentations, all of which are compatible with each other. So if you find another violinist and a pianist or a cellist to play with, these collections are for you.

- *Violin Series,* **Third Edition (Frederick Harris Music), by The Royal Conservatory of Music:** This is a graded series (Introductory to Grade 8) of repertoire albums, from the earliest stages to an advanced level. These albums feature a great variety of repertoire and choice. I also recommend this series because I selected and edited many of the pieces!

✔ *Suzuki Violin School* (**Summy-Birchard Inc.**): The original mover and shaker of the renowned Suzuki method, Shinichi Suzuki, compiled ten books of repertoire that are still the most popular method books in use in the world today. Although the books are geared to young students who take weekly lessons and group classes with their teacher, they come with CDs so you can hear every piece — an immense advantage. Some of the available CDs feature two versions of each piece, one with piano and violin together and one with just the piano accompaniment, so that you can play independently while enjoying the music all together. In addition to the pieces in *Violin For Dummies,* you can probably enjoy playing pieces in *Suzuki* Volumes 1, 2, and 3.

Participating in Festivals

A festival is an occasion to celebrate and be, well, *festive.* So you can be as enthusiastic as you like! You can participate in festivals in two ways: as a player or as part of an audience.

Local music festivals (competitive and noncompetitive)

Local music festivals provide opportunities for performances of all kinds, from music to ballet or even acting. Visiting adjudicators come to town for the festival and provide written and verbal feedback on each performance, awarding marks and placements in the competitive sections. Music festivals are geared mostly to kids, but they often include *classes* (festival-speak for a "section") for adults or classes where families can perform together. Usually, these classes are noncompetitive and pretty light-hearted affairs, meant for fun and the enjoyment of playing, rather than for playing louder and faster than little Samantha or Joshua. And then while you're there as a participant, you can stay and listen to a few other classes, to hear what everyone else is up to. And festivals often need volunteers, too, to sell tickets and help the competitors get organized.

International music festivals

International festivals provide an opportunity for you to be in the audience to hear some great performances by seasoned artists. Bigger festivals centered around concerts or operas happen in all kinds of places, so you can connect with one that seems attractive to you. For example, famous festivals take place in Bayreuth, Germany (Wagner operas); Montreal, Canada (The

International Jazz Festival); Edinburgh, Scotland (music, theater, opera, dance); Tanglewood, Massachusetts (classical and jazz); and Aspen, Colorado (a nine-week summer festival where great performers, both soloists and chamber ensembles, come to teach talented students and perform concerts; student orchestras also give exciting performances at a very high level). But many more festivals, big and small, happen all over the world, and with Internet access, you can check out the ones that interest you. If you want to attend a festival that's far away, you may even find a travel company (one that specializes in music tours) that's organizing a trip to the festival. And if cost is an issue, cities sponsor all kinds of outdoor, free concerts in their parks during the summer — they're just waiting for you and your picnic!

Building a CD Collection

A trip to any record store or to a music Web site offers you a huge selection of CDs. In addition, most of the magazines mentioned in this chapter suggest ideas for building a collection. At first, choosing one or two CDs featuring your favorite composer or violinist is a good start and makes for very enjoyable listening.

Check out these links for CD reviews and recommendations. Or just browse to see what's available:

- ✔ **www.amazon.com:** This online bookstore has an impressive selection of CDs for sale. Browse their bestseller list, and read online customer reviews.

- ✔ **www.gramophone.co.uk:** Find plenty of CD reviews and articles about musicians on this useful Web site.

- ✔ **www.grigorian.ca:** Canada's specialist store also ships to anywhere in the world from its extensive catalog of classical and jazz music listings. Look at detailed and helpful descriptions of CDs on their Web site.

For those of you who prefer their music collections compact and portable, you can buy MP3s of some great classical recordings from Web sites such as Apple's iTunes Store. You can usually listen to a short sample of the tracks before you buy too.

Collecting Videos and DVDs

If you work with the CD-ROM that accompanies *Violin For Dummies,* you're aware of how much you can find out from watching other violinists play their instruments — and how much you'd enjoy seeing your own home "concerts," performed by great artists. A trip to the local library may give you access to classical music performances on videos that you can borrow. Otherwise, you can head for a well-stocked music store to check out what's available, or look online at the big specialty retailers' sites. From grand opera to penny flutes, it's on DVD for you to watch.

Just to get you started, here are a few suggestions:

- *The Art of Violin* **(NVC Arts):** This compendium of footage of renowned violinists of the twentieth century is a fascinating two-hour program. Included are Heifetz, Kreisler, Menuhin, Perlman (read about their achievements in Chapter 18), and many others.

- *The Red Violin* **(Universal Studios):** An award-winning film about a priceless violin and its dramatic history. Pluses are the gorgeous sound-track composed by John Corigliano and the brilliant performances by violinist Joshua Bell.

- *Music of the Heart* **(Miramax):** An inspirational true story of a teacher's quest to teach violin to kids in a Harlem school. The film stars Meryl Streep.

- *Stradivari* **(Beverly Hills Video):** The life story of the celebrated violin maker of Cremona, with Anthony Quinn in the title role.

- *The Art of Henryk Szeryng* **(Video Artists International):** Video examples of the art of this giant of the violin world.

- *Gil Shaham Mozart Violin Sonatas* **(EuroArts):** A beautiful violinist playing the music of Mozart. Now who could ask for more?

Visiting Competitions

It's not quite like the Roman arena, with lions waiting in the wings to eat the losers, but violin competitions do draw some of the finest young players from all over the world. These players are all hoping to win and carry off both the financial prize and the concert engagements that go with winning. You can hear some truly wonderful playing in competitions.

That being said, some of the best players around never participated in any competition, or they took part but didn't win first prize. And then some grand prize winners have disappeared without making their mark on the world, or they've succumbed to other pressures that have prevented them from fulfilling their potential. Just like sports, an element of chance always exists, but if you don't participate, you won't win. In fact, just being there is a huge learning experience for all the participants. So if a competition is going on near you, take the opportunity to go to some of the rounds. Not all competitions are international. You can possibly find local events going on at your university, at a symphony hall, or in a city near you.

The most famous violin competitions, where many winners have continued on to significant careers, are the following:

- **Queen Elizabeth Competition, Brussels:** Founded in its current incarnation in 1951, the competition was originally set up by Queen Elizabeth of Belgium in memory of Eugène Ysaÿe (1858–1931), a great Belgian violinist, composer, and conductor. Winners include David Oistrakh, Leonid Kogan, Jaime Laredo, and Vadim Repin, all of whom have gone on to international solo careers.

- **International Tchaikovsky Competition, Moscow:** Founded in 1958, this competition takes place in Moscow every four years, and it features violin, piano, cello, and singing categories. Winners include Gidon Kremer, Elmar Oliveira, and Viktoria Mullova. Musicians apply from all over the world to participate in this rigorous competition, which usually features about 50 violinists in the first rounds and ends with six prizewinners — if someone actually wins the first prize, which doesn't always happen.

- **Wieniawski Competition, Warsaw:** Every five years, violinists gather in Poland to compete for the laurels in this well-established competition. The Wieniawski Competition has been happening regularly since 1952, after an original 1935 competition and the long interruption by the Second World War, which devastated Poland. Founded in memory of the Polish virtuoso violinist and composer Henryk Wieniawski (1835–1880), winners include incredible French violinist Ginette Neveu (whose remarkable career was cut tragically short at age 30, when her plane crashed en route to a concert engagement). In fact, Neveu beat out the great Soviet violinist David Oistrakh for first place in 1935. But Oistrakh's son Igor won first prize in the 1952 competition — a talented family!

Performing at Hospitals and Seniors' Homes

After you have some tunes under your fingers, what better way to share the music than to visit a hospital or seniors' home? Most institutions have an events organizer, who's your first contact in setting up a visit. Make your first visit short and sweet, just two or three songs is plenty. Then, if you like the idea and your audience enjoys the music, you can decide what else you have to offer. For example, you can play carols at Christmas, old music hall ballads, favorite classics — you may evoke some happy memories and even a sing-along or two!

Chapter 20

Ten Tips on Finding a Teacher

*F*inding a teacher to work with is a great step to move beyond this book, both to find out more and to enjoy some helpful feedback on your practicing. A whole lot of teachers are out there. Finding the right teacher for you involves a combination of finding someone who knows their stuff and having a good dose of the right chemistry — you and your teacher really need to get along well and to enjoy your time together too. You don't have to be best buddies with your teacher, but you do have to respect one another, and the lessons have to feel productive. This chapter is all about what to look for in a teacher and where to find the right teacher for you.

Networking

Networking is a big buzzword today, and when you're looking for a teacher, this is an excellent method. Talking to people and asking for recommendations may lead you to your perfect music teacher.

Perhaps you have friends who already take violin lessons. If your friends like their teachers, asking for a recommendation can be a good place to begin your inquiries. The element of trust is a major factor in having a good relationship with your music teacher, so just knowing a bit about the teacher and knowing that your friends like and trust this person is reassuring.

If you happen to know some professional musicians, mentioning your quest to them is another good place to start. For sure, some names will come up, and then you can assemble a list of a few possibilities. One caveat: Professional musicians may recommend a very good player, but if the player is very busy with concerts and gigs, teaching you may be low on the priority list. Make sure your teacher likes teaching and has time to see you regularly.

Qualities of a quality teacher

No matter what the subject — violin, math, pottery, whatever — good teachers all have a few common characteristics. Think about this list when you're assessing a potential violin teacher. Does this person have the following qualities?

- ✔ **A love of teaching:** Someone who truly enjoys what he does will do it well.

- ✔ **Expertise:** Preferably, your teacher has undergone teacher training or taken violin pedagogy at a university or music school.

- ✔ **Pleasant personality:** Is the teacher calm and relaxed? Does she smile? Although a fine teacher can occasionally become intense when trying to communicate an important musical idea, you don't want to take lessons from someone who is cranky or impatient.

- ✔ **The ability to put him/herself in your shoes:** The teacher should understand your occasional frustrations and help you work through them.

- ✔ **Punctuality:** A teacher who misses lessons or is often late may not respect your time.

- ✔ **Imaginative, thorough teaching methods:** You won't get the most out of lessons if the teacher uses a cookie-cutter approach where an adult student gets exactly the same lesson and materials as a 10-year-old student.

- ✔ **Connections:** A good teacher suggests ways to connect students to people and activities to further their studies and take their musical knowledge beyond weekly lessons.

You may also try checking in the phonebook or on the Internet for violin teachers in your area. I know that making cold calls when you're job hunting is a chore, but in this case, you're *offering* some work instead, so don't feel shy to call a few teachers or music schools to ask questions.

Just like other professionals, musicians have specialties, and even violin teachers have particular areas of teaching that they enjoy the most. Teaching adults is a specialized area, so finding someone who's open to teaching adults (or has experience doing so) and can adjust the lessons accordingly is a bonus. Also be sure your teacher can teach you the style of music that most interests you. If you feel drawn to fiddle music (refer to Chapter 15), finding a teacher who's open to working in nonclassical styles is important.

Calling the Local Orchestra

I use the term "local" very broadly. If you live in Smalltown, Remotestate, you may not have a local orchestra. But an orchestra in a town 50 or even 100 miles away from you may include a violinist who lives in your area, or who comes out once a week to a town near you to teach at a music school or community college. Musicians often travel a long way to get to the gig.

Professional associations

The American String Teachers Association (ASTA) is a national professional body offering all kinds of support and professional development to string teachers across the United States, Canada, and South America. The ESTA, its European counterpart, offers a similar set of services on the other side of the Atlantic. One of the services is a listing of teachers who are members. The list is arranged by area and by specialty. The Suzuki Association of the Americas (SAA) has a similar listing of teachers who have qualified as Suzuki teachers.

Visit these useful Web sites to help you on your quest for a great teacher:

- ✔ **ASTA:** www.astaweb.com
- ✔ **ESTA International:** www.esta-int.com
- ✔ **ESTA British Branch:** www.estaweb.org.uk
- ✔ **Suzuki Association of the Americas:** www.suzukiassociation.org
- ✔ **International Suzuki Association:** www.internationalsuzuki.org

Suzuki associations also exist in Australia, New Zealand, Asia, and Japan, with similar mandates and purpose to the ones I list here.

Thanks to the Internet, most orchestras have Web sites with contact information. You can probably find the name and phone number of the personnel manager or general administrator. Likely, the manager won't just hand out names and contact information for the orchestra violinists, but she may take your name and then put someone in touch with you.

If you feel uncomfortable doing this long distance, why not go to a concert to hear the orchestra play? You have the chance to hear some great music, and you can get a sense of who's around. Sometimes, orchestras have receptions after concerts, where you can circulate, meeting the members of the orchestra. From there, take the small step to finding out who teaches.

Inquiring at Music Schools

Music schools come in all shapes and sizes, but if you look around, you may find one that offers a good string program for adult beginners — or for people who have come back to violin after a gap of many years.

Calling Fred's Accordion School won't yield you a violin teacher right away. But if Fred's is the only school in town, Fred may have a brother or a friend who teaches violin very well. Give any available resource a try, if need be.

Most music schools are private businesses operating out of large old houses, from studios in music stores, or in strip malls, where the parking is easy. Look in the *Yellow Pages* or on the Internet for listings.

You may think that Suzuki schools (I talk about the Suzuki method in Chapter 19) offer lessons only to young children, but in fact, your local Suzuki school may also provide adults with a very good program. Parents of children enrolled in the schools often take lessons along with their children, or they become interested and take parent classes, which eventually evolve further into an adult program . . . and sometimes even adult chamber groups or orchestras. Suzuki teachers should have taken training with the Suzuki Association of the Americas, so ask about their accreditation.

Checking Out Community Colleges

You may typically expect community colleges to offer workplace-related subjects, such as skilled trades or computer qualifications. But many community colleges have plenty of arts programs as part of their commitment to continuing education. Even if your local college doesn't have instrumental instruction, it may offer some interesting courses about music history or theory for you to broaden your scope. When you're enrolled in a course, you meet people who are interested in music, and maybe some other string players who already study or . . . well, you get the picture.

Perhaps just thinking about conservatories evokes memories of a disastrous Grade 2 exam long ago, or images of pianists pounding away for ten hours a day. Well, you'll be glad to know that nowadays even large conservatories — which are mostly devoted to professional training — have adult courses on evenings and weekends. Lots of adults are enjoying music in addition to their day jobs. Check out brochures and Web sites for larger institutions, and enquire about summer programs too.

Your local high school (and elementary school) probably has a music program. The music teacher at a local school may be able to help you with suggestions for violin teachers, or if you're very lucky, you may find an actual violinist teaching at your local school — one who is happy to show you more about playing.

Asking at the University

Universities provide a rich resource of possibilities in music. If a university near you has a faculty or department of music, call the administrator and ask about violin lessons. Then, you have two possible avenues: finding a professional faculty member who may also teach a few students who aren't enrolled in the degree courses, or an upper-year student who's interested in doing some teaching. What a student lacks in experience he sometimes amply compensates for in enthusiasm — and the price is often right. Some students are already doing some teaching and may have Suzuki qualifications or violin pedagogy courses under their belts. And if the administrator doesn't help you, you can find a notice board where you can leave a note for students to see. You'll certainly get some replies.

A more expensive lesson isn't necessarily better. All kinds of factors go into setting a rate, but the price has to be something you can live with. Find out what music teachers (not just violin teachers) are charging, and add up what you can manage in your budget. Think carefully before you pay top dollar for a lesson, unless you recently won a lottery, because it may not be worth it for you — and the worry and resentment can get in the way of learning happily. Ask a few places for rates, and evolve a sense of what's a middle-of-the-road price in your area. Try to get a sense of the teacher's track record and qualifications. Be careful about studying with a teacher who seems to be charging more (or less) than his or her qualifications indicate.

Hearing Students Play

Most teachers hold student recitals as part of their program. If they don't hold formal recitals, they may schedule adult performance classes or visits to seniors' homes at Christmas, for example, as opportunities for their students to perform. Ask a teacher if you can attend a recital at some point.

If you go to a student recital, you can tell a lot about the teacher's effectiveness and the quality of the student-teacher relationships from hearing the students perform. Naturally, most students aren't prodigies, nor indeed are they intending to enter the highly competitive world of professional music. But you may gain a few important clues from the event:

- ✔ Is the recital well organized and at a suitable venue, and does it have a clear program of events?
- ✔ Does each student play reasonably fluently, with a sense of being thoroughly prepared?
- ✔ Does the accompanist deal well with the students?
- ✔ Does the teacher help and encourage the students?
- ✔ Do the students treat each other with respect and encouragement?

If the event is chaotic, with breakdowns and tears, if people don't treat one another with respect, or if the atmosphere is odiously competitive, you're in the wrong place.

Many towns hold music festivals, where students can perform in different classes according to their age and stage. Most festivals nowadays hold competitive and noncompetitive *classes* (sections where students at similar levels are grouped to perform in order at a particular time) and family classes or adult classes too, for those who have come to music later in life. These events are fun to watch for an hour or two, and you can hear the students of most of the local teachers. Take mental notes as you watch the performances, and maybe ask some questions afterwards:

- ✔ Do the students enjoy music?

- ✔ Do the students stay with the teacher for a number of years? (Four to eight years is a good time span.)

- ✔ Do the students continue to play after finishing their formal instruction?

- ✔ Do the students participate in suitable activities, such as orchestras, small chamber groups, musicianship classes, or choirs, outside of the private lessons?

- ✔ If the teacher is with a college or university, what are the graduates of this class doing now? A good percentage should have found jobs playing and teaching, or otherwise using their musical skills.

Asking at the Music Store

Most music stores have a notice board, and some even keep a registry devoted to making the business cards of local teachers available to customers at the store — a sort of unofficial referral association. Even though anyone may put up a business card or flyer at the store, the people who work there may be able to tell you which teachers they know — and possibly a little about each teacher — to help you decide who to approach.

Mentioning Your Quest Everywhere

Once you've decided to seek a teacher, mention it to your friends, neighbors, and colleagues. The most unexpected leads can occur — perhaps your office's computer guru was a professional violinist in the old country and can teach you a whole lot, or the guy next door who's putting a new tire on his car has a cousin who plays violin and likes his teacher. So mention it to everyone, and keep track of the leads you get. Being creative and very persistent are two qualities that serve you well in playing the violin too!

Looking at learning styles

You know how some people can read something once and remember it forever, while others remember something only if they do it themselves? That's because each person has a characteristic learning style that needs to be respected in the lessons. Most people have a combination of the following styles, but usually one or two are dominant.

So which learning style are you? Find the description that fits you best, and discover how to use your characteristic style to get the most out of your lessons.

✔ **Copying someone else:** If you've done sports or ballet at some point in life, you may be attuned to picking up movements from watching someone go through a particular sequence of actions and then copying them. Musicians who are good at this skill can progress quickly, and anyone who can summon up visual antennae finds this method very useful.

✔ **Doing:** You internalize best through hands-on experience and repetition. If this is you, try going over the motions of a particular technique a few times. Then try repeating the movements later, and at regular intervals over the next while, until your body is comfortable and familiar with the patterns.

✔ **Following explanations:** You like detailed descriptions and step-by-step instructions to help you understand something new. When you begin new movements, ask questions to clear it all up in your mind as you turn the words into actions. You need a teacher who can provide plenty of response on a verbal level during the lesson.

✔ **Hearing:** Listening to sounds and reproducing them is probably the oldest musical skill. This method works for more than just playing the notes of a song, because you can apply it also to shaping the sounds of bow strokes and becoming sensitive to all kinds of subtleties.

✔ **Reading off a page:** You're one of those few independent souls who like to work a lot out for themselves and then receive some advice and instruction when they have a song pretty much formulated in their minds and fingers. Having a teacher who interrupts or disregards this process may not be comfortable for you.

Even though most people have a stronger sense of one or two of these learning styles, a good teacher knows how to weave in to help develop the other styles too, just to fill in any details that haven't been covered in the first round.

And if after all this, you're still without a teacher — maybe because you live somewhere very remote, or because you weren't happy with the local teacher — you can always pursue your music at summer schools and programs. (Refer to Chapter 19 for more about summer courses and camps.)

Looking for a Good Gut Feeling before You Start

You can fulfill all kinds of criteria and check off little boxes for expectations. But in the end, if you don't feel right about your teacher, the lessons won't be productive. So this is where your gut is useful. No antacids required! After going through all the definitions of what a "good" teacher is, you may find someone outside the description who turns out to be a good choice. And you may also find someone very well qualified whom you simply don't connect with, or whose style doesn't suit yours.

The difference in personality isn't always the problem; sometimes it's the interaction between the two personalities. Here's one possible scenario: If you're a very instinctive, free kind of person, and your teacher is a very rule-bound and inflexible person, trouble can arise from the differences — unless you're willing to make an effort to be punctual, and your teacher is willing to adjust lesson plans to suit you too. The willingness of both people to accommodate their differences is the key.

If everything about a potential teacher seems fine, but you're still not quite sure if the person is the right teacher for you, just sign up for a few lessons — say till the end of the calendar year, if you begin in September. Then if you don't feel you're learning well, trying to undo an arrangement that's cast in stone won't be necessary. If the teacher signs people up only by the full academic year — which may happen, because teachers have to pay the rent too — ask yourself if you can accommodate that idea, and then go with your gut. You may be able to sign up for a lesson every two weeks, a gentle pace, and then move to every week when you feel more confident of your arrangement. Often, beginning jitters calm down, and then you settle in just fine with a carefully chosen teacher.

Meeting a Teacher for the First Time

Ideally, by the time you meet a potential teacher, you've had a phone call or exchanged e-mails to go over a few questions and to get a general sense of one another. The first meeting should take place before either of you has made a commitment, and not after you've signed up for a year of lessons. Bring along your violin and some music you want to play for your teacher. Make sure you allow plenty of time to get to the meeting so that you can arrive calmly and punctually.

Auditioning

At your first meeting, the teacher should ask you about what you've done so far on the violin. The purpose of this question is to establish your level of experience and to gain a bit of background information, such as whether you studied the piano as a child, can read music, and have time to practice — there's a lot to know about. If the teacher doesn't ask, make a mental note, because your teacher needs to know about you but may just be putting the moment off.

You can offer up some of the information I mention, but you shouldn't find it arduous. If you have to try too hard to communicate with your teacher, the situation may not be interactive enough for good learning to take place.

You should then play some songs, scales, and bits of favorite pieces (maybe from *Violin For Dummies?*) for your prospective teacher, to show what you've already accomplished.

Planning lessons

After you play, the teacher should provide you with some feedback about what you have accomplished and suggest a plan for your next steps, at least over the next few months. If you feel happy about the meeting and the plan, commit to lessons.

After your initial meeting with a prospective teacher, he's able to assess your needs more easily. After hearing you play and learning about your musical interests, the teacher might recommend another teacher he thinks is a better match, or someone whose schedule works better with your schedule. Teachers have choices too.

If you haven't decided to commit to lessons, you can thank the teacher for the meeting and offer to pay for the consultation. Say you're still not sure about the time commitment, but you'll be in touch. Then you need to follow up with a call or e-mail to let the teacher know your plans.

Don't burn any bridges when you decide not to pursue lessons from a violin teacher. You may want to study with this person at some other stage in your violin playing, even if you can't imagine it right now, so keep things pleasant and clear in your dealings.

Making business arrangements

Make sure you've discussed the duration of a lesson (half an hour is a good starting point; ask for a longer lesson as you progress), the cost of the lessons, and the method of paying your teacher. Some teachers ask for ten lessons to be paid in advance, some settle up at the end of each month (the easiest method, in my opinion), and so on. Make sure you both like the arrangement, and then stick to it.

Appendix

How to Use the CD-ROM

I've crammed a lot of music into *Violin For Dummies*; so much, in fact, that it doesn't fit on an audio CD! That's why I've put all of the more than 150 songs and exercises in handy MP3 format on the disk that accompanies this book. Pop the CD-ROM into your computer or transfer the files to your portable MP3 player, and play along with me for more than an hour of music.

As an added bonus, I demonstrate the trickier techniques in video, so you can see just how they're done.

Relating the Text to the CD-ROM

Hearing the audio tracks

When you see written music in the book and want to hear it played, check out the box in the upper-right corner. This box tells you the track number and start time (in minutes and seconds).

To get to the desired track, use the *track skip* control on the front panel of your MP3 player. If necessary, fast-forward to the exercise's start time by using the *cue/review* function. When you get to the proper time (as displayed in minutes and seconds), release the cue button to play the example.

Every exercise on the disk is preceded by a full measure of count-in, to help you get a sense of the exercise's tempo. This click track continues throughout each exercise, to help you stay on the beat.

The songs on the CD-ROM are accompanied by piano. For those songs, the pianist plays a brief introduction, and then the music that's printed in this book begins. These tracks sound quite polished — they would make the ideal material for a concert for your family and friends!

If you want to play along with the CD-ROM, give yourself a few seconds' lead time so that you're properly holding the violin before the song or exercise starts.

Watching the video clips

Whenever you see an "On the CD-ROM" icon in the text and I mention that you can watch me demonstrate an exercise, pop the CD-ROM into your computer. Navigate to the appropriate chapter on the disk's easy-to-use point-and-click interface, and select the appropriate video clip to watch. Your computer's media player opens and starts playing the clip.

System Requirements

Make sure that your computer meets the minimum system requirements shown in the following list. If your computer doesn't match up to most of these requirements, you may have problems using the software and files on the CD. For the latest and greatest information, please refer to the ReadMe file located at the start of the CD-ROM.

- A PC running Microsoft Windows 98, Windows 2000, Windows NT4 (with SP4 or later), Windows Me, Windows XP, or Windows Vista.
- A Macintosh running Apple OS X or later.
- A PC with a sound card
- A CD-ROM drive
- A media player (such as RealPlayer or iTunes) to view video clips and play MP3s

Using the CD with Microsoft Windows

To hear the MP3 tracks or watch the video clips, follow these steps.

1. **Insert the CD into your computer's CD-ROM drive. The license agreement appears.**

   Note to Windows users: The interface won't launch if you have autorun disabled. In that case, click Start⇨Run (For Windows Vista, Start⇨All Programs⇨Accessories⇨Run). In the dialog box that appears, type D:\Start.exe. (Replace D with the proper letter if your CD drive uses a different letter. If you don't know the letter, see how your CD drive is listed under My Computer.) Click OK.

   Note for Mac Users: The CD icon will appear on your desktop, double-click the icon to open the CD, and double-click the "Start" icon.

2. **Read through the license agreement, and then click the Accept button if you want to use the CD.**

   The CD interface appears. The interface allows you to look at the MP3 tracks or browse through the video clips with just a click of a button (or two).

You can also access the MP3 files and video clips directly by clicking the Explore button. That button will open a window that displays the different folders on the CD-ROM. This is handy if you want to transfer the MP3 files onto your hard drive or a portable player.

What You Find on the CD-ROM

MP3 audio tracks

Here is a list of the MP3 files on the CD-ROM along with the figure numbers that they correspond to in the book. You can put these files on your portable player!

Track (Time)		Figure Number	Song Title/Description
1		n/a	Tuning Reference
2		n/a	Dvorak's New World Symphony
3		n/a	"Jingle Bells"
4		n/a	"I've Been Workin' on the Railroad"
5		n/a	"Asian Mood"
6		n/a	"Octave Ping-Pong"
7		n/a	"Jingle Bells"
8		n/a	"Shortenin' Bread"
9	(0:00)	6-3	Finger marching exercise on the A string
	(0:42)	6-4	Finger hopping exercise on the A string
10	(0:00)	6-5a	Exercises for changing to higher strings, in 4/4
	(0:22)	6-5b	Exercises for changing to higher strings, in 3/4
	(0:39)	6-6	Exercises for changing to lower strings
	(1:01)	6-8	Crossing strings using fingers

Track (Time)		Figure Number	Song Title/Description
11	(0:00)	6-10	Climbing up the A string
	(0:10)	6-11	Climbing up the D string
	(0:21)	6-12	Climbing up and down the G string
	(0:36)	6-13	Climbing up and down on the E string
12		n/a	"Hot Cross Buns"
13		n/a	"Frère Jacques"
14		n/a	"Pachelbel Canon"
15		n/a	"Boil the Cabbage Down"
16		n/a	"Ode to Joy"
17	(0:00)	8-3	First two phrases of Pachelbel Canon in whole notes
	(1:01)	8-5	Pachelbel Canon in half notes
	(1:37)	8-7	Exercise with quarter notes
	(2:00)	8-10	Exercise with eighth and quarter notes
	(2:20)	8-12	Exercise with sixteenth notes
	(2:40)	8-14	Exercise with triplets and quarters
18	(0:00)	8-15	Exercise with dotted half notes
	(0:19)	8-16	Exercise with dotted quarter notes and eighth notes
	(0:31)	8-17	"Dot's All for Now, Folks!"
19		n/a	"Little Brown Jug"
20		n/a	"Boiling the Cabbage Further Down"
21		n/a	"Nutcracker Sweet"
22	(0:00)	9-5	Four 4/4 bars with 8ths, 16ths, and triplets
	(0:19)	9-7	Four bars of 4/4 for counting
	(0:38)	9-8	Exercise with rests
	(0:57)	9-9	Two versions of "O Come, All Ye Faithful"
23		9-12	Metronome exercise
24		n/a	"Old MacDonald"
25		n/a	"Pachelbel Canon"
26	(0:00)	9-13	Four 3/4 bars
	(0:16)	9-14	Bowing in 3/4 time

Track (Time)		Figure Number	Song Title/Description
27		n/a	"Pussycat, Pussycat, Where Have You Been?"
28		9-15	Four 2/4 bars
29		n/a	"Twinkle, Twinkle, Little Star"
30	(0:00)	9-16	Counting in 6/8 time
	(0:25)	9-17	A verse of "The Irish Washerwoman"
31		n/a	"Theme from Symphony No. 1 by Brahms"
32		n/a	"Old French Folk Song"
33		n/a	"Simple Gifts"
34		n/a	"Oranges and Lemons"
35	(0:00)	10-3	A major scale ascending
	(0:21)	10-4	A major scale descending
36	(0:00)	10-5	G major scale, upper octave
	(0:22)	10-6	G major scale, both octaves
37		10-8	E major scale
38		10-9	A major scale, two octaves
39		10-10	F major scale
40	(0:00)	10-13	A melodic minor, ascending and descending
	(0:22)	10-15	A harmonic minor
41	(0:00)	10-16	A natural minor
	(0:22)	10-17	Pentatonic scale
	(0:39)	10-18	Chromatic scale
	(1:11)	10-19	A major arpeggio
	(1:26)	10-20	A minor arpeggio
42		n/a	"Mozart Clarinet Quintet"
43		n/a	"Aunt Rhody becomes 'A Minor'"
44		n/a	"Bach's G Minor Gavotte"
45		12-3	"The Cancan" in broken chords
46		12-5	"Joshua Fit the Battle of Jericho" in major and minor broken chords
47		12-7	Broken chord dominant sevenths

Track (Time)		Figure Number	Song Title/Description
48		12-9	"Brahms Lullaby," accompanied by a dominant seventh
49	(0:00)	13-2	Slurring from an open string to a finger
	(0:22)	13-3	Slurring between fingers
	(1:00)	13-4	A major and B flat major scales with slurs
50		n/a	"Mary Had a Little Lamb"
51	(0:00)	13-5	Slurs across strings from an open string to a finger
	(0:23)	13-6	Slurs across strings and between fingers
	(1:01)	13-7	G major scale with slurs
52		n/a	"Asian Mood"
53	(0:00)	13-9	Three-note slurs with open strings
	(0:29)	13-10	Three-note slurs from finger to finger
	(0:52)	13-11	Three-note slurs across the strings
	(1:22)	13-12	A major, D major and G major arpeggios with 3-note slurs
54		n/a	"Old French Folk Song"
55	(0:00)	13-14	Exercise with four-note slurs
	(0:39)	13-15	G major two-octave scale with slurs
56	(0:00)	13-16	Bow division exercise
	(0:24)	13-17	More bowing decisions
57	(0:00)	13-18	Bow division by note length
	(0:23)	13-19	Short notes followed by a long note
	(0:37)	13-20	Adjusting the amounts of bow for dynamics
58		13-22	"Homage to Kreutzer" with accents
59		n/a	"Surprise Symphony"
60		13-24	"Homage to Kreutzer" in martelé
61		n/a	"Grand Old Duke of York"
62		13-26	"Homage to Kreutzer" in slurred staccato
63		n/a	"Drink to Me Only"
64		13-28	"Homage to Kreutzer" with brush strokes
65		13-30	"Homage to Kreutzer" in spiccato

Track (Time)		Figure Number	Song Title/Description
66		n/a	"Magic Flute Overture"
67		13-31	"Homage to Kreutzer" in pizzicato
68	(0:00)	14-1	Bowing on two open strings at the same time
	(0:14)	14-2	Double stops with fingers on the strings
	(0:37)	14-3	Going from a single string to a double stop and back again
	(1:10)	14-4	Going from one string to two strings and back again
	(1:42)	14-5	Double stops with a fingered lower string and open string upper note
	(2:18)	14-6	Double stops where both notes are stopped
69		n/a	"Hunting Horn Song"
70	(0:00)	14-7	Four 3-note chords
	(0:21)	14-8	Two 4-note chords
71		n/a	"Grand Finale"
72	(0:00)	14-11	F major scale in second position
	(0:18)	14-12	"Joy to the World" in second position
73	(0:00)	14-15	G major scale in third position
	(0:18)	14-16	"Joy to the World" in third position
74	(0:00)	14-19	A major scale in fourth position
	(0:18)	14-20	"Joy to the World" in fourth position
75		14-22	D major arpeggio, two octaves
76	(0:00)	14-23	Same-finger shift exercise
	(0:24)	14-24	Intermediate note shifts
	(1:06)	14-25	"My Dame Hath a Lame Tame Crane"
77	(0:00)	14-26	Exercise with finger substitution shifts
	(0:11)	14-27	Trio from Mozart's "Haffner" symphony
78		14-28	Changing position and going to a different string
79		n/a	"Speed, Bonnie Boat"
80		14-29	Vibrato impulses on the D string
81		n/a	"Pachelbel Canon"

Track (Time)		Figure Number	Song Title/Description
82	(0:00)	14-30	Exercise with Trills
	(0:29)	14-31	Trilling from finger to finger
	(0:45)	14-32	Changing positions to trill
	(1:06)	14-33	Trilling on a dotted quarter note
	(1:21)	14-34	Playing trills with a sharp and natural
83		n/a	"A Trill a Minuet"
84	(0:00)	15-2	Shuffling up and down the D major scale
	(0:14)	15-3	Double stops
	(0:27)	15-4	Slides
	(0:45)	15-5	"Shave and a haircut, two bits"
85		n/a	"Cripple Creek"
86		n/a	"Chicken Reel"
87	(0:00)	15-6	G major scale with syncopation
	(0:23)	15-7	*Sul ponticello*
	(0:36)	15-8	Swinging rhythm
	(0:46)	15-9	Blues scale
88		n/a	"Country Club"
89		n/a	"Sweet Georgia Brown"
90	(0:00)	15-10	Gypsy scale
	(0:18)	15-11	Glissando effects
	(0:46)	15-12	Tremolo
91		n/a	"Kalinka"
92		n/a	"Hungarian Dance No. 1"

Video clips

Here's a list of the video files on the CD-ROM along with the figure numbers that they correspond to in the book.

Clip	Figure Number	Description
1	2-3	Taking the violin and bow out of its case
2	n/a	Putting the violin and bow in its case
3	2-4	Tuning with the fine tuners
4	2-5	Tuning with the pegs

Clip	Figure Number	Description
5	3-1	Holding the violin; swinging it up into playing position.
6	3-2	Sitting position with the violin in resting position and playing position.
7	n/a	Setting up and putting on a bracket shoulder rest
8	n/a	Setting up and putting on a cushion shoulder rest
9	4-2	Tightening the bow
10	n/a	Loosening the bow
11	4-4	Putting rosin on the bow hair.
12	4-5	The "famous diva" bow hold method
13	4-6	The "hidden treasure" bow hold method
14	n/a	Finger tapping exercise
15	5-2	Getting your fingers into line
16	5-8	Shaping up for pizzicato
17	n/a	Crossing between two neighboring strings
18	n/a	Crossing between two non-neighboring strings
19	6-5	Exercises for changing to higher strings
20	6-6	Exercises for changing to lower strings
21	6-7	Arm steering
22	6-8	Crossing the strings using fingers
23	6-9	Walking your fingers across the fingerboard
24	6-10	Climbing up the A string
25	6-12	Climbing up and down the G string
26	n/a	Longer bow strokes on the "Pachelbel Canon" strings
27	n/a	Dynamic exercise
28	n/a	Conducting in 4/4 time
29	10-6	G major scale, two octaves
30	10-8	E major scale

Clip	Figure Number	Description
31	10-9	A major scale, two octaves
32	n/a	Hand exercises
33	10-10	F major scale
34	10-11	A melodic minor scale, ascending and descending
35	10-15	A harmonic minor
36	10-18	Chromatic scale
37	10-19	A major arpeggio
38	10-20	A minor arpeggio
39	13-2	Slurring from an open string to a finger
40	13-3	Slurring between fingers
41	13-4	A major and B flat major scales with slurs
42	13-5	Slurs across strings from an open string to a finger
43	13-6	Slurs across strings and between fingers
44	13-11	Three-note slurs across the strings
45	13-14	Four-note slurs
46	13-17	More bowing decisions
47	13-18	Bow division by note length
48	13-20	Adjusting the amounts of bow for dynamics
49	13-24	"Homage to Kreutzer" in martelé
50	13-26	"Homage to Kreutzer" in slurred staccato
51	13-28	"Homage to Kreutzer" in brush strokes
52	13-30	"Homage to Kreutzer" in spiccato
53	n/a	Pizzicato when you have time to prepare
54	n/a	Pizzicato for a few notes
55	n/a	Pizzicato when you can put the bow down
56	14-1	Bowing on two open strings at the same time

Clip	Figure Number	Description
57	14-3	Going from a single string to a double stop and back again
58	14-4	Going from one string to two strings and back again
59	14-5	Double stops with a fingered lower string and open string upper note
60	14-7	Four 3-note chords
61	14-8	Two 4-note chords
62	14-12	"Joy to the World" in second position
63	14-15	G major scale in third position
64	14-19	A major scale in fourth position
65	n/a	Shifting positions
66	14-22	D major arpeggio, two octaves
67	14-23	Same-finger shift exercise
68	14-24	Intermediate note shifts
69	14-26	Exercise with finger substitution shifts
70	14-28	Changing position and going to a different string
71	14-29	Vibrato impulses on the D string
72	14-30	Exercise with trills
73	14-32	Changing positions to trill
74	14-33	Trilling on a dotted quarter note
75	15-4	Slides
76	15-7	*Sul ponticello*
77	15-11	Glissando effects
78	15-12	Tremolo
79	n/a	Octave harmonics
80	n/a	Third-finger harmonics
81	17-3	Cleaning the strings and fingerboard with rubbing alcohol
82	17-4	Unwinding the peg, removing the string

Troubleshooting

I tried my best to ensure that this CD-ROM would work on most computers with the minimum system requirements. Alas, your computer may differ, and may not play the files properly for some reason.

The two likeliest problems are that you don't have enough memory (RAM) for the programs you want to use, or you have other programs running that are affecting installation or running of a program. If you get an error message such as `Not enough memory` or `Setup cannot continue`, try one or more of the following suggestions and then try using the software again:

- ✔ **Turn off any antivirus software running on your computer.** Installation programs sometimes mimic virus activity and may make your computer incorrectly believe that it's being infected by a virus.

- ✔ **Close all running programs.** The more programs you have running, the less memory is available to other programs. Installation programs typically update files and programs; so if you keep other programs running, installation may not work properly.

- ✔ **Have your local computer store add more RAM to your computer.** This is, admittedly, a drastic and somewhat expensive step. However, adding more memory can really help the speed of your computer and allow more programs to run at the same time.

If you have trouble with the CD-ROM, please call the Wiley Product Technical Support phone number at (800) 762-2974. Outside the United States, call 1(317) 572-3994. You can also contact Wiley Product Technical Support at `http://support.wiley.com`. John Wiley & Sons will provide technical support only for installation and other general quality control items. For technical support on the applications that play the MP3 and video files, consult the program's vendor or author.

Index

• *T* •

Notes

Notes

MUSIC

9780764599040

9780764578380

Also available:
- Banjo For Dummies 9780470127629
- Classical Music For Dummies 9780764550096
- Composing Digital Music For Dummies 9780470170953
- Home Recording For Musicians For Dummies 9780764588846
- Music Composition For Dummies 9780470224212

- Piano For Dummies 9780764551055
- Singing For Dummies 9780764524752
- Songwriting For Dummies 9780764554049

DIET & FITNESS

9780764541490

9780764578519

Also available:
- Conquering Childhood Obesity For Dummies 9780471791461
- Nutrition For Dummies 9780471798682
- Exercise Balls For Dummies 9780764556234
- Pilates For Dummies 9780764553974

- Power Yoga For Dummies 9780764553424
- Stretching For Dummies 9780470067413
- Weight Training For Dummies 9780471768456
- Workouts For Dummies 9780764551246

HEALTH

9780764554407

9780764568206

Also available:
- AD/HD For Dummies 9780764537127
- Arthritis For Dummies 9780764570742
- Breast Cancer For Dummies 9780764524820
- Diabetes Cookbook For Dummies 9780764584503
- Food Allergies For Dummies 9780470095843

- Healthy Aging For Dummies 9780470149751
- High Blood Pressure For Dummies 9780470137512
- Living Gluten-Free For Dummies 9780471773832
- Understanding Autism For Dummies 9780764525476

Available wherever books are sold. For more information or to order direct: U.S. customers visit www.dummies.com or call 1-877-762-2974. U.K. customers visit www.wileyeurope.com or call 0800 243407. Canadian customers visit www.wiley.ca or call 1-800-567-4797.

HOBBIES/CRAFTS/GAMES

9780764554766

9780764553950

Also available:
- Manga For Dummies
  9780470080252
- Photography For Dummies
  9780764541162
- Sewing For Dummies
  9780764568473
- Bridge For Dummies
  9780471924265

- Chess For Dummies
  9780764584046
- Home Decorating For Dummies
  9780764541568
- Texas Hold'em For Dummies
  9780470046043

LANGUAGE/MATH/SCIENCE

9780764551949

9780764524981

Also available:
- French For Dummies
  9780764551932
- Italian For Dummies Audio Set
  9780470095867
- Signing For Dummies
  9780764554360
- Algebra For Dummies
  9780764553257

- Astronomy For Dummies
  9780764584657
- Basic Math & Pre-Algebra For
  Dummies 9780470135372
- Evolution For Dummies
  9780470117736
- Forensics For Dummies
  980764555800
- Global Warming For Dummies
  9780470840986

HOME & BUSINESS COMPUTER BASICS

9780471754213

978047018061

Also available:
- Blogging For Dummies
  9780471770848
- Excel 2007 For Dummies
  9780470037379
- Macs For Dummies
  9780470048498

- Office 2007 For Dummies
  9780470009239
- Outlook 2007 For Dummies
  9780040038307
- PCs For Dummies 9780470137284
- Upgrading & Fixing PCs For
  Dummies 9780470121023

INTERNET & DIGITAL MEDIA

9780764598029

9780470174746

Also available:
- eBay For Dummies 9780470045299
- iPhone For Dummies 9780470174692
- The Internet For Dummies 9780470121740
- Expert Podcasting Practices For Dummies 9780470149263
- Home Networking For Dummies 9780470118061
- MySpace For Dummies 9780470095294
- Smart Homes For Dummies 9780470165676
- YouTube For Dummies 9780470149256

SPORTS, PARENTING, RELIGION & SPIRITUALITY

9780471768715

9780764544835

Also available:
- The Bible For Dummies 9780764552960
- Catholicism For Dummies 9780764553912
- Coaching Hockey For Dummies 9780470836859
- Curling For Dummies 9780470838280
- Rugby For Dummies 9780470153277
- Spirituality For Dummies 9780764552984
- Teaching Kids to Read For Dummies 9780764540431

TRAVEL

9780470837399

9780470069325

Also available:
- Alaska For Dummies 9780471945550
- Cancun and the Yucatan For Dummies 9780470120033
- Cruise Vacations For Dummies 9780471788638
- Europe For Dummies 9780470069332
- Ireland For Dummies 9780470105726
- Las Vegas For Dummies 9780470104446
- London For Dummies 9780470165621
- New York City For Dummies 9780471945505
- Paris For Dummies 9780470085844
- Walt Disney World & Orlando For Dummies 9780470134702

SELF-HELP & RELATIONSHIPS

9780470018385

9780764554476

Also available:
- Anger Management For Dummies 9780470037157
- Body Language For Dummies 9780470512913
- Dating For Dummies 9780471768708
- Dream Dictionary For Dummies 9780470178164
- Meditation For Dummies 9780471777748
- Neuro-Linguistic Programming For Dummies 9780764570285
- Sex For Dummies 9780470045237

BUSINESS

9780764576522

9780470037164

Also available:
- Advanced Selling For Dummies 9780470174678
- Call Centers For Dummies 9780470835494
- Doing Business in China For Dummies 9780470049297
- Managing For Dummies 9780764517716
- Project Management For Dummies 9780470049235
- Technical Writing For Dummies 9780764553080

PETS

9780764584183

9780470068052

Also available:
- Birds For Dummies 9780764551390
- Boxers For Dummies 9780764552854
- Cockatiels For Dummies 9780764553110
- Ferrets For Dummies 9780470127230
- Golden Retrievers For Dummies 9780764552670
- Horses For Dummies 9780764597978
- Puppies For Dummies 9780470037171

John Wiley & Sons Canada Ltd., End-User License Agreement

READ THIS. You should carefully read these terms and conditions before opening the software packet(s) includedwith this book ("Book"). This is a license agreement ("Agreement") between you and John Wiley & Sons Canada Ltd. ("Wiley Canada"). By opening the accompanying software packet(s), you acknowledge that you have read and accept the following terms and conditions. If you do not agree and do not want to be bound by such terms and conditions, promptly return the Book and the unopened software packet(s) to the place you obtained them for a full refund.

1. **Licence Grant.** Wiley Canada grants to you (either an individual or entity) a nonexclusive license to use one copy of the enclosed software program(s) (collectively, the "Software") solely for your own personal or business purposes on a single computer (whether a standard computer or a workstation component of a multiuser network). The Software is in use on a computer when it is loaded into temporary memory (RAM) or installed into permanent memory (hard disk, CD-ROM, or other storage device). Wiley Canada reserves all rights not expressly granted herein.

2. **Ownership.** Wiley Canada is the owner of all right, title, and interest, including copyright, in and to thecompilation of the Software recorded on the disk(s) or CD-ROM ("Software Media"). Copyright to the individual programs recorded on the Software Media is owned by the author or other authorized copyright owner of each program. Ownership of the Software and all proprietary rights relating thereto remain with Wiley Canada and its licensers.

3. **Restrictions on Use and Transfer.**

   (a) You may only (i) make one copy of the Software for backup or archival purposes, or (ii) transfer the Software to a single hard disk, provided that you keep the original for backup or archival purposes. You may not (i) rent or lease the Software, (ii) copy or reproduce the Software through a LAN or other network system or through any computer subscriber system or bulletin-board system, or (iii) modify, adapt, or create derivative works based on the Software.

   (b) You may not reverse engineer, decompile, or disassemble the Software. You may transfer the Software and user documentation on a permanent basis, provided that the transferee agrees to accept the terms and conditions of this Agreement and you retain no copies. If the Software is an update or has been updated, any transfer must include the most recent update and all prior versions.

4. **Restrictions on Use of Individual Programs.** You must follow the individual requirements and restrictions detailed for each individual program in Appendix A, "About CD," of this Book. These limitations are also contained in the individual license agreements recorded on the Software Media. These limitations may include a requirement that after using the program for a specified period of time, the user must pay a registration fee or discontinue use. By opening the Software packet(s), you will be agreeing to abide by the licenses and restrictions for these individual programs that are detailed in the "About the CD" appendix and on the Software Media. None of the material on this Software Media or listed in this Book may ever be redistributed, in original or modified form, for commercial purposes.

5. **Limited Warranty.**

   (a) Wiley Canada warrants that the Software and Software Media are free from defects in materials and workmanship under normal use for a period of sixty (60) days from the date of purchase of this Book. If Wiley Canada receives notification within the warranty period of defects in materials or workmanship, Wiley Canada will replace the defective Software Media.

   (b) **WILEY CANADA AND THE AUTHOR OF THE BOOK DISCLAIM ALL OTHER WARRANTIES, EXPRESS OR IMPLIED, INCLUDING WITHOUT LIMITATION IMPLIED WARRANTIES OF MERCHANTABILITY AND FITNESS FOR A PARTICULAR PURPOSE, WITH RESPECT TO THE SOFTWARE, THE PROGRAMS, THE SOURCE CODE CONTAINED THEREIN, AND/OR THE TECHNIQUES DESCRIBED IN THIS BOOK. CDG DOES NOT WARRANT THAT THE FUNCTIONS CONTAINED IN THE SOFTWARE WILL MEET YOUR REQUIREMENTS OR THAT THE OPERATION OF THE SOFTWARE WILL BE ERROR FREE.**

   (c) This limited warranty gives you specific legal rights, and you may have other rights that vary from jurisdiction to jurisdiction.

6. **Remedies.**

   (a) Wiley Canada's entire liability and your exclusive remedy for defects in materials and workmanship shall be limited to replacement of the Software Media, which may be returned with a copy of your receipt to the following address: Software Media Fulfillment Department, Attn.: Violin For Dummies, Wiley Publishing, Inc, 10475 Crosspoint Blvd, Indianapolis, Indiana 46256, or call 800-762-2974. Please allow three to four weeks for delivery. This Limited Warranty is void if failure of the Software Media has resulted from accident, abuse, or misapplication. Any replacement Software Media will be warranted for the remainder of the original warranty period or thirty (30) days, whichever is longer.

   (b) In no event shall Wiley Canada or the author be liable for any damages whatsoever (including without limitation damages for loss of business profits, business interruption, loss of business information, or any other pecuniary loss) arising from the use of or inability to use the Book or the Software, even if Wiley Canada has been advised of the possibility of such damages.

   (c) Because some jurisdictions do not allow the exclusion or limitation of liability for consequential or incidental damages, the above limitation or exclusion may not apply to you.

7. **General.** This Agreement constitutes the entire understanding of the parties and revokes and supersedes all prior agreements, oral or written, between them and may not be modified or amended except in a writing signed by both parties hereto that specifically refers to this Agreement. This Agreement shall take precedence over any other documents that may be in conflict herewith. If any one or more provisions contained in this Agreement are held by any court or tribunal to be invalid, illegal, or otherwise unenforceable, each and every other provision shall remain in full force and effect.